BULLETPROOFING
TCP/IP-BASED
WINDOWS NT/2000
NETWORKS

BULLETPROOFING TCP/IP-BASED WINDOWS NT/2000 NETWORKS

Gilbert Held

4-Degree Consulting
Macon, Georgia, USA

JOHN WILEY & SONS, LTD

CHICHESTER · NEW YORK · WEINHEIM · BRISBANE · SINGAPORE · TORONTO

Other Wiley Editorial Offices

John Wiley & Sons, Inc., 605 Third Avenue,
New York, NY 10158-0012, USA

Wiley-VCH Verlag GmbH,
Pappelallee 3, D-69469 Weinheim, Germany

Jacaranda Wiley Ltd, 33 Park Road, Milton,
Queensland 4064, Australia

John Wiley & Sons (Canada) Ltd, 22 Worcester Road,
Rexdale, Ontario M9W 1L1, Canada

John Wiley & Sons (Asia) Pte Ltd, 2 Clementi Loop #02-01,
Jin Xing Distripark, Singapore 129809

Library of Congress Cataloging-in-Publication Data

Held, Gilbert, 1943–
 Bulletproofing TCP/IP-based Windows NT/2000 networks/Gilbert Held.
  p. cm
 Includes bibliographical references and index.
 ISBN 0-471-49507-7 (pbk. : alk. paper)
 1. TCP/IP (Computer network protocol 2. Microsoft Windows NT. I. Title.

 TK5105.585.H44696 2001
 004.6'2--dc21   00-068507

British Library Cataloguing in Publication Data

A catalogue record for this book is available from the British Library

ISBN 0 471 49507 7

Typeset in 10 on 12.5 pt Bookman Light by Dobbie Typesetting Limited.
Printed and bound in Great Britain by CPI Antony Rowe, Eastbourne.
This book is printed on acid-free paper responsibly manufactured from sustainable forestry, in which at least two trees are planted for each one used for paper production.

CONTENTS

PREFACE

The purpose of this book is to provide you with detailed information concerning different types of TCP/IP network-based attacks and host-based attacks oriented towards Windows NT/200 computers. In addition, this book will provide you with knowledge concerning methods you can use to secure your network and networked hosts. While there are a number of books providing coverage of TCP/IP based network attacks and other books that focus on Windows security, those books look at each area as a separate entity. In this book we will examine both threats to a network and threats to individual Windows NT/2000 hosts. In doing so we will note that protection for a network and protection for individual hosts on the network go literally hand in hand. That is, a secure network may not by itself be sufficient to prevent host break-ins. Similarly, secure hosts may lose their ability to provide requested information if the network is compromised. Thus, it is extremely important to consider the network and the hosts connected to the network as an entity when examining methods to ensure your user environment is not adversely affected by malicious or inquisitive persons that should not be doing what they are doing or attempting to do.

Although the word 'bulletproof' is in the title of this book, there is probably no such thing as a completely bulletproof network and networked host. The complexity of modern routers and operating systems as well as the basic insecure design of the TCP/IP protocol stack creates vulnerabilities that persons commonly exploit. In fact, in the first chapter this author will acquaint you with a very insidious security hole that was exploited on Web sites of two large companies. This attack, which is probably being announced for the first time in conjunction with the publication of this book, can result in a significant financial expenditure for an organization. What is even more significant is the fact that when done correctly this type of attack may go undetected for day, months, and possibly years!

Hopefully, the information presented in this book will allow you to determine if your organization is vulnerable to this new type of attack, as well as to understand functions you can employ to mitigate its effect.

In the first series of chapters in this book we will primarily focus our attention upon different types of network attack, how they occur, and techniques you can consider to minimize their effect. However, before we get to specifics the first chapter in this book will introduce us to the concept of social engineering (a new term for a con artist) and how this technique can be used to overpower the best defense obtained from equipment and software available to secure your network and network resources. In addition, as previously discussed, the first chapter of this book will alert us to a new type of attack method discovered by this author that, if unchecked, can significantly affect the bottom line of your organization.

Once we have examined network attack methods, we will turn our attention to the operation of a series of network protection devices, to include the router, firewall and virus scanner. By examining the operation and utilization of each protection device we will become familiar with their capabilities and limitations. This will provide us with a foundation for examining how different methods by which a host located on a network can be compromised, and techniques we can employ as protective measures. In concluding this book we will examine the role of intrusion detection software. Although long popular for checking for network-based loopholes, the use of scanning software to check the security of Windows-based hosts is gaining in popularity and will also be covered.

Although the objective of this book is to assist you in hardening your network and network resources against attack, this author would be remiss if he did not mention the fact that the only totally secure host is one that has no outside connection and which is kept in a locked room. Once you connect a host to a network you can open it up to an unlimited potential for attack, especially when your network is connected to the Internet. Thus, while the information presented in this book will surely assist you in hardening your network and network resources against unauthorized access, it should be viewed as a starting point and not as an end to potential problems and security breaches. Unfortunately, many persons who seek to do harm to our network resources or to profit from obtaining confidential data are bright individuals who periodically develop new methods or learn to exploit weaknesses in existing software. Thus, security is a never-ending battle and you should periodically consult the references listed in this book to obtain information concerning new threats and potential solutions to those threats.

As a professional author I greatly value readers' comments. Please feel free to contact me through my publisher whose address is on the jacket of this book, or you can send an email directly to me at gil_held@yahoo.com. I welcome your comments, corrections and suggestions for potential enhancements for a future edition of this book.

Gilbert Held
Macon, GA

ACKNOWLEDGEMENTS

Over the years I have written a series of books for John Wiley & Sons, in which I noted that the work involved in the publication process represents a team effort. This book is no exception and a number of persons in addition to this author are responsible for its publication.

Once again I am indebted to Ann-Marie Halligan and Laura Kempster for backing another of my writing projects and preparing the necessary paperwork for the presentation and approval of the John Wiley & Sons book proposal review committee.

Once my written proposal had been accepted the fun began, requiring this author to research and review numerous network and host computer operational details to ensure their validity. This required many long nights and weekends of work that put a crimp on family quality time. Thus, once again, I truly appreciate the understanding of my wife Beverly for the weeks and months when I had to hibernate in my laboratory to verify key concepts and approaches presented in this book.

As an old-fashioned author I favor pen and paper over notebooks, especially due to the fact that I never have the correct electrical receptacle plug when I travel. It takes true talent to turn my handwritten pages and drawings into a professional manuscript. Thus, once again I am indebted to Mrs Linda Hayes for her fine effort in preparing the professional manuscript that resulted in this book.

Last but not least, the book production process is a key element that cannot be overlooked. I would like to thank the entire John Wiley & Sons production staff for their efforts in converting my manuscript into the book you are reading.

1

INTRODUCTION

There is an old adage that says 'we learn from experience'. There is another adage that says 'if we forget the past we are prone to repeat it'. Recognizing the validity of these statements forms the rationale for authoring a book that describes and discusses different types of network and networking device attack methods as well as techniques and tools we can use to minimize the effect of such attacks.

The need to secure your network and hosts residing on your network has been graphically illustrated time and again by the exploits of numerous hackers. Although the hype over the so-called millennium attack proved to be much more of a media quest for nightly news stories than any actual attack, it is quite possible that the publicity and the resulting extra vigilance by different government agencies, commercial organizations, and academia also contributed to a decision by hackers to party rather than penetrate. In any event, now is not the time to lower our guard, especially when connecting a private network to the Internet or migrating to the newest release of Windows, Windows 2000.

In this introductory chapter we will briefly examine the rationale for establishing different network and host computer security measures. In doing so we will also cover a popular method used by some persons to gain confidential or restricted information that can open up your best barriers like a can opener applied to a can of soup. The method we will discuss is referred to as social engineering and its use has resulted in many hackers being able to circumvent years of effort and the expenditure of millions of dollars on security-related hardware and software. Although social engineering is an important tool of hackers, we will only focus our attention upon this topic in this introductory chapter. The reason for this is the fact that the results of social engineering can be considered akin to a wedge used by a lever. Once you have provided a hacker with key corporate information the ultimate effect is difficult to predict. Thus, the remainder of this book is focused upon different attack methods and the creation of barriers to prevent those attacks that may or may not emanate from the use of social engineering. Once we have completed our discussion of social engineering we will focus our attention upon a new type of network attack discovered as a result of the curiosity of this author. Referred to as the 'Script-Form Attack,' as we will note this attack method can result in a significant waste of funds by the organization being targeted. After discussing this new attack method we will briefly note the key elements of the primary American federal law against computer fraud and abuse. Although this author is not an attorney and cannot provide legal advice he will discuss a couple of potential holes in the law which make it possible for some types of attack to go unpunished.

We will conclude this chapter with a preview of the other chapters. This information will provide you with a road map of the direction of this book.

1.1 RATIONALE FOR SECURITY MEASURES

Today we live in a technologically driven era, with advances in communications and computing continually appearing. Along with the benefits of technological advances we also become exposed to the antics of malicious and curious persons that want to penetrate our network, read our email, scan our databases, alter organizational records, infect our storage with viruses, and perform other harmful acts. Although we can physically control access to a building or an area within a building, once a LAN is connected to the Internet our organization becomes a possible area of exploration for tens of millions of visitors, mostly welcome visitors, but probably a handful or more representing potential threats to the integrity of information vital for the well-being of our organization.

1.1.1 No organization may be safe

During 1999 and continuing through 2000 there were numerous well-publicized successful penetrations of computer servers. Web servers operated by many branches of the United States Federal Government, including the Federal Bureau of Investigation (FBI), and other agencies were penetrated and had Web pages defaced. On a more serious note, a commercial organization that sells audio CDs was the recipient of a well-publicized extortion, with a Russian-based hacker accessing and transferring approximately

300,000 credit card numbers and billing records. When the CD retailer refused to pay a bribe for the return of the stolen credit card numbers, the hacker posted them on several Web sites and it required the intervention of the FBI and several court orders to remove the private information from public access. While I sincerely hope you will never face this or a similar situation, the truth of the matter is that no network or host computer may be totally secure. Thus, we must learn from the past to construct applicable policies and barriers as well as to stay abreast of technological developments. Doing so will ensure we have the knowledge to close loopholes as they are discovered in the complex technology environment in which we work. Concerning that technology environment, there are tens of millions of lines of coding in most modern operating systems. Those systems, which include routers, firewalls, workstations and servers, may have one or more security holes unknown at the present time but which may be discovered tomorrow. If you follow the history of Microsoft service packs it is obvious that no operating system is embedded in concrete, and we must maintain our guard concerning the possibility that one or more unknown holes will be exploited in the future.

1.1.2 Effect of attacks

While the defacing of a government Web site may appear to represent a prank it has serious connotations that effect every organization that operates a Web server. If a person can break into a server and alter a page, it is also within the realm of possibility that they can retrieve credit card numbers used by customers or access other types of confidential records. Even if your site encrypts such records the publicity that results from the break-in of a different site can, and probably will, affect your organization's Web site. The primary reason for this is the fact that each time one or more persons breaks into a Web site and their exploits are publicized it makes consumers wary of performing e-commerce transactions.

In addition to the potential for lost revenue when someone is successful in attacking another location, there are more serious problems your organization can face from a direct attack upon its network and host computers connected to the network. Those effects can run the gamut from the inability of users to obtain timely access to information to the destruction of records and, perhaps more sinister, the altering of records that may not be noticeable for days or weeks after a break-in. Regardless of the type of penetration and illegal activity performed, we can summarize the overall effect in three words: access, time and money. Concerning access, users could be blocked by a denial of service (DoS) attack or the destruction of files on a server. This illustrates an important concept. That is, an attack does not have to be very sophisticated to shut down the ability of an organization to serve their user population. In fact, to the end-user the inability to perform a transaction or access information represents the key problem and they normally do not care about the cause of the problem, although the network manager certainly should.

Once an unauthorized person gains access to prohibited resources it is difficult to predict what they will do. Some persons are simply motivated by the challenge, with their goal to post a message similar to 'Kilroy was here'. Other persons unfortunately take pleasure in altering information, infecting computers with a virus or performing another destructive act. Because it takes employee time to right the wrong and your employees could be doing other productive work, we can say that an attack is paid for by time and money. Thus, the overall effect of both successful and non-successful attacks can be summarized by the words access, time and money. Hopefully the preceding information provides us with an appreciation for the necessity to use different types of hardware and software product to protect our network and hosts residing on that network. To continue our examination of security, let us discuss an often-overlooked mechanism by which many persons gain information necessary to breach the best barriers we can construct. That mechanism is commonly referred to as social engineering.

1.1.3 Social engineering

As briefly discussed earlier in this chapter, the term social engineering represents a salesperson-type ability to con information from persons within an organization, that can facilitate their ability to penetrate your network defense. One of the earliest social engineering techniques was to use the TCP/IP finger command to obtain information about the users logged onto a computer. Some organizations that support finger structure their application to respond with the name of the employee, their user ID, telephone number, and department. A favorite technique of some social engineering activists is to use finger to obtain the previously mentioned information concerning one or more employees of the target organization. Using that information the social engineering activist might call Ms Brown, with the conversation similar to the following between Fred, the activist, and Ms Brown, the target.

Fred:	'Hello—Ms Brown?'
Ms Brown:	'Yes, this is Ms Brown.'
Fred:	'This is Fred in network control. I need to ask you for a favor. We are experiencing some network problems and need to pinpoint the location where failures are occurring. Can you help us?'
Ms Brown:	'I only have five or ten minutes right now—will that be sufficient?'
Fred:	'Oh, yes, that would be fine. I need you to log off and log back in. When you do so please tell me exactly every key you press. This shouldn't take more than 60 seconds and your effort will significantly help us.'
Ms Brown:	'OK, Fred, I'm logging back on, I'm entering my user ID which is . . .'

Within a few minutes Ms. Brown has provided Fred, obviously not his real name nor a member of the technical control center, with enough information to begin his attack. Perhaps Fred will wait until 5:00 p.m. or a Friday afternoon and begin his odyssey of exploration over a weekend?

Another popular social engineering technique is to call a department manager who you know will undoubtedly be busy or, if you are even luckier, has just left on a business trip or vacation. Sometimes the receptionist will provide you with the name of the associate manager or another department employee. With a bit of chutzpah the conversation between Fred and Joe, the latter a department employee, might be as follows:

Fred:	'Hi, Joe, this is Fred Muggs. I was given your name by Mike Abrams before he left for Chicago.'
Joe:	'Yes, Fred, what can I do for you?'
Fred:	'Mike told me you had a copy of the router configuration file and could email it to me.'
Joe:	'No problem, what's your email address?'

If the preceding exchange appears to be a bit farfetched, it might be of interest to note that a very similar conversation between a hacker and an employee of a cellular telephone manufacturer was reported on the CBS 60 Minutes news program. The end result of the conversation was the transmission via email of the source code used for the operation of a particular cellular telephone to a well-known hacker.

1.1.4 Dumpster diving

Prior to moving forward, another area related to social engineering deserves mention. That area is commonly referred to as dumpster diving, although it is also applicable to other types of facility. Under dumpster diving a person literally goes into a company's trash containers, searching for information that could be of value. In one famous case a hacker went through the trash at a large West Coast telephone company office and located their telephone installer manuals. Those manuals included the codes to use to access the main telephone company switch for the placement of long distance calls. After a few hours of reading and probably a shower or two, the hacker was able to make free long distance calls to virtually any location in the world.

While there is no need to become paranoid about the potential of social engineering and dumpster diving they do illustrate the need for the education of employees. Unfortunately, the best hardware and software is often no substitute for the failure of organizational employees to guard their 'crown jewels' as well as other important information that can form a foundation for enabling illegal activity to occur. That said, this will basically end our discussion of social engineering and the need to protect company information from the eyes, ears and hands of unauthorized persons. To paraphrase another adage, if they can see no evil, hear no evil and touch no evil, it will make their ability to do evil a lot more difficult.

1.1.5 The script-form attack

This author has been blessed with the widespread acceptance of many of his books that were adopted by institutions of higher education and commercial organizations. About two years ago Cisco Systems purchased a very large quantity of one of this author's books. Cisco offered the book in a promotion for its 1750 Modular Access Router which includes a feature described in general terms in the book.

Being inquisitive, this author fired up his Web browser and went to the Cisco URL that offered his book. The initial screen display of the applicable Web page is shown in Figure 1.1.

If you scroll down the Web page shown in Figure 1.1 you will encounter a box to click on to register for a copy of the author's book. Quite naturally, being inquisitive this author clicked on the box to begin the registration process.

Since logic might imply that Cisco Systems would think twice about sending a copy of the author's book to the author, this author decided to complete the form with a bit of 'tongue in cheek' response. Since this author was holding a pen in one hand as he was staring at the form, a quick thought turned 'pen' into 'Benny' while a scan of the screen display resulted in 'Asterisk' becoming the last name used for the book request. Figure 1.2 illustrates the top portion of the registration screen that this author was filling in to obtain a copy of his book.

In examining Figure 1.2 you will note an asterisk located to the right of the name of the first two fields. The asterisk indicates that an entry is required. The entire form has ten required fields you must complete. Those fields require you to enter your first and last name, organization, job title, address, city, state, zip code, country and email address. Although this may appear to be a lot of information for obtaining a $55.00 book, in actuality it is probably a 30 second process to enter the first series of field entries. As we will shortly note, those entries can then be easily modified by a script, over and over again, such that a ton of books could be flowing through the postal service.

Once a form has been completed the cgi script used by Cisco will display the information you previously entered and ask you to verify your entries.Figure 1.3 shows the initial portion of the verification screen while Figure 1.4 shows the lower portion of the screen. Note that the lower portion of the screen envelope indicates how the mailed package containing the requested book will be addressed.

In examining Figure 1.4 note that for your book to be processed you must click on the 'CONTINUE' hyperlink. If you make a mistake in completing the form the bottom portion of the verification screen informs you to use the back button of your browser to edit previously entered items. While this suggested action may appear to be benign, it is one of a series of oversights in creating this form that makes it very suitable for a script attack. As we will shortly note, a series of small oversights makes it a relatively easy task to request a book, either via a script or even manually. This can result in book after book, all of which Cisco, as a highly automated organization, will bag, label and send via Priority Mail whose postage alone exceeds $3.00 per book.

When you click on the hyperlink labeled CONTINUE Cisco displays a nice 'Thank You' as illustrated in Figure 1.5. At this time Cisco would probably hope for you to move from the screen shown in Figure 1.5 to a list of authorized re-sellers or obtain information about the 1750 router or the Cisco Resource Network. However, you can also click on the back button on your browser. When you do so you notice the fact that instead of clearing the previous screen it is presented in all its glory. In fact, if you initiate another click on your browser's back button you will return to the form you initially completed.

Because you can easily return to the previously completed form, let us discuss a manual operation and then note how it can be

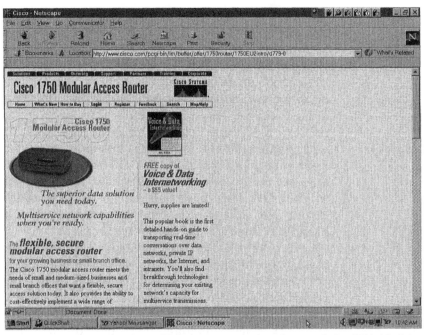

Figure 1.1 The main Cisco Web page promoting the vendor's 1750 Modular Access Router as well as providing visitors with the opportunity to obtain a free copy of a book previously written by the author of this book

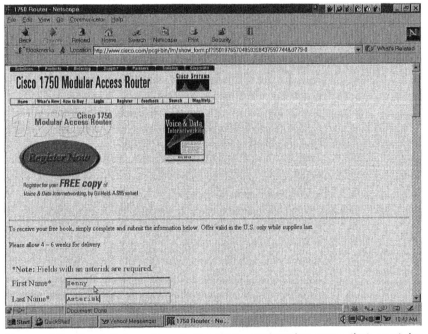

Figure 1.2 The initial portion of the Cisco registration page that must be completed to obtain a free book

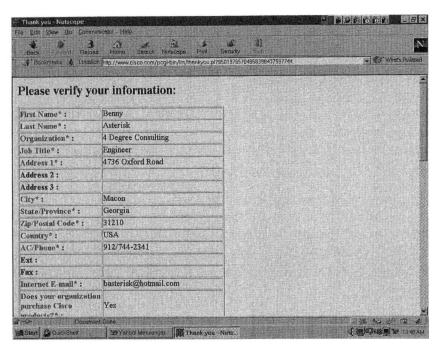

Figure 1.3 The top portion of the Cisco verification screen

automated via a script. If we click twice on the back button to return to the initially completed form, let us now change 'Benny' to 'Charlie'. Once this is accomplished we now only need to scroll down to the bottom of the screen and click on CONTINUE to generate another book request. Figure 1.6 illustrates the new package that will be mailed to Charlie Asterisk!

Although it is logical to assume that somebody at Cisco might notice hundreds or thousands of books shipped to a single address, this author decided to 'push the envelope' to a degree with a script. The script developed by the author accessed a database containing a series of ten first names, ten last names and five addresses (his, his mother's, his brother's and those of several friends). Since a telephone number and email address were also required, these were made up. Next, because it was felt that it would be too obvious to request book after book after book, a delay was built into the script. Using a random number generator to obtain a number and multiplying it by 1000 resulted in a number between 1 and 1000. This number was used as a timer between requests being automatically generated. That is, the random number represented the delay in minutes between requests. The random number was also smoothed to a value between 1 and 10 to select the first and last names to be used and again smoothed to a number

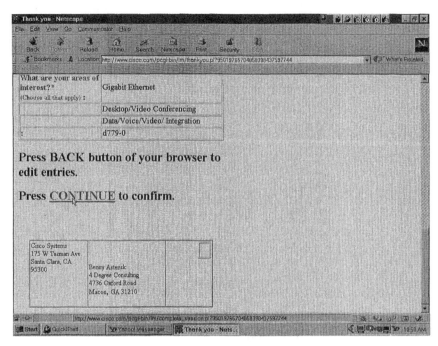

Figure 1.4 You must scroll down to the bottom of the verification screen and click on CONTINUE for your book request to be processed

between 1 and 5 to select an address. Note that if you multiply 10 by 10 by 5 you obtain 500 unique names and addresses.

After a bit of testing and some fine-tuning, the script-form attack was unleashed. Since this author did not want to bite the hand that feeds him (since Cisco has purchased large quantities of several of his books), the script was only executed periodically over a short period of time. During that short period of time, however, approximately 100 books were received, indicating that this is a significant weapon which organizations must guard against.

For those 'Doubting Thomas' persons, Figure 1.7 illustrates the stack of books received by this author, which he piled on the side of his car to illustrate the potential effect of this type of attack. It should be noted that since this author was teaching a course on Voice over IP at Georgia College and State University (where he is a member of the adjunct faculty) the books received were provided to students for use in the course.

With a few modifications the previously mentioned script was run against an automobile manufacturer whose motto is 'the relentless pursuit of perfection'. This action resulted in this author receiving several hundred multicolor, beautifully printed brochures for luxury cars, indicating that their computer operation is anything

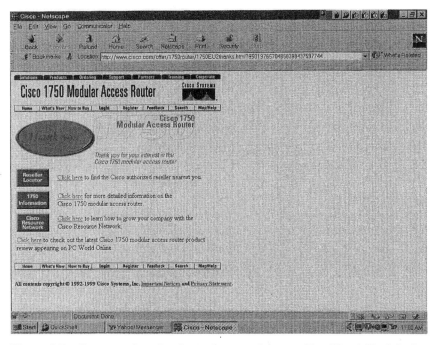

Figure 1.5 Once your form has been processed the resulting 'Thank You' display allows you to return to the previously completed form

but perfect. After a bit more searching, several additional Web sites were identified that were easy candidates for a script-form attack.

While it may appear that the previously described actions are representative of a childhood prank, they illustrate the vulnerability of highly automated computer systems. In fact, if a terrorist compiled a list of a large number of Web sites offering brochures, he or she could easily flood the distribution system of the Postal Service. Because many brochures are sent via Priority Mail, it is within the realm of possibility that if performed near Christmas the Postal Service could be overwhelmed!

Counter measures

There are several counter measures that organizations should consider to make it much more difficult for manual or automated attacks against forms. First, the form should be cleared once it is completed. Secondly, in addition to checking the telephone number or email address the back end of the form should capture the IP address of the originator to preclude repeated attacks from persons with a direct connection. Similarly, software should examine

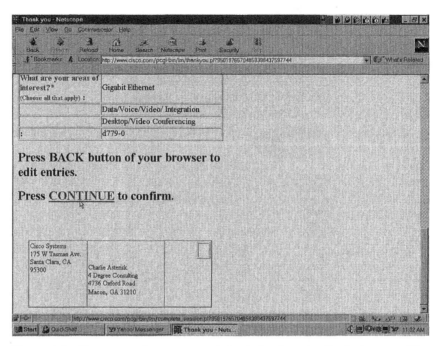

Figure 1.6 The new package prepared simply by changing the first name of the book requester

addresses within a city. Is it really wise to mail brochures to the same address with different names on the request? Last, but not least, too much automation makes your organization highly vulnerable for exploitation. For example, when this author ran his script he used a real telephone number for one location that was connected to an answering machine. Periodically, when he checked the machine he would hear message after message addressed to fictional employees. Sometimes it was hard not to laugh as the caller left messages for different variations of the name of this author's pets. I guess because they probably received a printout of names and phone numbers they assumed all was well, even though nobody ever answered the telephone. This action indicates another key security-related area you must consider. That is, consider everything, as a malicious person who may not stop at 100 or 1000 requests but continue their script-form attack. Within a short period of time the cost of the mailing envelopes, the cost of the premium or brochures contained in the premium and the cost of the actual mailing and handling can easily exceed $1,000 to $20,000. With a script-form attack this can be viewed as a minor wound that if unchecked can slowly bleed an organization into a bad state of fiscal health.

Figure 1.7 A portion of books written by this author which were shipped by Cisco as a result of a script-form attack

Now that we have an appreciation for how the curiosity of a person can result in a potential computer attack, let us turn our attention to the primary law that guards American society against computer fraud and abuse and provides a mechanism for punishing certain types of activity. As we will note, the law may have a few loopholes that could make it possible for certain activities to go unpunished.

1.1.6 The Computer Fraud and Abuse Act

No discussion of potential computer security related problems would be complete without mentioning the law. Unfortunately, there are many laws relating to the criminal use of computers, ranging from state and local laws to national laws. In this section we will turn our attention to United States Federal law in the form of the Computer Fraud and Abuse Act of 1986. Although this law is rather old, it is currently the primary law by which persons committing computer crimes that cross state boundaries can be prosecuted in the United States. As you might surmise, other countries may or may not have legal statutes concerning computer crime, and when criminal acts cross national boundaries it is presently unknown what laws would be applicable for prosecution. While this author does not claim to be knowledgable about the law and certainly will refrain from providing any legal advice, he will review the key provisions of the Act of 1986 as well as indicating where he believes a key loophole resides.

The Computer Fraud and Abuse Act of 1986 can be considered to represent a reaction to several well-publicized hacking operations. Those hacking operations include the use of what was then a relatively recently developed PC used with low-speed modems to provide a mechanism for persons to break into corporate merchandise-ordering files, government agency documents and—perhaps the straw that broke the proverbial camel's back—the White House switchboard. Concerning the latter, one group of hackers was able to penetrate the White House switchboard to obtain toll-free access to overseas joke lines. While the hackers may have considered this to be funny, legislatures did not, resulting in the Computer Fraud and Abuse Act being signed into law by then President Ronald Reagan on October 16, 1986.

Major provisions

The Act prohibits gaining unauthorized access to computers with respect to committing seven crimes. Those crimes are:

*Espionage
*Accessing unauthorized information
*Accessing non-public government computers
*Fraud by computer
*Damage to computer
*Trafficking in passwords
*Threats to damage a computer

Under the Act unauthorized access of a computer with intent to commit fraudulent theft is considered a felony. Another felony involves altering information in, or preventing the use of, a computer. Here a malicious damage violation has to result in the loss to the victim of $1000 or more, except in cases involving the alteration of medical records where this action is a felony regardless of the value of the loss.

Another interesting provision of the Act is the term Federal interest computer. This term is used to represent a computer used by a financial institution or the US Government or a computer which is one of two or more computers used in the offense, not all of which are located in the same state. Under this definition only federal and interstate computer crimes appear to be addressed. Thus, if a hacker runs a Denial of Service attack against a Web server in the same state they are located in, it appears that there would have to be a state law against this offense for the hacker to be prosecuted.

Another apparent problem with the Act is the fact that its provisions are primarily oriented towards unauthorized access and malicious damage, with the latter occurring via altering information. The Act does not define the spreading of damaging code nor does it have severe penalties for second-time offenders. In addition, the Act does not appear to address the manual or automated entry of data into forms on Web servers that allow persons to request free books, brochures, and similar information. Because the form is available for anybody to use and the Web sites do not have any published restrictions (such as 'only one copy per person'), it would appear that it is currently legal, although highly unethical, for a person to continuously fill in a form and request brochure after brochure or book after book. If the target Web site does not check addresses and the person requests delivery to one or a few addresses of willing participants, it appears that there is no law to block a poor form fulfillment process.

1.2 BOOK PREVIEW

In the remainder of this chapter we will turn our attention to obtaining a preview of the focus of material to be presented in succeeding chapters in this book. You can use this information either by itself or in conjunction with the index to locate information of particular interest. It should be noted that where possible each chapter was written in a modular fashion, independent of preceding and succeeding chapters. However, to obtain the maximum benefit it is recommended that if possible you should read this book in the order in which chapters are presented. The reason for this is due to the fact that, while this author attempted to make each chapter independent of preceding and succeeding chapters, there is no escape from the fact that knowledge is cumulative and the sequence of chapters provides a foundation of knowledge that may not be obvious if you jump to a particular chapter.

1.2.1 The TCP/IP protocol suite

The purpose of Chapter 2 is to provide a general overview of the TCP/IP protocol suite. In doing so we will review layer 3 and layer 4 protocols including IP, TCP and UDP. In addition, we will discuss the operation of ICMP as well as several TCP/IP applications. Besides providing a general overview of the TCP/IP protocol suite, we will describe and discuss several network vulnerabilities as we review the protocol suite. These vulnerabilities will be further addressed in succeeding chapters as we probe deeper into network attack methods and techniques available to block or minimize the effect of such methods. Thus, we can consider Chapter 2 as the chapter which provides a foundation of knowledge concerning the Transmission Control Protocol/Internet Protocol for those of us requiring a bit of tutorial information that will make subsequent chapters more meaningful.

1.2.2 Network attack methods

The third chapter in the book can be considered to officially begin our exploration of bulletproofing methods to secure our network and hosts on that network. In this chapter we will describe and discuss several network attack methods, ranging from spoofing attacks to denial of service and router disturbance. For each network attack method we will describe and discuss its operation and indicate how we can either block or minimize the effect of the attack method. Because many of these network attack methods are resolved through the use of communications equipment whose operations are described in detail in succeeding chapters, we will primarily describe network attack prevention methods in general terms in this chapter, referencing applicable chapters for detailed explanations of methods that can be used to block or minimize different types of network attack.

1.2.3 The security role of the router

In Chapter 4 we begin our examination of several communications devices that can be used to enhance network security. In this chapter we turn our attention to the router which due to its location as a gateway between networks results in the device becoming your first line of network defense. In discussing the security role of the router we will focus our attention upon two key areas, router access and packet filtering which is accomplished through the use of access lists.

Because most organizations with geographically separated networks cannot afford to have communications specialists physically located at each site, routers are primarily controlled remotely. This is a two-edged sword, as it allows remote administration, which significantly enhances employee productivity, while at the same time opening up the possibility that an unauthorized person could take control of your router. Thus, we will discuss in detail access control methods in the first portion of Chapter 4.

In the second portion of Chapter 4 we will turn our attention to router access lists, which provide a mechanism to perform packet filtering. In this second part of Chapter 4 we will examine the different types of access list that are supported by Cisco routers, since that vendor has approximately 70 percent of the market for this category of communications device. As we discuss and describe different types of Cisco access lists, we will also examine applicable configuration examples. While the use of access lists represents the first line of defense of a network there are certain actions and activities they cannot prevent. Thus, we will conclude Chapter 4 by discussing some of the limitations of access lists that will form the basis for our coverage of firewalls, which are presented in the next chapter in this book

1.2.4 The role of the firewall

Recognizing the limitations of router access lists makes coverage of firewalls a logical progression to the prior chapter. Thus, in Chapter 5 we will discuss and describe how firewalls operate and where they should be located for maximum effect. We will then illustrate some examples of how they are configured.

Similarly to router access lists, firewalls also have certain limitations. Two of those limitations are primarily in the area of virus checking and encryption, which are commonly supported on other devices. Thus, another natural progression is to examine these two areas in the next chapter, which is what we will do.

1.2.5 The role of virus scanners and encryption

In Chapter 6 we will turn our attention to the role of virus scanners and encryption. In doing so we will examine the use of centralized and decentralized products that provide these functions as well as the advantages and disadvantages associated with each approach to providing these functions.

1.2.6 Host attack methods

In Chapter 7 we begin our coverage of Windows NT/2000 security-related topics. Because it is quite possible that all our good intentions and efforts could come to naught by a sophisticated hacker or, for that matter, by an equipment failure, we will begin this chapter by discussing the role of the emergency repair disk and backup. Once this has been accomplished we will describe and discuss several common host attack methods as well as protection methods that can be employed to attempt to bulletproof your host computer.

1.2.7 Working with Windows

Because a key to preventing unauthorized network access or finding out your host is under attack is obtained from the Windows user account system, we will turn our attention to this topic in Chapter 8. In this chapter we will first review the different types of account supported by Windows NT/2000, the creation of applicable passwords that are difficult to compromise, and how we can perform auditing and observe the results of this action in an appropriate computer log.

No discussion of Windows security would be complete without a discussion of the Windows file system. Thus, we will also discuss this topic, examining the different types of file system supported and the advantages and disadvantages of their use with respect to security.

1.2.8 The role of the scanner

In the concluding chapter of this book we recognize that it is quite possible that our best efforts and intentions may result in one or more holes in our defensive barriers. Although we should check and recheck our work, we should also consider using scanning software that examines our network and hosts for potential vulnerabilities. This software is the focus of Chapter 9. In this chapter we will describe and discuss the role of scanning software and how the use of an appropriate product may save us from future embarrassment or much worse, having to reconstruct one or more databases due to an unexpected penetration.

2

THE TCP/IP PROTOCOL SUITE

The audience that reads a book consists of persons with a wide variety of knowledge and experience. Recognizing this fact, the purpose of this chapter is to provide readers with diverse backgrounds with the ability to obtain a common level of knowledge concerning the TCP/IP protocol suite. In this chapter we will initially focus our attention upon the relationship of the TCP/IP protocol suite to the ISO Reference Model. Once this has been accomplished we will examine TCP/IP layer 3 and layer 4 protocols in detail, noting the operation of IP, TCP, UDP and ICMP as well as the key topic of IP addressing.

2.1 COMPARISON TO THE ISO REFERENCE MODEL

TCP/IP represents one of the earliest developed layered protocol suites and it preceded the development of the International Standards Organization's (ISO's) Open System Interconnect (OSI) Reference Model by approximately 20 years. Although it predates the OSI Reference Model we can obtain an appreciation of the protocol suite by comparing it to that model.

Similar to the ISO Reference Model, the TCP/IP protocol suite is subdivided into distinct layers, commencing at the network layer. Although the protocol suite does not include equivalents to the lower two layers of the ISO Reference Model it provides a mechanism to translate addressing from the network layer of the reference model to Media Access Control (MAC) addresses used by LANs at the lower portion of the data link layer. This enables the TCP/IP protocol suite to use the physical layer supported by different LANs.

A second key difference between the ISO Reference Model and the TCP/IP protocol suite occurs at the top of the suite. TCP/IP

ISO Layers   The TCP/IP Protocol Suite

5-7	FTP	Telnet	SMTP	HTTP	SNMP	NFS	BOOTP
4	TCP				UDP		
3	ICMP IP ARP						
2	Ethernet	Token-Ring		FDDI		. . .	
1	Physical Layer						

Figure 2.1 Comparing the TCP/IP Protocol Suite to the ISO Reference Model. ARP: Address Resolution Protocol; BOOTP: Bootstrap Protocol; FTP: File Transfer Protocol; HTTP: HyperText Transmission Protocol; NFS: Network File System; SNMP: Simple Network Management Protocol

applications can be considered to represent the equivalent of layers 5 through 7 of the OSI Reference Model. Based upon the preceding, Figure 2.1 provides a general comparison of the TCP/IP protocol suite and the ISO Reference Model. Note that as previously mentioned the TCP/IP protocol suite commences at the equivalent of layer 3 of the ISO Reference Model. Thus, the dashed lines surrounding Ethernet, Token-Ring and FDDI layer 2 protocols and their physical layers indicate that they are not actually part of the TCP/IP protocol suite. Instead, the Address Resolution Protocol (ARP) which can be viewed as a facility of the Internet Protocol (IP) provides the translation mechanism which enables IP addressed packets to be correctly delivered to workstations that use MAC addresses. In fact, the TCP/IP protocol suite can also run over ATM, with a special type of address resolution used to resolve IP to ATM addresses. Thus, address resolution enables the TCP/IP protocol suite to be transported by other protocols and to use the physical layer specified by those protocols.

Now that we have an appreciation for the general relationship between the TCP/IP protocol stack and the ISO's Open System Interconnection Reference Model, let us turn our attention to the actual layers of the protocol suite.

2.2 THE NETWORK LAYER

The Internet Protocol (IP) represents the network layer protocol employed by the TCP/IP protocol suite. IP packets are formed by the addition of an IP header to the layer 4 protocol data entity which is either the Transport Control Protocol (TCP) or the User Datagram Protocol (UDP).

IP headers contain 32-bit source and destination addresses that are normally subdivided to denote a network address and host address on the network. In actuality, the host address is really an interface on the network since a host can have multiple interfaces, with each having a distinct address. However, over the years the terms host address and interface address have been used synonymously although this is not technically correct. Later in this chapter we will examine the IP header in detail.

2.3 ICMP

The Internet Control Message Protocol (ICMP) represents a diagnostic testing and error reporting mechanism that enables devices to generate various types of status and error reporting message. Two of the more popularly employed ICMP messages are the Echo Request and Echo Response packets generated by the Ping application.

Although Figure 2.1 indicates that ICMP is a layer 3 protocol, from a technical perspective an ICMP message is formed by the addition of an IP header to an ICMP message with the Type field within the IP header set to indicate that it is transporting an ICMP message. When we examine IP later in this chapter we will also turn our attention to the Internet Message Control Protocol.

2.4 THE TRANSPORT LAYER

The designers of the TCP/IP protocol suite recognized that two different types of data delivery transport protocol would be required. This resulted in two transport protocols supported by the protocol suite.

2.4.1 TCP

TCP is a reliable, connection-oriented protocol used to transport applications that require reliable delivery and for which actual data should not be exchanged until a session is established. From Figure 2.1 you will note that FTP, Telnet, SMTP, and HTTP are transported by TCP.

Because TCP is a connection-oriented protocol this mean thats actual data will not be transferred until a connection is established.

While this makes sense when you are transmitting a file or Web pages it also delays actual data transfer.

2.4.2 UDP

A second transport protocol supported by the TCP/IP protocol suite is UDP. UDP represents a connectionless protocol that operates on a best effort basis. This means that instead of waiting for confirmation that a destination is available, UDP will commence actual data transfer, leaving it to the application to determine if a response was received. Examples of applications that use UDP include SNMP, NFS and BOOTP.

The use of UDP and TCP results in the prefix of an appropriate header to application data. When TCP is used as the transport layer protocol, the TCP header and application data are referred to as a TCP segment. When UDP is used as the transport layer protocol, the UDP header and application data transported by UDP is referred to as a UDP datagram.

2.5 PORT NUMBERS

Because TCP and UDP were designed to transport multiple types of application data between a source and the same or different destinations, a mechanism was needed to distinguish one type of application from another. That mechanism is obtained by port number fields contained in TCP and UDP headers and explains how a Web server can also support FTP and other applications. Once again, we should note that later in this chapter we will turn our attention to the composition of TCP/IP transport protocol headers and the use of different port numbers.

2.6 APPLICATION DATA DELIVERY

In concluding this section we will examine the use of TCP/IP and LAN headers to facilitate the delivery of application data from a host on one network to a host on another network. Figure 2.2 illustrates the manner by which a LAN frame containing TCP/IP application data is formed. The LAN frame header uses a MAC destination address to direct the frame to a router. The router removes the LAN header and trailer and uses a wide area network

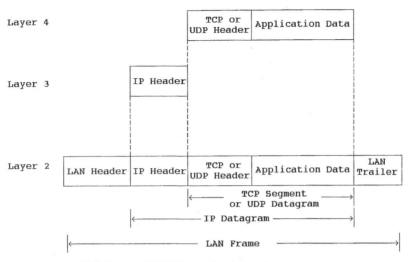

Figure 2.2 LAN delivery of TCP/IP application data

(WAN) protocol to transport the IP datagram. At the destination network another router receives the inbound packet, removes the WAN header and trailer, and encapsulates the IP datagram into a LAN frame for delivery to the appropriate IP address. However, since LAN frames use MAC addresses and TCP/IP applications use IP addresses, the router will either check its memory to determine if it previously discovered the MAC address associated with the destination IP address, or will use the Address Resolution Protocol (ARP) to discover the MAC address. Once the destination MAC address is known, the router can complete the formation of the LAN frame and transmit it onto the network for delivery to the appropriate device.

Now that we have an appreciation of the relationship of the TCP/IP protocol suite to the ISO's OSI Reference Model and an overview of the suite's main components, let us move up the protocol suite. To do so we will commence our detailed examination of the suite with the Internet Protocol (IP).

2.7 THE INTERNET PROTOCOL

In this section we continue to acquire a foundation of knowledge concerning the TCP/IP protocol suite by focusing attention upon the network layer in the suite. The Internet Protocol (IP) represents both the network layer protocol in the TCP/IP protocol suite as well as the data delivery mechanism which enables packets to be routed from source to destination.

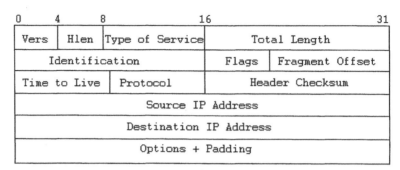

Figure 2.3   The IPv4 Header

In this section we will first examine the composition of the fields within the IP header. This will include a detailed examination of IP addressing since many network-related problems can be traced to this area. Because ICMP messages are transported via IP we will also examine the Internet Control Message Protocol.

2.7.1 The IPv4 header

The current version of the Internet Protocol is version 4. Fields in the IPv4 header are illustrated in Figure 2.3. In examining that illustration note that the header contains a minimum of 20 octets of data. Also note that the width of each field is shown in Figure 2.3 with respect to a 32-bit word.

In this chapter and succeeding chapters we will synonymously use the terms octet and byte to refer to the width of different header fields. The term octet was employed by standards organizations to explicitly refer to 8 bits operated upon as an entity at a time when computers were manufactured with different numbers of bits per byte. To alleviate potential confusion when referring to a group of eight bits, standards organizations turned to the term octet. Today essentially all computers use eight bit bytes and the terms byte and octet are commonly used synonymously. To obtain an appreciation for the functions performed by the IPv4 header, let us turn our attention to reviewing the functions of each of the fields in the header.

2.7.2 Vers field

The Vers field consists of four bits which identify the version of the IP protocol used to create the datagram. The current version of the IP protocol is 4 and the next generation of the IP protocol is assigned version number 6.

2.7.3 Hlen and Total Length fields

The second and fourth fields in the IPv4 header indicate the length of the header and the total length of the datagram, respectively. The Hlen field indicates the length of the IPv4 header in 32-bit words. In comparison, the Total Length field indicates the total length of the datagram including its header and higher layer information, such as a following TCP or UDP header and application data following either of those headers. Because the Total Length field consists of 16 bits, an IP datagram can be up to 2^{16}, or 65,535 octets in length.

2.7.4 Type of Service field

The Type of Service (TOS) field is one octet or 8 bits in length. The purpose of this field is to denote the importance of the datagram (precedence), delay, throughput and reliability requested by the originator.

Figure 2.4 illustrates the assignment of bit positions within the TOS field. Because the TOS field provides a mechanism to define priorities for the routing of IP datagrams it would appear that the TOS field could be used to provide a quality of service (QoS) for IP. Applications can set the appropriate values in the TOS field to indicate the type of routing path they would like. For example, a file transfer would probably request normal delay, high throughput and normal reliability. In comparison, a real time video application would probably select low delay, high throughput and high reliability. While this concept appears to provide a QoS, this is not the case as it does not provide a mechanism to reserve bandwidth. For example, ten stations, each requiring 512 Kbps, could all define an immediate priority for flowing through a router connected on a T1 circuit operating at 1.544 Mbps. Another problem associated with the TOS field is the fact that many routers ignore its settings. This is due to the fact that to support the TOS field a router would have to construct and maintain multiple routing tables which in the era of relatively slow processors when the Internet evolved was not an attractive option with router manufacturers. Thus, although this field provides a precedence definition capability, its use on a public network can be limited. Recognizing this limitation, plans were being developed to reuse

```
       0  1  2    3   4   5   6   7      bit positions
      ┌──────────────┬───┬───┬───┬──────────┐
      │  PRECEDENCE  │ D │ T │ R │  UNUSED  │
      └──────────────┴───┴───┴───┴──────────┘
```

```
Bits 0-2: Defines precedence
                    111 - Network control
                    110 - internetwork control
                    101 - Critic/ECP
                    100 - Flash override
                    011 - Flash
                    010 - Immediate
                    001 - Priority
                    000 - Routine
      Bit 3 Delay:          0 = normal, 1 = low delay
      Bit 4 Throughput:     0 = normal, 1 = high
      Bit 5 Reliability:    0 = normal, 1 = high
      Bits 6 and 7:         Reserved for future use (set to 0)
```

Figure 2.4   The Type of Service field

the TOS field as a mechanism to differentiate services requested when a data stream enters a network. This action resulted in a proposal to rename the TOS byte as a Diff Service field and an RFC was being developed to define its use when this book was written.

2.7.5 Identification field

The Identification field is two octets or 16 bits in length. This field is used to identify each fragmented datagram and is one of three fields that govern fragmentation. The other two are the Flags field and the Fragment Offset field.

IP fragmentation results when data flow between networks encounters different size maximum transmission units (MTUs). The MTU is commonly set when a device driver initializes an interface and represents the payload portion of a frame, i.e. the frame length less frame overhead. Most protocol stacks support MTUs up to 64K−1 octets (65,535). Another MTU is a per route MTU which represents the MTU that can be used without causing fragmentation from source to destination. Per route MTUs are usually maintained as a value in a host's routing table and set either by manual configuration or via a discovery process. When a route has interfaces with different MTUs and a large datagram must be transferred via an interface with a smaller MTU, the routing entity will either fragment the packet or drop it. As we will note in the next section, if the DON'T_FRAGMENT bit is set in the flag field the router will drop the datagram. This will result in the

Table 2.1 Flag field bit values.

_____

Bit 0 Reserved (set to 0)
Bit 1 0 = may fragment, 1 = don't fragment
Bit 2 0 = last fragment, 1 = more fragment(s) follow

_____

router generating an ICMP 'Destination Unreachable — Fragmentation Needed' message to the originator which will cause the MTU discovery algorithm to select a smaller MTU for the path and subsequent transmissions.

2.7.6 Flags field

This three-bit field indicates how fragmentation will occur. Bit 0 is reserved and set to zero, while the values of bits 1 and 2 define whether or not fragmentation can occur and if the present fragment is the last fragment or if one or more fragments follow. Table 2.1 lists the values associated with the three bits in the Flags field.

2.7.7 Fragment Offset field

The third field in the IPv4 header that is involved with fragmentation is the Fragment Offset field. This field is 13 bits in length and indicates where the fragment belongs in the complete message. The actual value placed in this field is an integer which corresponds to a unit of 8 octets and provides an offset in 64-bit units.

IP fragmentation places the burden of effort upon the receiving station and the routing entity. When a station receives an IP fragment it must fully reassemble the complete IP datagram prior to being able to extract the TCP segment, resulting in a requirement for additional buffer memory and CPU processing power at the receiver. In doing so it uses the values in the Fragment Offset field in each datagram fragment to correctly reassemble the complete datagram. Because the dropping of any fragment in the original datagram requires the original datagram to be present, most vendor TCP/IP protocol stacks set the DON'T_FRAGMENT bit in the Flag field. Setting that bit causes oversized IP datagrams to be dropped and results in an ICMP 'Destination Unreachable — Fragmentation Needed' message transmitted to the originator. This action results in the MTU discovery algorithm selecting a smaller MTU for the path and using that MTU for subsequent transmissions.

2.7.8 Time to Live field

The Time to Live (TTL) field is one octet in length. This field contains a value which represents the maximum amount of time a datagram can live. The use of this field prevents a mis-addressed or mis-routed datagram from endlessly wandering the Internet or a private IP network.

The value placed in the Time to Live field can represent router hops or seconds, with a maximum value for either being 255. Because an exact time is difficult to measure and requires synchronized clocks, this field is primarily used as a hop count field. That is, routers decrement the value in the field each time a datagram flows between networks. When the value of this field reaches zero the datagram is sent to the great bit bucket in the sky. The current recommended default Time to Live value for IP is 64.

2.7.9 Protocol field

The purpose of the Protocol field is to identify the higher layer protocol being transported within an IP datagram. By examining the value of this field, networking devices can determine if they have to look further into the datagram or should simply forward the datagram towards its destination. For example, a router that receives an IP datagram whose Protocol field value is 6 and which indicates that the higher layer protocol is TCP would simply forward the datagram towards its destination.

The eight bit positions in the Protocol field enable up to 256 protocols to be uniquely defined. Table 2.2 lists the current assignment of Internet protocol numbers. Although TCP and UDP by far represent the vast majority of upper layer protocol transmissions, other protocols can also be transported that govern the operation of networks, such as the Exterior Gateway Protocol (EGP) and Interior Gateway Protocol (IGP) that govern the interconnection of autonomous networks. In examining the entries in Table 2.2 note that a large block of numbers are currently unassigned. Also note that the evolving IPv6 uses a Next Header field in place of the Protocol field but uses the values contained in the table.

2.7.10 Checksum field

The tenth field in the IPv4 header is the Checksum field. This 16-bit or two-octet field protects the header and is also referred to as the Header Checksum field.

Table 2.2 Assigned Internet Protocol Numbers.

Decimal	Keyword	Protocol
0	HOPOPT	IPv6 Hop-by-Hop Option
1	ICMP	Internet Control Message
2	IGMP	Internet Group Management
3	GGP	Gateway-to-Gateway
4	IP	IP in IP (encapsulation)
5	ST	Stream
6	TCP	Transmission Control Protocol
7	CBT	CBT
8	EGP	Exterior Gateway Protocol
9	IGP	any private interior gateway (used by Cisco for their IGRP)
10	BBN-RCC-MON	BBN RCC Monitoring
11	NVP-II	Network Voice Protocol Version 2
12	PUP	PUP
13	ARGUS	ARGUS
14	EMCON	EMCON
15	XNET	Cross Net Debugger
16	CHAOS	Chaos
17	UDP	User Datagram
18	MUX	Multiplexing
19	DCN-MEAS	DCN Measurement Subsystems
20	HMP	Host Monitoring
21	PRM	Packet Radio Measurement
22	XNS-IDP	XEROX NS IDP
23	TRUNK-1	Trunk-1
24	TRUNK-2	Trunk-2
25	LEAF-1	Leaf-1
26	LEAF-2	Leaf-2
27	RDP	Reliable Data Protocol
28	IRTP	Internet Reliable Transaction
29	ISO-TP4	ISO Transport Protocol class 4
30	NETBLT	Bulk Data Transfer Protocol
31	MFE-NSP	MFE Network Services Protocol
32	MERIT-INP	MERIT Internodal Protocol
33	SEP	Sequential Exchange Protocol
34	3PC	Third Party Connect Protocol
35	IDPR	Inter-Domain Policy Routing Protocol
36	XTP	XTP
37	DDP	Datagram Delivery Protocol
38	IDPR-CMTP	IDPR Control Message Transport Protocol
39	TP++	TP++ Transport Protocol
40	IL	IL Transport Protocol
41	IPv6	Ipv6
42	SDRP	Source Demand Routing Protocol

Continued

Table 2.2 *Continued*

Decimal	Keyword	Protocol
43	IPv6-Route	Routing Header for IPv6
44	IPv6-Frag	Fragment Header for IPv6
45	IDRP	Inter-Domain Routing Protocol
46	RSVP	Reservation Protocol
47	GRE	General Routing Encapsulation
48	MHRP	Mobile Host routing Protocol
49	BNA	BNA
50	ESP	Encap security Payload for IPv6
51	AH	Authentication Header for IPv6
52	I-NLSP	Integrated Net Layer Security
53	SWIPE	IP with Encryption
54	NARP	NBMA Address Resolution Protocol
55	MOBILE	IP Mobility
56	TLSP	Transport Layer Security Protocol (using Kryptonet key management)
57	SKIP	SKIP
58	IPv6-ICMP	ICMP for IPv6
59	IPv6-NoNxt	No Next Header for IPv6
60	IPv6-Opts	Destination Options for IPv6
61		any host internal protocol
62	CFTP	CFTP
63		any local network
64	SAT-EXPAK	SATNET and Backroom EXPAK
65	KRYPTOLAN	Kryptolan
66	RVD	MIT Remote Virtual Disk Protocol
67	IPPC	Internet Pluribus Packet Core
68		any distributed file system
69	SAT-MON	SATNET Monitoring
70	VISA	VISA Protocol
71	IPCV	Internet Packet Core Utility
72	CPNX	Computer Protocol Network Executive
73	CPHB	computer Protocol Heart Beat
74	WSN	Wang Span Network
75	PVP	Packet Video Protocol
76	BR-SAT-MON	Backroom SATNET Monitoring
77	SUN-ND	SUN ND PROTOCOL-Temporary
78	WB-MON	WIDEBAND Monitoring
79	WB-EXPAK	WIDEBAND EXPAK
80	ISO-IP	ISO Internet Protocol
81	VMTP	VMTP
82	SECURE-VMTP	SECURE-VMPT
83	VINES	VINES
84	TTP	TTP
85	NSFNET-IGP	NSFNET-IGP

Continued

Table 2.2 *Continued*

Decimal	Keyword	Protocol
86	DGP	Dissimilar Gateway Protocol
87	TCF	TCF
88	EIGRP	EIGRP
89	OSPFIGP	OSPFIGP
90	Sprite-RPC	Sprite RPC Protocol
91	LARP	Locus Address Resolution Protocol
92	MTP	Multicast Transport Protocol
93	AX.25	AX.25 Frames
94	IPIP	IP-within-IP Encapsulation Protocol
95	MICP	Mobile Internetworking Control Protocol
96	SCC-SP	Semaphore Communications Sec. Protocol
97	ETHERIP	Ethernet-within-IP Encapsulation
98	ENCAP	encapsulation Header
99		any private encryption scheme
100	GMTP	GMTP
101	IFMP	Ipsilon Flow Management Protocol
102	PNNI	PNNI over IP
103	PIM	Protocol Independent Multicast
104	ARIS	ARIS
105	SCPS	SCPS
106	QNX	QNX
107	A/N	Active Networks
108	IPPCP	IP Payload Compression Protocol
109	SNP	Sitara Networks Protocol
110	Compaq-Peer	Compaq Peer Protocol
111	IPX-in-IP	IPX in IP
112	VRRP	Virtual Router Redundancy Protocol
113	PGM	PGM Reliable Transport protocol
114		any 0-hop protocol
115	L2TP	Layer Two Tunneling Protocol
116	DDX	D-II Data Exchange (DDX)
117–254		Unassigned
255		Reserved

2.7.11 Source and Destination address fields

Both the Source and Destination address fields are 32 bits in length. Each field contains an address that normally represents both a network address and a host address on the network. Because it is extremely important to understand IP addressing, this topic will be covered in detail in as a separate entity in this chapter.

2.7.12 Options and Padding fields

The Internet Protocol includes a provision for adding optional header fields. Such fields are identified by a value greater than zero in the field. Table 2.3 indicates IP Option field values based upon the manner by which the Option field is subdivided. That subdivision includes a one-bit copy flag, a two-bit class field, and a five-bit option number. The value column in Table 3.3 indicates the value of the eight-bit field. IP options are commonly referred to by this value.

Options whose values are 0 and 1 are exactly one-octet long which is their Type field. All other options have their one-octet Type field followed by a one-octet length field followed by one or more octets of option data. The optional padding occurs when it becomes necessary to expand the header to fall on a 32-bit word boundary.

2.7.13 IP addressing

IP addressing provides the mechanism which enables packets to be routed between networks as well as to be delivered to an appropriate host on a destination network. IPv4 uses 32-bit IP addresses to identify distinct device interfaces, such as interfaces that connect routers, workstations and gateways to networks, as well as to route data to those devices. Each device interface in an IP network must be assigned a unique IP address to enable it to receive communications addressed to the interface. Normally workstations have a single interface in the form of a LAN connection which would be assigned an IP address. However, routers typically have more than one interface and some high performance servers may have two network connections. In such instances each device interface would have a separate IP address.

2.7.14 Overview

The Internet Protocol was standardized in September 1981. At that time the standard included a requirement for each host connected to an IP-based network to be assigned a unique 32-bit address value for each network connection. This resulted in some networking devices that have multiple interfaces, such as routers, gateways and servers being assigned a unique IP address for each network interface.

Table 2.3 IP Option field values.

Copy	Class	Number	Value	Name
0	0	0	0	EOOL End of Options List
0	0	1	1	NOP No Operation
1	0	2	130	SEC Security
1	0	3	131	LSR Loose Source Route
0	2	4	68	TS Time Stamp
1	0	5	133	E-SEC Extended Security
1	0	6	134	CIPSO Commercial Security
0	0	7	7	RR Record Route
1	0	8	136	SID Stream ID
1	0	9	137	SSR Strict Source Route
0	0	10	10	ZSU Experimental Measurement
0	0	11	11	MTUP MTU Probe
0	0	12	12	TRUR MTU Reply
1	2	13	205	FINN Experimental Flow Control
1	0	14	142	VISA Experimental Access Control
0	0	15	15	ENCODE
1	0	16	144	IMITD IMI Traffic Descriptor
1	0	17	145	EIP
0	2	18	82	TR Traceroute
1	0	19	147	ADDEXT Address Extension
1	0	20	148	RTRALT Router Alert
1	0	21	149	SDB Selective Directed Broadcast
1	0	22	150	NSAPA NSAP Addresses

To illustrate the assignment of IP addresses to interfaces, consider Figure 2.5 which shows two bus-based Ethernet LANs connected by a pair of routers. Note that each workstation and server on each LAN has a single interface in this example. Thus, each of those devices would be associated with a single IP address by the assignment of one IP address to each device interface. Each router has two interfaces, with one connected to a LAN while a second represents a serial port used to interconnect routers via a WAN. Thus, each router would be assigned two IP addresses, one assigned to its LAN interface while the other would be assigned to its serial interface. Through the assignment of addresses to each device interface, this method of addressing enables datagrams to be correctly routed when a device has two or more network connections.

2.7.15 The basic addressing scheme

During the development of the TCP/IP protocol suite it was recognized that internetworking two or more networks required

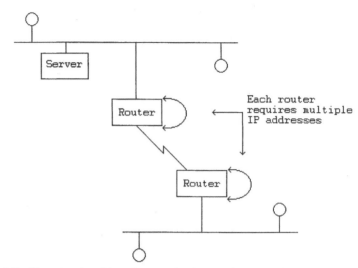

Figure 2.5 IP network addressing results in a unique 32-bit network address assigned to each device network interface. ○: workstations

distinct network addresses to differentiate one network from another. Because each host on a network also required a distinct address, a mechanism was required to identify a network as well as a host connected to a network. Although some protocols, such as NetWare's IPX, use separate network and host addresses, the designers of the TCP/IP protocol suite looked for a method to subdivide IP address space so that one address field in the IP header could identify the network and the host on the network, with the latter actually the interface since IP addresses are assigned to interfaces. The result was the development of a two-level addressing hierarchy which is illustrated in Figure 2.6.

Under the two-level IP addressing scheme all hosts on the same network must be assigned the same network prefix; however, each host must have a unique address to differentiate it from another host on the same network. Similarly, two hosts on different networks must be assigned different network prefixes; however, the hosts can have the same host address.

2.7.16 Address classes

The two-level IP addressing scheme illustrated in Figure 2.6 represents the most common method of routing data from source to destination over an IP network. However, as we will soon note, IPv4 supports other addressing schemes. Those schemes, as well

Under the two level IP addressing hierarchy, the 32-bit IP
address is subdivided into network and host portions. The
composition of the first four bits of the 32-bit word specifies
whether the network portion is 1, 2, or 3 bytes in length,
resulting in the host portion being either 3, 2, or 1 bytes in
length, respectively.

Figure 2.6 The two-level Internet Protocol (IP) addressing hierarchy

as the two-level IP addressing scheme, were developed in
recognition of the fact that the use of a single method of subdivision
of the IPv4 32-bit address space would be wasteful with respect to
the assignment of addresses. For example, if the address space was
split evenly into a 16-bit network and a 16-bit host number, the
result would be a maximum of 65,535 (2^{16}) networks, with up to
65,535 hosts per network. In actuality there are certain host
addresses that cannot be used which slightly reduces the number
of hosts that can reside on an IP network. Later in this section we
will turn our attention to those addresses. However, returning to
our address splitting example, the assignment of a network
number to an organization that only had 200 computers would
result in a waste of 65,334 host addresses that could not be
assigned to another organization. Recognizing this problem as well
as recognizing the need to obtain flexibility in assigning address
space to different organizations resulted in the subdivision of the
32-bit address space into different address classes. Today, IPv4
address space consists of five address classes that are referred to
as Class A through Class E. Of the five address classes, Class A
through Class C are subdivided into a network identifier and
host identifier. Class D and Class E do not incorporate two-level
addressing as they represent special IP addressing. Class D
addresses are used for IP multicasting, where a single message is
distributed to a group of hosts dispersed across one or more
networks that join a multicast group to receive the message.
Through IP multicasting a single voice or video data stream can be
transmitted to multiple recipients on the same or different networks, significantly reducing the use of precious bandwidth. Class
E addresses are reserved for experimental use. Although Class D
and Class E addresses are single level addresses, they are similar
to Class A through C addresses in that they are 32 bits in length
and are identified in the same manner.

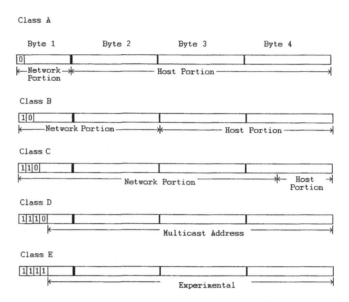

Figure 2.7 IPv4 address formats

2.7.17 Address formats

Figure 2.7 illustrates the five IPv4 address formats, including the bit allocation in the first byte of each format which identifies the address class. Once an address class is identified the subdivision of the remainder of the address into network and host address portions can be automatically noted.

Addresses within a specific address class are assigned by the Internet Network Information Center (InterNIC). To obtain an appreciation for the use of each address class let us first turn our attention to the composition and notation of IP address. Once this has been accomplished we will then examine special IP addresses and each address class.

2.7.18 Address composition and notation

IPv4 addresses are specified in terms of 32 bits for source and destination. Because we would prefer not to work with 32-bit strings, dotted decimal notation was developed as a method to facilitate specifying the IP address.

Under dotted decimal notation the binary value of an 8-bit byte is expressed as a decimal number between 0 and 255. Because a

32-bit IPv4 address is equivalent to four bytes, the use of dotted decimal notation permits four decimal numbers to be used in place of a 32-bit binary string. Since periods are used to separate each decimal number the term dotted decimal notation is used to reference the use of a string of four decimal numbers separated from one another by periods to represent a 32-bit binary IP address.

To illustrate the use of dotted decimal notation, consider the following IP address expressed as a 32-bit binary number:

11001111 00000010 10000000 10101010

If you remember, the bit values of a byte are as follows:

128 64 32 16 8 4 2 1

Then, the dotted decimal address for the above 32-bit binary IP address becomes:

207.2.128.170

2.7.19 Special IP addresses

There are several special IP addresses that have predefined functions. Those addresses and their meanings are listed in Table 2.4.

In examining the entries in Table 2.4 note that a subnet represents a subdivision of a network obtained by the expansion of the network portion of the address to the detriment of the host portion of the address. The expanded portion of the network address is used to denote a subnet which is only applicable internally within an organization's network structure. Later in this chapter we will examine subnets in detail.

Returning to Table 2.4, note that an IP address of either all 0's or all 1's has a special meaning. Because a host value of all 0's and all 1's is part of the first two special addresses in Table 2.4, it cannot be used for a host address. This means that when we compute the number of possible hosts on a Class A, B or C network we must reduce the total by two. Similarly, we must reduce the number of hosts on a subnet by two to take into account a host value of zero and a host value of all 1's that have special subnet meanings.

In examining Table 2.4 note that any address with all 0's in the network portion of the address is used to represent 'this' network. Also note that an old form of broadcasting known as the all 0's takes the form of 0.0.0.0. You should not use this old broadcasting

Table 2.4 Special IP Addresses.

Address	Description
Network = 0, Host = 00	This host on this network.
Network = 0all 1's, Host = 0 all 1's	Direct broadcast to network.
Subnet = 0all 1's, Host = 0all 1's	Direct broadcast to all subnets on the network.
Host = 0 all 1's on any subnet	Direct broadcast to all hosts on the specified subnet.
Network = 0127, Host = any	Internal host loopback address

address as that address is now used in a routing table to indicate a default route.

Finally, note that an address prefix of 127 represents an internal host loopback address and cannot be assigned to any host as a unique address. This address can be used to determine if a host's TCP/IP protocol stack is operational. For example, in a Windows NT/Windows 2000 environment you can Ping yourself by using 127.0.0.1. In fact, because 127.*anything* represents a loopback, you could also use 127.0.0.2 or even 127.255.255.255. Now that we have an appreciation for special IP addresses, let us turn our attention to the five IPv4 classes.

Class A

A Class A IPv4 address is defined by a 0-bit value in the high order bit position of the 32-bit address. This setting indicates that the address has the following 4-byte format:

<network number.host.host.host>

Because the network portion of the Class A address uses one bit for identification, only 7 bits in the first byte are available for network addressing. Out of the 128 combinations all 0's and all 1's cannot be used. This is because all 0's represent 'this host on this network' and all 1's provide an internal loopback address. Thus, a maximum of 126 network addresses are permitted. Those addresses range from 1 to 126.

The 3-byte host field of a Class A address cannot have all 0's nor all 1's. Thus, it supports $2^{24} - 2$ or 16,277,214 hosts per network. Due to the relatively small number of Class A networks that can be defined and the large number of hosts that can be supported per network, Class A addresses are primarily assigned to large organizations and countries that have national IP-based networks. Another use of Class A addresses is for use by Internet Service Providers as a mechanism to issue Classless InterDomain Routing Protocol (CIDR) addresses. CIDR addressing is covered later in this section.

Class B

The setting of the two high order bits in an IPv4 address to a value of '10' indicates a Class B address. This address takes the following form:

<network number.network number.host.host>

The network portion of a Class B address cannot use the first 2 bit positions as they identify the network class. Thus, the number of distinct networks becomes 2^{14} or 16,384 network numbers. Each network number is capable of supporting $2^{16}-2$ or 65,354 hosts.

Because the first two bits in the Class B address are set to a value of '10,' network numbers are restricted to the decimal range of 128 to 191 in the first portion of the dotted decimal notation for Class B addresses. Since a Class B address supports a large but not extravagant population of hosts, such addresses are normally assigned to relatively large organizations with tens of thousands of employees. Today just about all Class B addresses are allocated and only when a previously allocated Class B address is returned is it possible to obtain the use of this type of IPv4 address.

Class C

A Class C address is identified by the setting of the three high-order bits in a 32-bit IPv4 address to a value of '110', This results in the form of the Class C address being noted as follows:

<network number.network number.network number.host>

The use of three bits to identify the network address as a Class C address reduces the number of bits that can be used to identify a particular network address from 24 to 21. This enables 2^{21} or 2,097,152 possible network addresses to be supported. Because a Class C address uses eight bits for the portion of the host address, this means that each Class C address can support up to 2^8-2 or 254 hosts.

Because the first byte of a Class C address will always have the composition 110*xxxxx* where *x* represents any binary value, the allowable network range is decimal 192–233 in the first field used for dotted decimal representation of a Class C address. Class C addresses are primarily assigned for use by relatively small networks, such as an organizational LAN requiring a connection to the Internet. Because it is common for many organizations to have multiple LANs, it is also common for multiple Class C addresses to be assigned to organizations that require more than 254 host addresses.

Class D

The assignment of a value of '1110' to the first four bit positions in a 32-bit IPv4 address defines a Class D address. The remaining 28 bits in the address are used to define 2^{28} or approximately 268 million possible multicast addresses.

Multicasting is an addressing technique which allows a source to send a single copy of a datagram to a specific group of recipients through the use of a multicast address. Each recipient dynamically registers to join the multicast group. As multicast traffic flows through a network only recipients registered to receive an appropriate multicast session read the traffic denoted by the lower order 28 bits within a 32-bit Class D address. Other stations that are not members of a multicast group only have to read the first 4 bits of the address to note it is a Class D address and can then ignore the remainder of the address.

To obtain an appreciation for the manner by which a Class D address conserves bandwidth, consider a digitized audio or video presentation routed from the Internet onto a private network for which a dozen employees on the network wish to receive the presentation. Without a multicast transmission capability a dozen separate audio or video data streams would be transmitted onto the private network, with each stream containing packets with a dozen distinct host addresses. In comparison, the use of a multi-cast address allows one data steam to be routed to the private network on which each registered station reads appropriate traffic. Because audio or video data streams can require a relatively large amount of bandwidth, the ability to eliminate multiple data streams via multicast transmission can prevent networks from becoming saturated, as well as considerably reducing traffic on the Internet. Since the first four bits in a Class D address are set to a value of '1110', the range of Class D addresses lies between 224 and 239 for the first decimal position when the address is expressed as a dotted decimal number.

Class E

The assignment of the binary value '1111' to the first four bits in a 32-bit IPv4 address denotes a Class E address. This address is reserved for experimentation.

Class E addresses range between 240 and 254 in their first decimal position when the IPv4 address is expressed as a dotted decimal number. Table 2.5 summarizes IPv4 address classes based upon values permissible in the network or first byte portion of the address when expressed in dotted decimal notation.

2.7.20 Reserved addresses

No discussion of IPv4 address classes would be complete without focusing attention upon three blocks of reserved addresses. Such addresses were originally reserved for networks that would not be connected to the Internet and are defined in RFC 1918, 'Address Allocation for Private Internets'.

Table 2.6 lists the three address blocks defined in RFC 1918. The use of addresses in one or more address blocks defined by RFC 1918 is primarily based upon security considerations as well as the difficulty organizations can face in attempting to obtain relatively scarce Class B or Class A IPv4 addresses.

Because the use of any private RFC 1918 Internet address by two or more organizations connected to the Internet would result in addressing conflicts and the unreliable delivery of information, those addresses are not directly used. Instead, organizations either use a router with a network address translation (NAT) capability or a proxy firewall to provide an address translation capability between a large number of private Internet addresses used on the internal private network and a lesser number of assigned IP addresses. For example, an organization with a thousand work-stations could assign one RFC Class B address internally and translate those addresses to one Class C issued address, permitting up to 254 IP sessions at a time to be supported. In addition to enabling organizations to connect large internal networks to the Internet without having to obtain relatively scarce Class A or Class B addresses, NAT hides internal addresses from the Internet community. This action results in a degree of security as any hacker that attempts to attack a host cannot directly do so. Instead, he must attack an organization's router or proxy firewall which hopefully is hardened by the manufacturer to resist such attacks.

Table 2.5 Permissible IPv4 First Byte Values.

Class	Length of network address (bits)	Decimal values
Class A	8	0–127
Class B	16	128–191
Class C	24	192–223
Class D	N/A	224–239
Class E	N/A	240–254

Table 2.6 Reserved IPv4 addresses for private Internet use (RFC 1918).

Address Blocks
10.0.0.0–10.255.255.255
172.16.0.0–172.31.255.255
192.168.0.0–192.168.255.255

Although RFC 1918 addresses are a valuable feature for creating private internets whose addresses can be translated into valid IP addresses for routing over the Internet, they are also unfortunately a favorite for use in address spoofing. That is, when a hacker wants to attack a particular location they will commonly configure their protocol stack with an RFC 1918 source address. Other popular spoofed addresses include the use of a loopback address and the address of a host on the network to be attached. Later in this book we will discuss address spoofing and various counter-measures that can be employed in detail.

2.7.21 Subnetting and the subnet mask

The use of IP addresses represents a precious resource. Recognizing the limited number of network addresses available for use as well as the need of organizations to create more manageable networks, the IETF approved subnetting in RFC 950 as a mechanism to share a single network address among two or more networks. To better understand the need for subnetting, consider a Class B address. That address permits up to 65,535 hosts. However, it would be both a performance and an administrative nightmare to have one network with that number of hosts. Thus, subnetting provides users with the ability to subdivide a Class B network as well as Class A and Class C networks into more manageable entities.

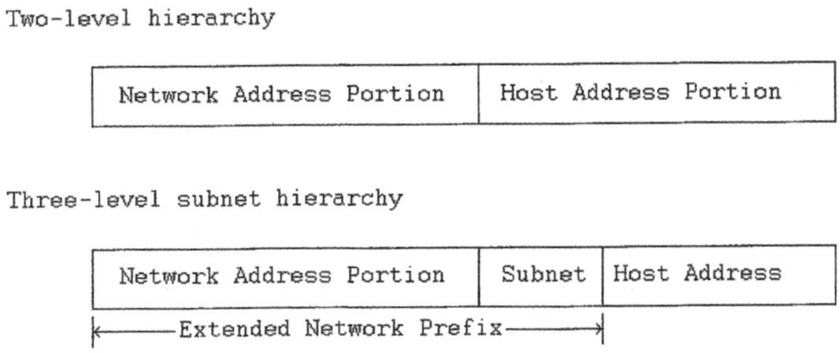

Two-level hierarchy

Network Address Portion	Host Address Portion

Three-level subnet hierarchy

Network Address Portion	Subnet	Host Address

|←————Extended Network Prefix————→|

Figure 2.8 Creating a subnet by extending the network prefix into the host address portion of a Class A, B or C address

Subnetting represents an extension of the network portion of a Class A, B or C address internally to an organization. Through the process of subnetting, the two-level IPv4 address hierarchy of Class A, B and C addresses is turned into a three-level hierarchy.

Figure 2.8 illustrates the creation of a subnet by the extension of the network address to the detriment of the host portion of an address. Note that the resulting action produces a subnet field and a reduced length host field, which reduces the number of hosts that can reside on each subnet.

Through subnetting a Class A, B, or C network address can be extended, with the extension divided into different subnet numbers. Each subnet number can be used to identify a different network internal to an organization. However, because the network portion of the address does not change, all subnets appear externally to be located on the same network. This means that routing tables on devices that form the backbone of the Internet need to recognize a lesser number of network addresses which simplifies routing. This also means that routers within an organization must be able to differentiate between different subnets.

To illustrate the subnet process consider an organization that within a building operates five Ethernet networks, with between 20 and 30 stations on each network. Although the organization could apply for five Class C addresses and assign one address to each network, doing so would waste precious Class C address space since each Class C address supports a maximum of 254 devices. In addition, the assignment of five Class C addresses would result in configuring numerous routers on the Internet to note those addresses. This in turn would adversely effect bandwidth utilization on the Internet, as five router table entries would be transmitted each time routers broadcast the contents of their routing tables.

```
Base Network:   11001101.10000011.10101111.00000000 = 205.131.175.0

Subnet #0:      11001101.10000011.10101111.00000000 = 205.131.175.0

Subnet #1:      11001101.10000011.10101111.00100000 = 205.131.175.32

Subnet #2:      11001101.10000011.10101111.01000000 = 205.131.175.64

Subnet #3:      11001101.10000011.10101111.01100000 = 205.131.175.96

Subnet #4:      11001101.10000011.10101111.10000000 = 205.131.175.128

Subnet #5:      11001101.10000011.10101111.10100000 = 205.131.175.160

Subnet #6:      11001101.10000011.10101111.11000000 = 205.131.175.192

Subnet #7:      11001101.10000011.10101111.11100000 = 205.131.175.224
```

Figure 2.9 Creating extended network prefixes via subnetting

Because we need to support five networks at one location, we would extend the network portion of one Class C address by 3 bit positions. This is because 2^3 provides 8 subnets, while 2^2 provides 4 which is insufficient. Because a Class C address uses one 8-bit byte for host identification, this also means that a maximum of five bit positions $(8-3)$ can be used for the host number. This reduces the number of hosts that can reside on each subnet to 2^5-2 or 30, which is sufficient for our example.

Let us assume we obtained the Class C network address 205.131.175.0 for our subnetting effort. To use that network we would extend its network prefix by three bit positions as illustrated in Figure 2.9.

In examining Figure 2.9 note that the top entry labeled 'Base Network', represents the Class C network address with a host address byte field set to all zeros. Because we previously decided to use three bits from the host portion of the Class C IPv4 address, the entries below the base network indicate the use of three bits from the host position in the address to create extended prefixes to identify all possible distinct subnets.

For each subnet there are several addressing restrictions that reduce the number of hosts, or more correctly, interfaces that can be supported. First, you cannot use a base subnet of all 0's or all 1's. Thus, for subnet 0 in Figure 2.9 valid host addresses would range from 1 to 30, while for subnet 1 valid host addresses would range from 33 to 61, and so on.

A second limitation on subnetting for Class A, B and C addresses concerns the subdivision of the last byte of an IP address. Because a subnet must be able to have some hosts residing on it, you can only use up to six bits in the last byte when you create a subnet mask. Thus, the maximum class C subnet would be 6 bits, while the maximum Class A and B subnets would be 22 and 14 bits, respectively.

Although the use of a three-bit subnet mask permits eight subnets to be defined, our requirement was to assign subnets to five LANs. Thus, we will use subnet 0 through subnet 4 shown in Figure 2.9 although we could select any five of the eight subnets. To the router connecting the organization's network to the Internet, all five subnets we will use would appear as the network address 205.131.175.0, with the router of our organization being responsible for directing traffic to the appropriate subnet. It is important to note that external to the organization there is no knowledge of the dotted decimal numbers shown in the right column of Figure 2.9, which represent distinct subnets. This results from the fact that routers external to the organization view the binary value of the first byte of each dotted decimal number and note that the first two bits are set. This informs each router that the address is a Class C address and that the first three bytes represent the network portion of the IPv4 address, while the last byte represents the host address. Thus, to the outside world the 205.131.175.32 address would not be recognized as subnet 1 on network 205.131.175.0. Instead, routers external to the organization would interpret the address as network 205.131.175.0 with a host address of 32. Similarly, subnet four would be recognized as a Class C network address of 205.131.175.0 with a host address of 128. However, within the organization internally each of the IPv4 addresses listed in the right column in Figure 2.9 would be interpreted and recognized as a subnet. Figure 2.10 illustrates the difference between viewing the network internally and externally.

2.7.22 Host addresses on subnets

Although we briefly discussed some subnet addressing rules we have yet to denote how we assign host addresses to devices connected to different subnets nor how routers can examine an IPv4 address so it can correctly route traffic to an appropriate subnet. Thus, let us turn our attention to these topics.

In Figure 2.9 we subdivided the host portion of the Class C address into a 3-bit subnet field and a 5-bit host field. Because we cannot use a host field address of all 0's nor all 1's this means each subnet can support a maximum of $2^5 - 2$ or 30 addresses. Thus, we

Subnet 2: <u>11001101.10000011.10101111.010</u>00000 = 205.131.175.64

Host 1:   <u>11001101.10000011.10101111.010</u>00001 = 205.131.176.65

Host 2:   <u>11001101.10000011.10101111.010</u>00010 = 205.131.176.66

            .   .   .   .   .   .

            .   .   .   .   .   .

            .   .   .   .   .   .

Host 30:   11001101.10000011.10101111.01011110 = 205.131.176.94

Figure 2.10 Assigning host addresses to Subnet 2

could use host addresses 1 through 30 on subnet 0, 33 through 62 on subnet 1, and so on. Remembering the restriction that we cannot use all 0's nor all 1's in the host portion of a subnet governs our ability to assign host addresses by subnet. This is illustrated in Figure 2.11, which indicates how we could assign host addresses to subnet 2 whose creation was previously indicated in Figure 2.9. In examining Figure 2.11 note that we commence our addressing operation with the subnet address 205.131.175.64 for which the first three bits in the fourth byte are used to indicate the subnet. Then, we use the remaining five bits to define the host address on each subnet. Thus, the address 205.131.175.64 represents the second subnet on the 205.131.175.0 network, while addresses 205.131.175.65 through 205.131.175.94 represent hosts 1 through 30 that can reside on subnet 2.

While the previously presented information explained how we can create subnets and host addresses on subnets, an unanswered question is how devices on a private network recognize subnet addressing. For example, assume that an IP datagram with the destination address of 205.131.175.65 arrives at your organization's router. How does that router know to route the datagram onto subnet 2? The answer to this question is the use of a subnet mask, so let us turn our attention to this topic.

2.7.23 The subnet mask

The subnet mask is a sequence of binary 1's that indicates the length of the network address, including any subnetting that has occurred. Thus, the subnet mask provides a mechanism that enables communications devices on a network to determine the

```
Subnet 2:  11001101.10000011.10101111.01000000 = 205.131.175.64

Host 1:    11001101.10000011.10101111.01000001 = 205.131.176.65

Host 2:    11001101.10000011.10101111.01000010 = 205.131.176.66

     .         .        .        .        .        .

     .         .        .        .        .        .

     .         .        .        .        .        .

Host 30:   11001101.10000011.10101111.01011110 = 205.131.176.94
```

Figure 2.11   Assigning host addresses to Subnet 2

separation of an IP address into its network, subnet and host portions.

To illustrate the use of the subnet mask, let us assume our network address is 205.131.175.0 and we need to develop a subnet mask that can be used to identify the extended network as well as the subnet and host on the subnet. Because we previously extended the network by 3 bits the subnet would become:

$$11111111.11111111.11111111.11100000$$

Note that the above mask can be expressed in dotted decimal notation as 255.255.255.224.

The subnet mask tells a communications device which bits in an IP address should be treated as an extended network address consisting of network and subnet addresses. Then, the remaining bits that are not set indicate the host on the extended network address. Because the first or first few bits in an IP address denote the address class, a communications device that examines those bits determines the number of bits in the network portion of the address. Subtracting that value from the number of bits in the subnet mask indicates the subnet field, allowing the device to note the subnet. For example, consider the IPv4 address 205.131.175.66 and the subnet mask 255.255.255.244. The address 205.131.175.66 has the first two bits in the address set, representing a Class C address which uses 3 bytes or 24 bits for the network address. Because the subnet mask represents 27 set bits, this indicates that the subnet is 27−24 or 3 bits in length and occurs in bit positions 25 through 27 in the IP address. Because bits 25 through 27 have the bit composition 010, this indicates that the subnet is subnet 2. Because the last five bits have the value 00010, this indicates host 2 on subnet 2. Figure 2.12 illustrates the previously described relationship.

To facilitate the ability to work with subnets, Table 2.7 contains a listing of the number of subnets that can be created for IPv4 Class B and C addresses, their subnet masks, the number of hosts that can reside on a network and the total number of hosts capable of being supported by a particular subnet mask. Thus, this table can be used as a guide for considering the extension of a network address internally to form a subnet. In examining the entries in Table 2.7 note that the total number of hosts can vary considerably based upon the use of different subnet masks, and it should be carefully considered prior to performing the subdivision of a network.

In Table 2.8 you will find an additional subnet mask reference. This table indicates the dotted decimal value associated with the use of different numbers of subnet bits in the last byte of a subnet mask.

2.7.24 Configuration examples

There is an old adage that states 'the proof of the pudding is in its eating'. We can apply this adage to the information previously discussed about IP addressing by turning our attention to the manner by which workstations and servers are configured to operate on a TCP/IP network.

When configuring a workstation or server to operate on a TCP/IP network, most operating systems will require you to enter a minimum of three IP addresses and an optional subnet mask. The three IP addresses you will normally configure include the IP address assigned to the interface of a workstation or server, the IP address of the gateway responsible for relaying packets with a

```
IP address:      205.131.175.66      11001101.10000011.10101111.01000010
Subnet mask:     255.255.255.224     11111111.11111111.11111111.11100000

Extended Network Address                 |———— 27 bit positions ————→|

First 2 bits of IP address            = 11
   Indicates Class C address

Network portion of Class C address    |←—24 bit positions ————→|

Subnet field = Extended Address  - Network Portion of Address  |←3→|
   Value of subnet = 010 = 2                                     bits
Host portion of subnet is 8 - 3 bits                          |←—5→|
   Value of host on subnet 2 is 00010 or 2                      bits
```

Figure 2.12   The relationship between an IP address, its subnet mask, subnet value, and host value on the subnet

Table 2.7 Subnet mask reference.

Number of subnet bits	Subnet mask	Number of subnetworks	Hosts/subnet	Total number of hosts
Class B				
1	—	—	—	—
2	255.255.192.0	2	16382	32764
3	255.255.224.0	6	8190	49140
4	255.255.240.0	14	4094	57316
5	255.255.248.0	30	2046	61380
6	255.255.252.0	62	1022	63364
7	255.255.254.0	126	510	64260
8	255.255.255.0	254	254	64516
9	255.255.255.128	510	126	64260
10	255.255.255.192	1022	62	63364
11	255.255.255.224	2046	30	61380
12	255.255.255.240	4094	14	57316
13	255.255.255.248	8190	6	49140
14	255.255.255.252	16382	2	32764
15	—	—	—	—
16	—	—	—	—
Class C				
1	—	—	—	—
2	255.255.255.192	2	62	124
3	255.255.255.224	6	30	180
4	255.255.255.240	14	14	196
5	255.255.255.248	30	6	170
6	255.255.255.252	62	2	124
7	—	—	—	—
8	—	—	—	—

destination address different from the local network off the local network, and the address of a name resolver. The gateway represents an old term for the modern router. The resolver is a computer responsible for translating host addresses entered in a browser, FTP or Telnet client applications, or another application into its IP address as routing in a TCP/IP environment is based upon IP addresses. The name resolver is also referred to as a Domain Name Server or DNS.

Figure 2.13 illustrates the first configuration screen in a series of screens displayed by the Windows 95 TCP/IP properties dialog box. In the example illustrated in Figure 2.13 note that we entered an IP address of 205.131.175.66 and a subnet mask of 255.255.255.224. This informs the protocol stack that the workstation is a Class C address since a 205 value in the first byte

Table 2.8 Subnet masks.

Subnet bits	Host bits	Decimal mask
0	8	0
1	7	128
2	6	192
3	5	224
4	4	240
5	3	248
6	2	252
7	1	254
8	0	255

indicates this fact. Because the subnet mask has 27 set bits (224 decimal is 11100000 in binary) and the network portion of a Class C address is 24 bits, the protocol stack knows that the first three bits in the fourth byte of the IP address represents the subnet. Because decimal 66 has a binary value of 01000010, this indicates that the workstation resides on subnet 2. Similarly, because the last five bits in the fourth byte of the IP address represent the host on the subnet a decimal value of 66 indicates host 2 on subnet 2. Because we previously specified in this section we would use a 3-bit subnet, a subnet mask of 255.255.255.224 was entered in Figure 3.11. The last decimal digit corresponds to the 3-bit subnet entry in Table 2.8 and indicates how you can use that table if you have an aversion to working with binary numbers.

Returning to the TCP/IP properties display shown in Figure 2.13, note that by clicking on different tabs you can display different configuration screens. For example, clicking on the tab labeled 'Gateway' results in the display shown in Figure 2.14. In this screen you would enter the IP address of one or more gateways so the TCP/IP protocol stack on the workstation will know where to send IP datagrams whose destination addresses are not on the local network.

A third configuration screen which is used to specify the address of the name resolver is shown in Figure 2.15. At this level clicking on the tab labeled DNS Configuration provides you with the ability to specify your computer's host and domain name as well as the IP address of one or more DNS servers. In Figure 2.15 the host name is shown entered as 'gil' while the DNS domain name was entered as 'feds.gov'. This informs the domain server at the indicated address that requests to access the host address gil.feds.gov should be routed to the IP address previously entered into the IP

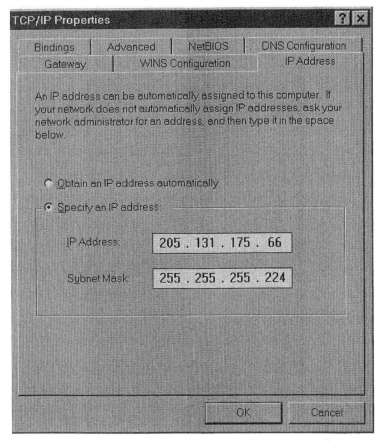

Figure 2.13   The first configuration screen in a series of screens displayed by the Windows 95 TCP/IP Properties dialog box

configuration screen. If no network users will be addressing a computer by its host name you can leave those entries blank.

2.7.25 Classless networking

Although the term classless normally refers to a person without taste, when applied to IPv4 addressing it represents a technique to more efficiently assign addresses to organizations. Classless networking is a technique which does away with network classes, enabling the inefficiencies associated with allocating Class A, B and C addresses to organizations that have a limited number of devices to be overcome.

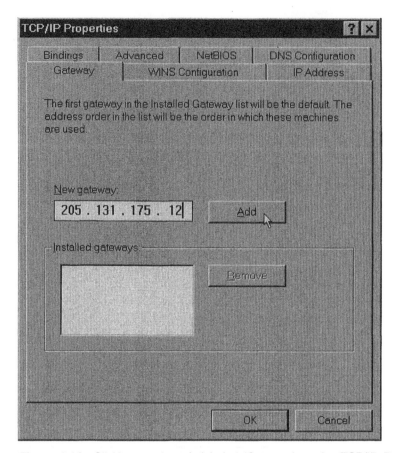

Figure 2.14 Clicking on the tab labeled 'Gateway' on the TCP/IP Properties dialog box results in this display

Under classless networking an organization is assigned a number of bits for use as the local part of its address that best corresponds to the number of addresses it requires. For example, assume your organization requires 4000 IP addresses. Because 2^{12} provides 4096 distinct addresses that best correspond to your organization's requirements, you would be assigned 12 bits for use as the local portion of your organization's address. The remaining 20 bits in the 32-bit IPv4 address space are then used as a prefix to denote what is referred to as a supernetwork. Thus, the format of a classless address is as follows:

Supernetwork address: network address

The forward slash is used to denote the network portion of a classless network. That character is then followed by the number of

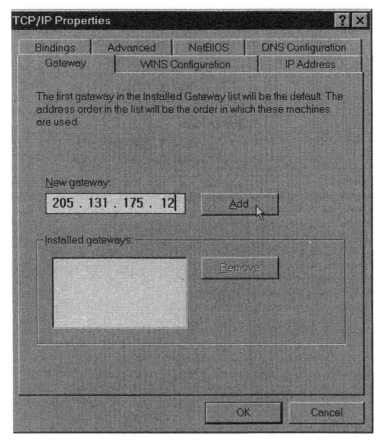

Figure 2.15 A third configuration screen which is used to specify the address of the name resolver

bits in the network address. Thus, the previously described classless network would be denoted as /20.

Address allocations employed for classless networking are taken from available Class C addresses. This means that obtaining a 20-bit classless network prefix to support up to 4096 devices is equivalent to obtaining 16 continuous Class C addresses. Table 2.9 provides a list of classless address blocks that can be assigned from available Class C address space.

Another key advantage of classless networking concerns the use of router tables and router performance. Under classless addressing a router becomes able to forward traffic to an organization using a single routing entry. This permits a reduction in router table entries which in turn allows the router to perform lookup operations faster. Thus, classless addressing provides a mechanism to extend

Table 2.9 Classless network address assignments.

Network part	Local bits	Equivalent number of Class C addresses	Distinct addresses
124	8	1	256
123	9	2	512
122	10	4	1024
121	11	8	2048
120	12	16	4096
119	13	32	8192
118	14	64	16284
117	15	128	32768

the availability of IP addresses in a more efficient manner, as well as enabling routers to operate more efficiently until IPv6 is deployed.

2.7.26 ICMP and ARP

In concluding this section on the Internet Protocol we will turn our attention to two special protocols that facilitate the operation of the Internet Protocol: the Internet Control Message Protocol (ICMP) and the Address Resolution Protocol (ARP).

2.7.27 ICMP

The Internet Control Message Protocol (ICMP) represents an error-reporting mechanism which is transported via IP datagrams. The format of an ICMP message and its relationship to an IP datagram is illustrated in Figure 2.16. Note that although each ICMP message has its own format, they all begin with the same three fields: an 8-bit Type field, an 8-bit Code field, and 16-bit Checksum field.

Similarly to IP, there are two versions of ICMP, ICMPv4 and ICMPv6. In this section we focus our attention upon the values of the Type and Code fields associated with ICMPv4 since it may be many years until ICMPv6 is in widespread use.

The ICMPv4 header

When ICMPv4 is used to transport control messages, an IPv4 header precedes the ICMP header. This results in the use of 32-bit IPv4 addressing for the routing of datagrams.

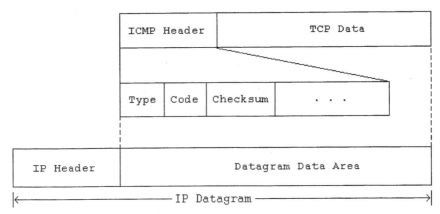

Figure 2.16 The creation of an ICMP message

Type field

The ICMP Type field defines the meaning of the message as well as its format. Perhaps the two most familiar ICMP messages are Type 0 and Type 8. A Type field value of 8 represents an Echo Request, while a Type 0 ICMP message denotes an Echo Reply. Although their official names are Echo Reply and Echo Request, most persons are more familiar with the term Ping which is used to refer to both an ICMP Echo Request and ICMP Echo Reply. Table 2.10 lists the values of the ICMP type fields that identify specific types of ICMP messages.

Code field

The second field common to each ICMP header is the Code field. The Code field provides additional information about the message and may not be meaningful for certain messages. For example, both Type field values of 0 and 8 always have a Code field value of 0. In comparison, a Type field value of 3 (Destination Unreachable) can have one of 16 possible code field values which further defines the reason why the destination was unreachable.

Table 2.11 lists the Code field values presently assigned to ICMPv4 based upon their Type field values. As we will note when we discuss security issues later in this book, many firewalls and routers provide administrators with the ability to filter all or selected ICMP messages. You could use this feature to prevent malicious Pinging either as an attempt by a hacker to learn the devices on your organization's internal network or as a mechanism to deny service to a host by flooding it with Pings.

2.7.28 ARP

The Address Resolution Protocol (ARP) was developed as a mechanism to translate layer 3 addresses such as the Internet Protocol used by the TCP/IP protocol suite into layer 2 addresses used primarily by

Table 2.10 ICMP Type field values.

Type	Name
0	Echo Reply
1	Unassigned
2	Unassigned
3	Destination Unreachable
4	Source Quench
5	Redirect
6	Alternate Host Address
7	Unassigned
8	Echo Request
9	Router Advertisement
10	Router Selection
11	Time Exceeded
12	Parameter Problem
13	Timestamp
14	Timestamp Reply
15	Information Request
16	Information Reply
17	Address Mask Request
18	Address Mask Reply
19	Reserved (for Security)
20–29	Reserved (for Robustness Experiment)
30	Traceroute
31	Datagram Conversion Error
32	Mobile Host Redirect
33	IPv6 Where-Are-You
34	IPv6 I-Am-Here
35	Mobile Registration Request
36	Mobile Registration Reply
37	Domain Name Request
38	Domain Name Reply
39	SKIP
40	Photuris
41–255	Reserved

LAN delivery systems, such as Ethernet, Token-Ring and FDDI. Technically ARP is not a layer 3 protocol as it does not run on top of IP and its format as we will note is conspicuous by the absence of an IP header. Although ARP actually operates on top of the datalink layer, its translation of layer 2 to layer 3 address results in most authors discussing it after IP. This also explains why a diagram of the TCP/IP protocol suite when compared to the ISO OSI Reference Model typically shows ARP above layer 2, usually as a small block within the network layer portion of the protocol suite.

Popular LANs such as Ethernet and Token-Ring use six byte source and destination addresses that represent universally or locally administrated addresses. A three-byte universally admini-strated address prefix is assigned by the IEEE to vendors who burn a six-byte address into network adapter cards they manufacture. The first three bytes have a fixed value which identifies the manufacturer of the network adapter card and is obtained from the IEEE. The values for the last three bytes are altered by the adapter manufacturer to uniquely identify each adapter produced. When software is used to override the burnt-in address on the adapter with a locally generated address, the addressing technique is referred to as a locally administrated address.

Need for address resolution

To understand the need for address resolution consider a station on a network that operates a TCP/IP protocol stack and needs to transmit a packet to the Internet via a router connected to the Internet and the local network. The workstation's TCP/IP stack is configured to set an IP address to the interface on the network. Similarly, the router is configured so that its interface on the local network is assigned another IP address. When the workstation needs to transfer a packet to an IP address that is not located on the local network where it resides, it must forward the packet to the router. While this appears to be a simple process, it is not. This is because data flows on the LAN in frames that use layer 2 addresses. Thus, while the workstation knows the router's IP address, it needs to determine the router's MAC address so it can transmit one or more LAN frames containing the layer 3 packet to the router. A similar but opposite problem occurs when a communications device knows an IP address but needs to find the associated IP address. Both of these translation problems are handled by protocols developed to provide an address resolution capability. One protocol, known as the Address Resolution Protocol

Table 2.11 ICMP Code field values based on message type.

Message type	Code field values
3	**Destination Unreachable**
	Codes
	0 Net Unreachable
	1 Host Unreachable
	2 Protocol Unreachable
	3 Port Unreachable
	4 Fragmentation Needed and Don't Fragment was Set
	5 Source Route Failed
	6 Destination Network Unknown
	7 Destination Host Unknown
	8 Source Host Isolated
	9 Communication with Destination Network is Administratively Prohibited
	10 Communication with Destination Host is Administratively Prohibited
	11 Destination Network Unreachable for Type of Service
	12 Destination Host Unreachable for Type of Service
	13 Destination Host Unreachable for Type of Service
	14 Communication Administratively Prohibited
	15 Precedence cutoff in effect
5	**Redirect**
	Codes
	0 Redirect Datagram for the Network (or subnet)
	1 Redirect Datagram for the Host
	2 Redirect Datagram for the Type of Service and Network
	3 Redirect Datagram for the Type of Service and Host
6	**Alternate Host Address**
	Codes
	0 Alternate Address for Host
11	**Time Exceeded**
	Codes
	0 Time to Live exceeded in Transit
	1 Fragment Reassembly Time Exceeded
12	**Parameter Problem**
	Codes
	0 Point Indicates the Error
	1 Missing a Required Option
	2 Bad Length
40	**Photuris**
	Codes
	0 Reserved
	1 Unknown security parameters index
	2 Valid security parameters, but authentication failed
	3 Valid security parameters, but decryption failed

(ARP) translates an IP address into a hardware (layer 2) address. The Reverse Address Resolution Protocol (RARP), as its name implies, performs a reverse translation or mapping, converting a hardware layer 2 address into an IP address.

Operation

Figure 2.17 illustrates the format of an ARP packet. Note that the numbers contained in some fields represent the byte position when the field spans a four-byte boundary. When a station knows a destination IP address but needs to learn the destination layer 2 address associated with the destination IP address, it will transmit an ARP packet as a broadcast frame.

By setting the target IP address in the last field in the packet the sender provides a mechanism for each station on the network to determine if it has the desired IP address. If so, the station will return the packet to the originator after it fills in its hardware address, enabling the sender to create a frame using an appropriate MAC address to transport data to the desired IP address. Now that we have an overview of the manner by which ARP operates, let us turn our attention to each field in the header.

Hardware Type field

The first field in the ARP packet is a 16-bit Hardware Type field. A value is placed in this field to indicate the type of hardware

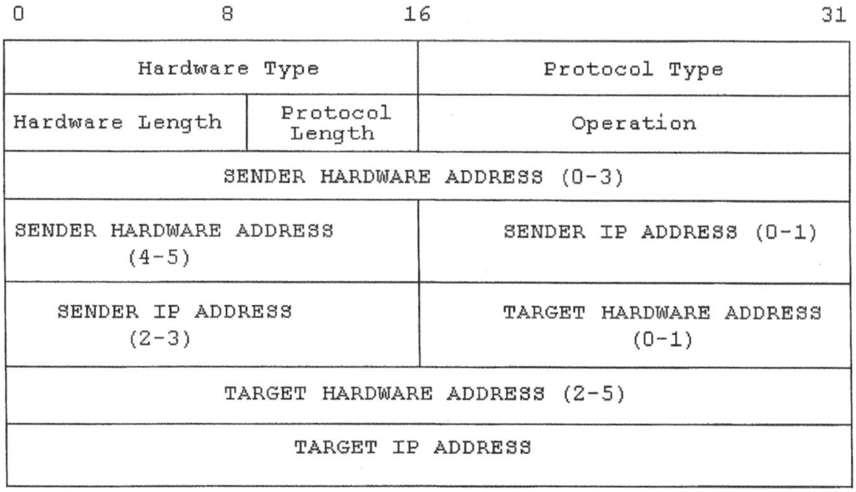

0	8	16	31

Hardware Type		Protocol Type	
Hardware Length	Protocol Length	Operation	
SENDER HARDWARE ADDRESS (0-3)			
SENDER HARDWARE ADDRESS (4-5)		SENDER IP ADDRESS (0-1)	
SENDER IP ADDRESS (2-3)		TARGET HARDWARE ADDRESS (0-1)	
TARGET HARDWARE ADDRESS (2-5)			
TARGET IP ADDRESS			

Figure 2.17 The Address Resolution Protocol (ARP) packet format

generating the ARP. Table 2.12 lists presently defined Hardware Type field values.

Protocol Type field

The Protocol Type field indicates the protocol for which an address resolution process is being performed. Thus, as you might surmise, ARP can be used to resolve addresses between many types of network protocol and hardware address. For IP the Protocol Type field has a value of hex 0800.

Hardware Length field

The Hardware Length field denotes the number of bytes in the hardware address. Similar to the Protocol Type field permitting

Table 2.12 ARP Hardware type field values.

Field value	Hardware type (hrd)
1	Ethernet (10Mb)
2	Experimental Ethernet (3Mb)
3	Amateur Radio AX.25
4	Proteon ProNET Token Rink
5	Chaos
6	IEEE 802 Networks
7	ARCNET
8	Hyperchannel
9	Lanstar
10	Autonet Short Address
11	LocalTalk
12	LocalNet (IBM PCNet or SYTEK LocalNET)
13	Ultra link
14	SMDS
15	Frame Relay
16	Asynchronous Transmission Mode (ATM)
17	HDLC
18	Fibre Channel
19	Asynchronous Transmission Mode (ATM)
20	Serial Line
21	Asynchronous Transmission Mode (ATM)
22	MIL-STD-188-220
23	Metricom
24	IEEE 1394.1995
25	MAPOS
26	Twinaxial
27	EUS-64

many types of network addresses to be resolved, the Hardware Length field permits many types of hardware product, including shared media LANs and ATM switch based networks, to be identified. The value of this field is 6 for both Ethernet and Token-Ring network adapter cards.

Protocol Length field

The Protocol Length field is similar to the Hardware Length field, indicating the length of the address in bytes for the protocol to be resolved. For IPv4 the value of this field is 4.

Operation field

The Operation field has a value of 1 for an ARP Request. When a target station responds, the value of this field is changed to 2 to denote an ARP reply. This explains how the same ARP packet can be transmitted as a broadcast to all stations on a LAN and returned with the resolved layer 2 address to the originator.

Sender Hardware Address field

The Sender Hardware Address field is 6 bytes in length. The entry in this field indicates the address of the station generating the ARP Request or ARP Reply.

Sender IP Address field

Because ARP is used to resolve an IP address, the station generating the ARP request must have an operational TCP/IP stack. Thus, the sender's IP address is placed in this field.

Target Hardware Address field

Because a station is attempting to determine the target hardware address, this field is set to a value of zero in an ARP request. When a destination station recognizes its IP address it enters its hardware address in this field.

Target IP Address field

The last field in the ARP packet is the Target IP Address field. A station requiring the hardware address associated with a particular IP address enters the IP address in this field. When this field is completed and returned in a packet with an Operation field value of 2, the address resolution process is completed.

Because the need for address resolution occurs quite frequently the broadcasting of frames transporting ARP packets and the appropriate ARP reply can adversely affect the utilization of the local network. To lower the level of network utilization as well as facilitate the prompt resolution of previously learned addresses, the originator of ARP requests maintains a table of resolved addresses referred to as an ARP cache. The use of the ARP cache allows subsequent datagrams with previously learned correspondences between IP addresses and MAC addresses to be quickly noted.

Under the ARP standard devices on a network also update their ARP tables with MAC and IP address pairs found in ARP replies that flow on the network. Most modern operating systems include an ARP command which provides you with the ability to view the contents of the ARP cache as well as to modify entries in the cache. In a Windows NT environment you can use its ARP command to both view and alter ARP cache entries. Figure 2.18 illustrates the format of the ARP command while Figure 2.19 illustrates the use of

```
C:\>arp

Displays and modifies the IP-to-Physical address translation tables used by
address resolution protocol (ARP).

ARP -s inet_addr eth_addr [if_addr]
ARP -d inet_addr [if_addr]
ARP -a [inet_addr] [-N if_addr]

  -a            Displays current ARP entries by interrogating the current
                    protocol data.  If inet_addr is specified, the IP and Physical
                    addresses for only the specified computer are displayed.  If
                more than one network interface uses ARP, entries for each ARP
                    table are displayed.
  -g            Same as -a.
  inet_addr     Specifies an internet address.
  -N if_addr    Displays the ARP entries for the network interface specified by if_addr.
  -d          Deletes the host specified by inet_addr.
  -s            Adds the host and associates the Internet address inet_addr
                    with the Physical address eth_addr.  The Physical address is
                    given as 6 hexadecimal bytes separated by hyphens.  The entry is
                permanent.
  eth_addr      Specifies a physical address.
  if_addr       If present, this specifies the Internet address of the
                    interface whose address translation table should be modified.
                    If not present, the first applicable interface will be used.

C:\>
```

Figure 2.18 Windows NT ARP command options

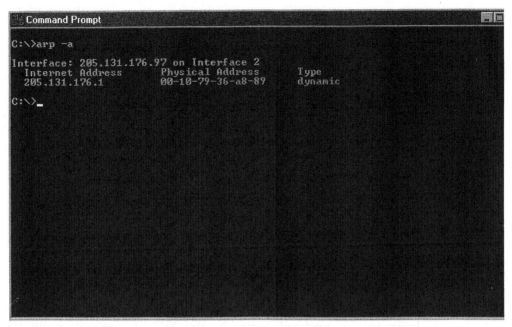

Figure 2.19 An illustration of the use of the ARP command with its — a option to view the contents of the ARP cache

the command with its — a option to view the contents of the ARP cache.

ARP notes

In concluding our examination of ARP there are two additional items that we should note. They are referred to as gratuitous ARP and proxy ARP.

A gratuitous ARP occurs when a communications device initializes its network connection. This type of ARP results in a device issuing an ARP request for its own IP address by entering its address in the Target IP Address field. While this action may appear silly (after all, the protocol stack needs to be configured with an IP address) assume a response occurs from a different hardware address contained in the Target Hardware Address field in the ARP Reply. This would indicate that another device on the network is using the IP address configured on the device and explains how the IP address conflict error message occurs.

The second ARP variation is a proxy ARP. A proxy ARP permits a device to answer an ARP Request on behalf of another device. To understand the rational for a proxy ARP consider a Class C network subdivided into two or more subnets via the use of a router. If the originating device erroneously had a standard Class C subnet mask of 255.255.255.0 it would assume that any address within its Class C network resides on its own physical network, and if powered on should respond to an ARP Request. If the destination was on the other side of the router it would not receive the ARP. However, because the router must be configured to note each subnet, it can answer an ARP Request on behalf of other devices on the destination subnet by entering its own layer 2 address in an ARP Reply. This results in the originating device placing the router's MAC address in its ARP cache and sending packets to the router which forwards them onto the correct subnet. However, it should be noted that not all routers support a proxy ARP capability and those that do may require you to enable this feature.

2.8 THE TRANSPORT LAYER

In concluding this chapter we will turn our attention to the fourth layer in the protocol suite. In the TCP/IP protocol suite the transport layer permits multiple applications to flow to a common destination, either from the same source or from different data originators. The transport layer resides between the network layer and the application layer, receiving application data, encapsulating the data with a transport header which identifies the type of application, and providing the encapsulated data and header to the network layer for transmission onto the network.

Included in the TCP/IP protocol suite are two transport layer protocols, the Transmission Control Protocol (TCP) and the User Datagram Protocol (UDP), both of which are the focus of this section. TCP represents a connection-oriented, reliable transport protocol which creates a virtual circuit for the transfer of information. In comparison, UDP represents a connectionless, best-effort transport layer protocol. As we turn our attention to each protocol in this section we will note their suitability for different applications. For example, a connection-oriented protocol requires a significant amount of setup time when used to transport small packets of information. Recognizing the fact that different applications will have different requirements concerning both the need to establish a connection prior to transmitting data, and the need to acknowledge the fact that data was delivered correctly and without error, resulted in the support of two transport protocols by the TCP/IP protocol suite. As we investigate each protocol it will become clearer that there are valid reasons for some applications using one transport protocol while other applications are designed to use a different transport protocol.

2.8.1 TCP

As previously noted, TCP represents a connection-oriented, reliable transport protocol. The need for this type of protocol was recognized when the TCP/IP protocol suite was being developed during the 1970s. At that time local area networks were in the conceptual phase of development and TCP/IP hosts communicated via analog serial lines that were prone to transmission errors. This meant that a transport protocol was required that could detect missing packets as well as transmission errors that occurred on the contents of a packet, resulting in TCP using sequence numbers to order packets and note when one or more became missing, as well as using an error detection algorithm and acknowledgments to detect errors occurring within a packet and then attempting to correct errors by requesting the retransmission of erroneous packets. Because an understanding of the manner by which the TCP protocol operates is facilitated by an understanding of the fields in the protocol header, we will turn our attention to the header prior to examining TCP's data flow.

2.8.2 The TCP header

We previously noted that IP does not provide a guaranteed delivery mechanism to enable datagrams to be correctly received with respect to their content and sequence. Instead, reliable delivery is provided at the transport layer through the use of the TCP protocol. As we will shortly note, the TCP header includes fields that are used to ensure datagrams are received correctly with respect to both their content and sequence. Another important function of the TCP header is to denote the type of application data carried by each datagram. This function is accomplished by the use of port fields which identify the process or application transported in the datagram. In actuality, the TCP header plus data is referred to as a segment, resulting in the port number identifying the type of data in the segment. When the IP header is prefixed to the TCP segment the resulting datagram contains the source and destination IP address and enables the segment to be delivered via the network. Concerning the TCP segment, at the transport layer TCP accepts application data in chunks up to 64 Kbytes in length. Those chunks are fragmented into a series of smaller pieces representing segments which become datagrams through the addition of IP headers. TCP segments are commonly 512 or 1024 bytes in length, with the actual length used dependent upon the length supported by source and destination networks as well as any intermediate networks. As we will note later in this chapter, the selection of an appropriate datagram length requires the TCP layer at each end to denote the maximum length they support and select the smallest mutually supported length. Figure 2.20 illustrates the fields of the TCP header. By examining the contents and utilization of each field in the header we can obtain an appreciation for various protocol functions that will be discussed and described once we have completed our examination of the header fields.

2.8.3 Source and destination port fields

The source and destination port fields are 16 bits in length. The source port contains a port number that theoretically denotes the application associated with the data generated by the originating station. The reason the term 'theoretically' was used is that in most transmissions the source port number is randomly generated by the originator. If the source port is not used, its value is set to 0. In comparison, the destination port field contains a port number that identifies a user process or application for the receiving station, enabling it to distinguish different applications transported from a common location. For example, when a station initiates a file transfer it might open FTP to transfer data using port number 1234

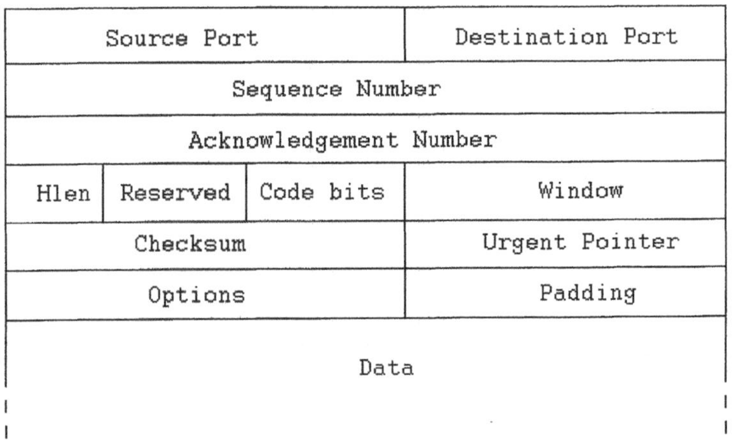

Source Port			Destination Port
Sequence Number			
Acknowledgement Number			
Hlen	Reserved	Code bits	Window
Checksum			Urgent Pointer
Options			Padding
Data			

Figure 2.20 The TCP header

as the source port, while later in the day a second file transfer might occur with the station using source port 2345. However, for all FTP transfers the destination port would be fixed at 21, which is the standard port number for which FTP incoming data is received. When the destination station receives the incoming data it responds by creating a segment and placing the source port number in the destination port field. This action enables the file originator to correctly identify the response to its datagram. As we will note later in this section, each TCP segment contained in an IP datagram has a segment number which enables the opposite end of the transmission to ensure that datagrams are received in their correct order and none are lost. Because there are three types of port number that can be used in the port fields, and both TCP and UDP headers have the same source and destination port fields, we will first turn our attention to the port number universe prior to continuing our examination of the fields in the TCP header.

2.8.4 Port numbers

Both TCP and UDP headers contain 16-bit source and destination port fields, permitting port numbers in the range of 0 through 65,535. This results in 65,536 distinct port numbers being available for utilization. This 'universe' of port numbers is subdivided into three ranges, referred to as well-known ports, registered ports, and dynamic or private ports.

2.8.5 Well-known ports

Well-known ports are also referred to as assigned ports as their assignment is controlled by the Internet Assigned Numbers Authority (IANA).

Well-known or assigned ports are in the range of 0 through 1023 and are used to indicate the transportation of standardized processes. Where possible, the same well-known port number assignments are used with TCP and UDP. Ports used with TCP commonly provide connections that transport relatively long-term conversations, such as file transfers and remote access. In dated literature references to well-known port numbers are specified as being in the range of values from 0 through 255. While that range was correct many years ago, the range for assigned ports managed and controlled by the IANA is now from 0 through 1023.

Table 2.13 provides a summary of some of the more popular well-known ports, including the service supported by a particular port

Table 2.13 Well-known TCP and UDP services and port utilization.

Keyword	Service	Port type	Port number
TCPMUX	TCP Port Service Multiplexer	TCP	1
RJE	Remote Job Entry	TCP	5
ECHO	Echo	TCP and UDP	7
DAYTIME	Daytime	TCP and UDP	13
QOTD	Quote of the Day	TCP	17
CHARGEN	Character Generator	TCP	19
FTD-DATA	File Transfer (Default Data)	TCP	20
FTP	File Transfer (Control)	TCP	21
TELNET	Telnet	TCP	23
SMTP	Simple Mail Transfer Protocol	TCP	25
MSG-AUTH	Message Authentication	TCP	31
TIME	Time	TCP	37
NAMESERVER	Host Name Server	TCP and UDP	42
NICNAME	Who Is	TCP	43
DOMAIN	Domain Name Server	TCP and UDP	53
BOOTPS	Bootstrap Protocol Server	TCP	67
BOOTPC	Bootstrap Protocol Client	TCP	68
TFTP	Trivial File Transfer Protocol	UDP	69
FINGER	Finger	TCP	79
HTTP	World Wide Web	TCP	80
KERBEROS	Kerberos	TCP	88
RTELNET	Remote Telenet Service	TCP	107
POP2	Post Office Protocol Version 2	TCP	109
POP3	Post Office Protocol Version 3	TCP	110
NNTP	Network News Transfer Protocol	TCP	119
NTP	Network Time Protocol	TCP and UDP	123
NETBIOS-NS	NetBIOS Name Server	UDP	137
NETBIOS-DGM	NetBIOS Datagram Service	UDP	138
NETBIOS-SSN	NetBIOS Session Service	UDP	139
NEWS	News	TCP	144
SNMP	Simple Network Management Protocol	UDP	161
SNMTTRAP	Simple Network Management Protocol Traps	UDP	162
BGP	Border Gateway Protocol	TCP	179
HTTPS	Secure HTTP	TCP	413
RLOGIN	Remote Login	TCP	513
TALK	Talk	TCP and UDP	517

and the type of port (TCP or UDP) for which the port number is primarily used. Note that such common applications as Telnet, file transfer protocol (FTP), and World Wide Web (HTTP) traffic are transported via the use of well-known ports.

2.8.6 Registered port numbers

Assigned port numbers range from 0 through 1023 out of the universe of 65,536 available numbers. Port numbers that exceed 1023 can be used by any process or application; however, doing so in a haphazard manner could create incompatibilities between vendor products. Recognizing this potential problem, the IANA permits vendors to register the use of port numbers. The result is the use of the range of port number values from 1024 through 49,151 for registered ports. Although an application or process may be registered, its registration does not hold legal implications and is primarily to enable other vendors to develop compatible products as well as to enable end users to set up equipment appropriately. For example, if a new application uses a registered port number, it is relatively easy to adjust a router access list or firewall to enable many compatible products behind the router or firewall to interact with the new application. Although developers can use any port number beyond 1023, many respect registered port numbers.

2.8.7 Dynamic port numbers

Dynamic port numbers are in the range from 49,152 through 65,535. Port numbers in this range are typically used by vendors implementing proprietary network applications, such as a method to transmit digitized voice. Another common use of dynamic port numbers includes the random selection of a port number by certain applications.

2.8.8 Sequence number field

The third field in the TCP header is a 32-bit sequence number field. Unless a bit in the code bit field known as the SYN bit is set, each TCP segment is assigned a number. That number reflects the number of bytes in a TCP packet as TCP represents a byte-oriented sequencing protocol. That is, a byte-oriented protocol results in every byte in each packet being assigned a sequence number. However, it is important to note that this does not mean that TCP transmits a packet containing a single byte. What this means is that TCP will transmit a group of bytes and assign the packet a sequence number based upon the number of bytes in the packet's data field. For example, assume that a station transmits three packets to the same destination with the first two packets each containing 512 bytes of data, while the third packet contains 1024 bytes of data. The first packet would have a sequence number of

512 while the second packet would have a sequence number of 1024. Then, the third packet would have a sequence number of 2048. At the receiving station the fact that the first packet was received with a sequence number of 512 and contains 512 bytes of data tells the receiver to expect the next sequence number to be 1024. Similarly, upon receipt of the second packet with a sequence number of 1024, the counting of 1024 data bytes results in the receiver expecting the next sequence number to be 2048.

2.8.9 Acknowledgment number field

The fourth field in the TCP header is the acknowledgment number field. This 32-bit field contains the number that indicates the next sequence number the destination expects to receive. Similar to the sequence number field, the acknowledgment number field value is based upon a data byte count, and it indicates the next byte the receiver expects to receive. Because it would be inefficient to acknowledge each datagram when transmission occurs over relatively error-free circuits, the TCP protocol supports a variable window. For example, returning an acknowledgment number field value of 2049 would indicate the receipt of all data that was transmitted by the prior three datagram examples consisting of 512, 512 and 1024 bytes of data. To ensure lost datagrams or lost acknowledgments do not place this transport protocol in an infinite waiting period, the originator will retransmit data if it does not receive a response within a predefined period of time. This period is controlled by one of several TCP timers whose operation will be described later in this chapter.

The use of the acknowledgment number field is referred to as Positive Acknowledgment or Retransmission (PAR). PAR requires that each unit of data must be explicitly acknowledged. If a unit of data is not acknowledged before the time the originator's time-out period is reached, the previous transmission is retransmitted. When the acknowledgment field is in use the second bit position in the code bit field, which is the ACK flag, is set.

2.8.10 Hlen field

The Hlen field is 4 bits in length and contains a value which indicates the length of the header in 32-bit words. Thus, the Hlen field denotes the location where the TCP header ends and data being carried by the protocol begins.

The rationale for the use of the Hlen field results from the fact that the potential inclusion of options results in a variable length header. Without a field that indicates where the header ends it would not be possible to support a variable length header. Because the minimum length of the TCP header is 20 bytes, the minimum value of the Hlen field is five 32-bit words. It should be noted that in many references to TCP the Hlen field is referred to as the Offset field.

2.8.11 Reserved field

Within the TCP header are six bits that are reserved for future use. The value of those bits are presently set to all zeros.

2.8.12 Code bit fields

There are six bits in the TCP header whose individual settings control different functions. These bits are collectively referred to as code bits. They are also upon occasion referred to as control flags.

Figure 2.21 illustrates the position of the individual bits in the code bit field. Those bits include an urgent pointer (URG), acknowledgment (ACK), push function (PSH), connection reset (RST), sequence number synchronization (SYN), and connection release (FIN).

URG bit

The urgent pointer bit or flag is set to denote an urgent or priority activity, such as when a user presses the CTRL-BREAK key combination. When a predefined urgent or priority activity occurs, the application sets the URG bit, which results in TCP immediately transmitting everything it has for the connection. If a destination station previously closed its Receive window, the setting of the URG bit tells the receiver to accept the packet. When the URG bit is set it also indicates that the urgent pointer field is in use. That field contains the offset in bytes from the current sequence number where the urgent data is located.

URG	ACK	PSH	RST	SYN	FIN

Figure 2.21 The flags in the code bit field. URG: Urgent pointer field significant; ACK: Acknowledgement field significant; PSK: Push function; RST: Reset the connection; SYN: Synchronize sequence numbers; FIN: Release the connection.

ACK bit

The second bit in the code bit field is the ACK bit. When set, this bit indicates that the segment contains an acknowledgment to a previously received datagram or series of datagrams.

PSH bit

The third bit in the code bit field is the PSH (push) bit. Setting this bit tells the receiver to immediately deliver data to the application and forgo any buffering.

RST bit

The fourth bit in the code bit field is the RST (reset) bit. The setting of this bit resets the current connection.

SYN bit

The fifth bit in the code bit field is SYN (synchronization) bit. This bit is set at TCP startup as well as to inform a receiver that a sequence number is being established to synchronize sender and receiver.

FIN bit

The sixth and last bit in the code bit field is the FIN (finish) bit. This bit is set to indicate the sender has no additional data to send and the connection should be released.

2.8.13 Window field

The eighth field in the TCP header is the window field. This field is 2 octets in length and contains the number of data octets beginning with the one indicated in the Acknowledgment field that the sender of this segment is willing to accept. Thus, the use of the Window field provides a method of flow control between the source and destination. A large value can significantly improve the TCP performance as it permits the originator to transmit more data without having to wait for an acknowledgment, while permitting the receiver to acknowledge the receipt of data carried in multiple segments with one acknowledgment.

The use of the window field permits a variable window to be created that governs the amount of data that can be transmitted prior to requiring an acknowledgment. A window can be established in each direction between sender and receiver since TCP is a full-duplex transmission protocol. This means that both ends of a transmission session can use the window field to provide a bi-directional flow control mechanism. For example, by reducing the value of the window field, one end of the conversation informs the other end to transmit less data.

2.8.14 Checksum field

The 16-bit checksum field provides an error detection and correction capability for TCP. Instead of computing the checksum over the entire TCP header, the checksum calculation occurs over what is referred to as a 12-octet pseudo header. This header extends into the IP header and consists of such key fields as the 32-bit Source and Destination address fields in the IP header, the 8-bit Protocol field, and a length field that denotes the length of the TCP header and data transported within the TCP segment. Thus, the checksum can be used to ensure data arrives at its correct destination, and the receiver has no doubt about the address of the originator nor the length of the header and types of application data transported by TCP.

2.8.15 Urgent pointer field

As previously noted, the setting of the URG bit in the code bit field indicates that the urgent pointer field is in use. This field contains the offset in octets from the current sequence number where the urgent data is located.

2.8.16 Options field

The options field is variable in length and enables a host to specify options required by the TCP protocol. For example, through the use of values in this field a host can specify the use of an alternative checksum, a maximum segment size, or the use of authentication.

Table 2.14 lists currently defined option numbers used to specify the use of optional header fields. In examining the entries in Table

Table 2.14 TCP options numbers.

Number	Length	Meaning
0	—	End of Option List
1	—	No—Operation
2	4	Maximum Segment Size
3	3	WSOPT—Window Scale
4	2	SACK Permitted
5	N	SAC
6	6	Echo (Obsoleted by option 8)
7	6	Echo Reply (Obsoleted by option 8)
8	10	TSOPT—Time Stamp Option
9	2	Partial Order Connection Permitted
10	3	Partial Order Service Profile
11		CC
12		CC.NEW
13		CC.ECHO
14	3	TCP Alternate Checksum Request
15	N	TCP Alternate Checksum Data
16		Skeeter
17		Bubba
18	3	Trailer Checksum Option
19	18	MD5 Signature Option

TCP Alternate Checksum Numbers

Number	Description
0	TCP Checksum
1	8-bit Fletchers' algorithm
2	16-bit Fletchers' algorithm
3	Redundant Checksum Avoidance

2.14 note that options 0 and 1 are exactly one octet in length. All other options have their one octet number field followed by a one octet length field, which in turn is followed by actual option data.

2.8.17 Padding field

Because the use of an option results in a variable length header, a padding field is included to ensure the header ends on a 32-bit boundary. If the options field is omitted or the use of an option results in the header following on a 32-bit boundary, the padding field is not used.

2.8.18 Operation

As briefly noted earlier in this section, TCP is a connection-oriented protocol. This means that a connection between source and destination must be established prior to the transmission of data between the two. Within a TCP/IP protocol stack applications such as FTP and Telnet initiate a connection request through the use of function calls. For example, an OPEN call will be requested by an application when a connection is required while a CLOSE call is requested to terminate a previously established connection.

2.8.19 Connection types

There are two types of connection that many applications can establish, active and passive. An active connection is initiated by the issuance of an OPEN call when a connection to a remote station is required. In comparison, a passive connection occurs when an OPEN call is issued to enable connections to be received from a remote station. Because there are limits on the number of passive OPENs that can be issued by an application, one hacker attack commonly used is to flood an application on a target host with requests from randomly generated IP addresses.

Figure 2.22 illustrates an example of the TCP connection establishment process. In this example the host at 205.131.175.10 is initiating an FTP session with the server at IP address 205.131.175.20. Here the station at the first IP address issues an active OPEN call to the server at the second address. To enable a connection to be made, the

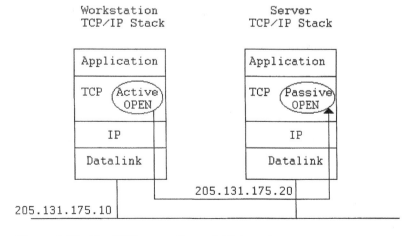

Figure 2.22 The TCP connection establishment process

server must have previously issued a passive OPEN request to enable incoming connections to be established. If a passive OPEN request was previously issued, the server's operating system will then generate a separate process to maintain the connection. Concerning this connection, the incoming datagram will contain the destination port number which tells the server the application the originator wishes to use on the server. Thus, a server that supports multiple applications can conceivable accept certain applications while rejecting other applications.

2.8.20 The three-way handshake

A TCP session begins with a 'three-way handshake'. Only after the source and destination exchange datagrams via the three-way handshake will a pending connection become active.

The three-way handshake results in the exchange of three messages: SYN, SYN/ACK and ACK. When a client application wants to establish a connection the application places an active OPEN call to TCP, requesting a connection to an application on a remote station. The client TCP creates a header, setting the SYN bit in the code bit field and assigning an initial sequence number that can start at any value, including 0. After setting values in other header fields, the client sets a timer and passes the TCP segment to IP. IP adds its header, generating a datagram that is transmitted onto the network to its destination.

At the destination, assuming an appropriate passive OPEN was issued, the receiver creates a segment in response to the inbound SYN segment. The responding segment includes the setting of the SYN and ACK bits in the code field in the TCP header and the setting of appropriate values in the Sequence number and Acknowledgment number fields. Concerning the values in those fields, the Sequence number field can be set to any value while the Acknowledgment number field must contain a value of the sequence number in the inbound segment plus one. The TCP header is then passed to IP, which creates what is referred to as a SYN/ACK packet that must be received by the originator prior to its timer expiring. At the client, the SYN/ACK packet is noted as an acknowledgment to its connection request. The client then creates a new TCP segment, setting the ACK bit in the code bit field, filling in the Acknowledgment number to an appropriate value, and sending the segment to IP for the creation of a datagram. This datagram, which represents a TCP ACK, completes the three-way handshake. The client also sets a retransmission timer based upon the round-trip delay occurring between the SYN and SYN/ACK datagrams. If succeeding data packets are not ACKed when the timer expires, this informs the client to retransmit a previously transmitted datagram.

Figure 2.23 illustrates an example of a three-way handshake between a client and server via the use of a time chart. In this example the client is shown setting the SYN bit in the code bit field and a value of 0 being placed in the sequence number field. The server is shown responding with an initial sequence number of 100 and sets the value of its acknowledgment number field to the received sequence number plus 1, or 1. The setting of the SYN and ACK bits in the TCP header's code bit field results in the response being referred to as a SYN/ACK response. In response to the SYN/ACK, the client constructs a

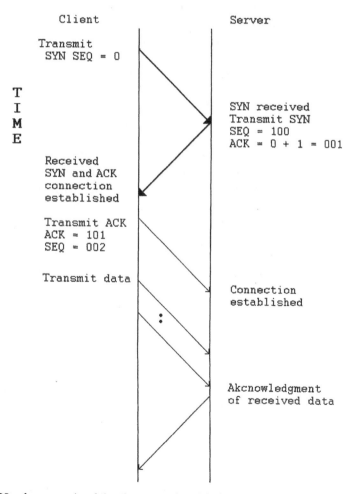

Figure 2.23   An example of the three-way handshake

response, setting the ACK bit in the code bit field, setting the acknowledgment number to one more than the received sequence number (101), and incrementing its sequence number from 0 to 1. Once the client has responded to the SYN/ACK with an ACK it can then transmit one or more data segments.

2.8.21 Segment size support

When TCP transmits data the number of segments that can be transmitted and the maximum length or size of each segment are governed by two different control mechanisms. The number of segments that can be transmitted depends upon the window field value which we will cover in the next section in this chapter. In comparison, the maximum segment size (MSS) is set during the establishment of each TCP connection and is determined independently by each station via the use of one of the following algorithms.

During the exchange of SYN and SYN/ACK segments each end station transmits their desired MSS to the remote endpoint. The desired MSS is the maximum transmission unit (MTU) of the interface being used minus the IP and TCP header overhead, typically 40 bytes. Each end station derives the MSS that will be used as the minimum of the MSS received in the SYN packet and the MTU of the local interface minus the IP and TCP header overhead. When two networks with differing MTUs are connected the resulting MSS used is the smaller of the two, permitting communications without requiring IP fragmentation. Now that we have an appreciation for the manner by which a segment size is selected, let us turn our attention to the use of the window field and how it can be used to control the flow of data on and between networks.

2.8.22 The window field and flow control

We briefly noted earlier in this section that the window field in the TCP header provides the mechanism which governs the number of segments that can be outstanding at any one point in time. Stations adjust the value in the window field based upon their ability to process a series of segments, in effect providing a mechanism to regulate the flow of data between source and destination.

As TCP processes data in memory, it places a window over the data as it is structured into segments. The movement of the window

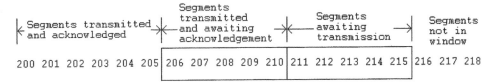

Figure 2.24 The TCP sliding window in operation

over data results in a sliding window as more and more data is processed into segments.

Figure 2.24 illustrates an example of a TCP sliding window. In this example segments used with sequence numbers 200 through 205 were both transmitted to their destination and acknowledged. Segments with sequence numbers 206 through 210 were transmitted but have yet to be acknowledged. Segments with sequence numbers 211 through 215 are still in the originating station and are waiting to be transmitted, while segments with sequence numbers 216 through 218 represent data to be sent that is not presently in the window.

It is important to note that the length of the sliding window is variable and controlled through the use of the window field in the TCP header. If the receiving station is running out of buffer space it can tell the originator to slow its transmission by reducing the value in the window field returned in an acknowledgment. By setting the value in the window field to 0 a receiving station informs the originator it cannot accept additional data. The receiving device will continue to send datagrams with a window field value of 0 until it cleans its buffer area to the point where it can again accept data. At that time it will transmit a datagram with a window field value other than zero, indicating it is now capable of receiving data.

2.8.23 Timers

TCP retransmissions as well as the termination of an existing connection are governed by different types of timer. Four key timers used by TCP are a delayed ACK, FIN-WAIT-2, Persist, and Keep Alive timers.

Delayed ACK timer

When TCP receives data that does not require an immediate acknowledgment it can set a delayed ACK timer. This timer can be set to a value up to 20 ms and enables TCP to form a segment of data that an be transmitted with the ACK, conserving bandwidth.

FIN-WAIT-2 timer

To gracefully terminate an existing connection TCP sets the FIN bit in the code bit field in the TCP header. Upon receipt of the datagram the destination station enters a FIN-WAIT-1 state. Because TCP supports a full-duplex connection the originator expects an acknowledgment. Upon receipt of the acknowledgment the originator enters a FIN-WAIT-2 state. At this time a FIN-WAIT-2 timer is set. The purpose of the timer is to avoid leaving the connection in a FIN-WAIT-2 state in the event that a final FIN is not received from the destination.

The FIN-WAIT-2 timers can be set to a value up to 10 minutes. Upon expiration it is reset to 75 seconds, after which the connection is dropped.

Persist timer

The Persist timer is set when the other side of a connection advertises a window size of zero, stopping TCP from transmitting additional data. Because it is possible that a datagram containing a window advertisement could be lost, TCP will transmit one byte of data after its Persist timer expires to see if the window opened up.

Keep alive

Once a connection has been established there can be periods of time when data is not exchanged. During such periods the Keep alive timer is used to detect if the connection is up. That is, if the connection is idle for a fixed period of time the Keep alive timer expires, resulting in a probe segment being transmitted to the other side of the connection in an attempt to elicit a response. If no response is received further attempts are optional and the connection will be closed.

2.8.24 Slow start and congestion avoidance

Early versions of the TCP/IP protocol stack enabled TCP to transmit multiple segments up to the window size generated by the receiver's acknowledgment during the initial phase of communications. While the ability to transmit a large amount of data when sender and receiver were on the same network rarely caused problems, if they were on different networks intermediate devices and transmission facilities such as routers and serial communications links could easily become saturated, causing router buffers to overflow, packets to be dropped and retransmissions to occur that would further compound an already bad situation. This potential situation resulted in the addition of a slow start mechanism to TCP as a method to avoid the generation of network congestion during and after startup.

Under slow start TCP initially sets the value in its window field to 1. Each time an ACK is received the value in the returned window field is increased exponentially. That is, the sender first transmits one segment and upon receipt of an ACK transmits two more. The next ACK results in the transmission of 4 segments, while the following ACK permits the sender to transmit 8 segments. The sender will continue to increase the number of segments transmitted at one time until the value reaches that provided during the initialization period. The value established during the initialization period is often referred to as the TCP advertised window value, while the value in the window field during the slow start process is often referred to as the congestion window value.

Once the sender has obtained the ability to transmit a group of segments that corresponds to the number advertised by the receiver, it will continue to do so until a time-out or duplicate ACKs is received. When either situation occurs the sender compares the size of the congestion window and the TCP advertised window, selects and halves the smaller of the two and stores it as a slow start threshold. The value stored must be a minimum of 2 segments; however, if a time-out occurred the value will be stored as 1, resulting in a slow start process commencing anew. If a value exceeding 1 is stored, a congestion avoidance algorithm is used which results in the potential linear growth in the number of segments that can be transmitted in response to each ACK. This algorithm first multiplies the segment size by 2. Next, it divides the resulting value by the value of the congestion window and then increases the resulting segment size using this algorithm each time an ACK is received. In comparison to slow-start the congestion avoidance algorithm results in a more controlled rate of growth in the number of segments that can be transmitted each time an ACK is received. Both slow start and congestion avoidance algorithms are now incorporated into modern TCP/IP protocol stacks.

Through the use of these algorithms a significant amount of network overloading is prevented; however, this is not without cost. The key cost associated with slow-start is the inability of the protocol to recognize that a higher transfer capability could be used due to available network bandwidth. This means that TCP transfers are always initially slow and only are enhanced as ACKs are received.

2.8.25 UDP

The User Datagram Protocol (UDP) represents the second network layer protocol in the TCP/IP protocol suite. UDP is based upon the datagram method of transport for applications for which an occasional lost packet is not considered serious. Thus, UDP represents a connectionless, unreliable, best-effort transport service. This means that UDP does not issue acknowledgments to the originator upon receipt of data nor provide order to incoming datagrams. Thus, UDP does not provide error detection nor the capability to recover from the situation where packets become lost. Instead, it is up to the application to detect lost or missing data, typically by noting the absence of a response within a predefined period of time and then, if appropriate, retransmitting the data that was presumed to be lost.

2.8.26 The UDP header

Figure 2.25 illustrates the fields in the UDP header. In examining the fields in the header you will note that it has a relatively low overhead in comparison to TCP which enables a higher level of data transfer. Also note the absence of a window field which results in UDP being unable to adjust its rate of data flow based on network conditions. Although UDP is similar to TCP in that it can transmit datagrams containing up to 65,535 bytes, unlike TCP there is no mechanism to communicate an MTU to a UDP stack. If a UDP datagram exceeds the MTU, IP fragmentation becomes necessary.

```
0               16                31
┌────────────────┬─────────────────┐
│  Source Port   │ Destination Port│
├────────────────┼─────────────────┤
│    Length      │    Checksum     │
└────────────────┴─────────────────┘
```

Figure 2.25 The UDP header

The ability of UDP to initiate transmission without first establishing a connection between source and destination results in a considerably faster data transfer capability. Examples of UDP applications include electronic mail, network management and voice over IP transmission. To obtain a better understanding of UDP, let us examine the use of each field in the header.

Source and destination port fields

The source and destination port fields in the UDP header are each two octets in length. Each field functions in a manner similar to the counterparts in the TCP header. That is, the source port field value is optional and can be either randomly selected or set to all 0's when not used. The destination port field contains a numeric which identifies the destination application or process.

Length field

The two octet length field indicates the length of the UDP datagram, including its header and user data. This field has a minimum value of eight which represents a UDP header without data.

Checksum field

The last field in the UDP header is the checksum field. This field is two octets in length and is used to validate the UDP header and key data. When used in this manner the checksum is computed on a pseudo header which covers the source and destination addresses and the protocol field from the IP header. By providing a mechanism to verify the two address fields in the IP header, the pseudo header checksum assures that the UDP datagram is delivered to the correct destination network and host. However, this checksum does not verify the contents of the datagram.

The use of the checksum field is optional. If not used the field is filled with 0's if the application does not require a checksum.

2.8.27 Operation

The simplified structure of the UDP header results in a simplified operating procedure, with error detection and correction left to the application layer. As a transport protocol UDP breaks application data into pieces for transport, appending a header which identifies the application and the length of the datagram. UDP passes the resulting datagram to IP for the addition of an IP header that identifies sending and receiving stations. Because there is no error detection and correction mechanism, delivery occurs on a best-effort basis; however, the avoidance of a slow-start procedure enables UDP to transfer data significantly faster than TCP. Due to this, UDP is well-suited for digitized voice applications.

3

NETWORK ATTACK
METHODS

This objective of this chapter is to become aware of a core set of network attack methods. As we discuss and describe each method we will become acquainted with their operation and potential effect on network resources. In examining each network attack method we will also turn our attention to tools and techniques we can use to minimize or block their effect. However, because we will describe and discuss the operation and utilization of routers, firewalls and other network security devices in subsequent chapters, we will concentrate on the manner by which different network attack methods are counteracted in this chapter. Of course, we will refer to the appropriate subsequent chapters in this book where you will find specific details concerning methods to block or minimize the effect of different types of network attack.

Because most hackers attempt to hide their identity we will commence this chapter with an overview of IP spoofing. As we discuss and describe IP spoofing we will also note common addresses used by hackers to hide their real IP address and methods we can use to minimize the ability of packets with spoofed addresses to flow through our network.

3.1 IP ADDRESS SPOOFING

IP address spoofing does not represent a network attack method. Instead, it represents a method of hiding the identity of the originator of a packet. Because the spoofing of an IP packet's source address makes it extremely difficult to determine who originated the packet, IP spoofing represents a popular technique used by hackers to hide their identity.

3.1.1 Background

The Internet Protocol (IP) represents a connectionless protocol that operates at layer 3, which is the network layer, in the Open System Interconnection (OSI) Reference Model. As indicated in Chapter 2 when we discussed the TCP/IP protocol suite, almost every type of current TCP/IP traffic is formed by prefixing an IP header to either a TCP segment or UDP datagram to form an IP datagram.

The goal of IP is to provide a mechanism for the routing of datagrams. To enable routing, IPv4 contains a 32-bit header field that holds the destination address of the datagram. Under IPv6 the destination address field is 128 bits. Although both IPv4 and IPv6 headers include a source address field whose width is the same as the destination address field, routers do not check the source address field for routing purposes. The source address field was included in IP datagrams as a mechanism to identify the originator of the datagram. Because neither routers nor the TCP/IP protocol stack check source addresses for other than ensuring that their configuration is within acceptable limits, this lack of checking enables you to configure your protocol stack to 'be anything you want to be'. To illustrate this fact let us use a series of common Windows operations to identify a Web site and attack the site, so that if the owner analyzed the attack he would think he was being attacked by a well-known U.S. government agency.

3.1.2 Obtaining an IP address to spoof

Figure 3.1 illustrates the use of two common utility programs built into Windows that enable you to obtain the IP address of a host. In the top portion of Figure 3.1 we used the Ping command to resolve the IP address for the Web server whose Uniform Resource Locator (URL) is www.fbi.gov. For readers beyond North America, this is the Web site for the U.S. Federal Bureau of Investigations. Note that because the target address used with the Ping command was a host address, the address is automatically resolved into an IP address (since all routing on the Internet is based upon destination IP addresses). Also note that instead of receiving a reply from the FBI Web server we obtained a 'destination not unreachable' message from the device whose IP address is 165.87.34.182. If we used the traceroute (called tracert under Windows) application with the host name www.fbi.com, we would obtain a similar result. This is because the router providing access to the FBI's network was configured to block pings. However, the router was not configured

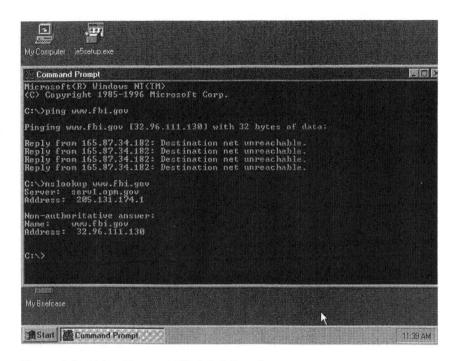

Figure 3.1 Using Ping and NSLOOKUP to determine the IP address of a host name

to avoid returning the message 'destination net unreachable' and the router's IP address.

In the lower portion of Figure 3.1 we used the nslookup utility program which used the local DNS server on our network to determine the IP address of the host name www.fbi.gov. Once again, we determined that the IP address of the FBI's Web server is 32.96.111.130.

3.1.3 Reconfiguring the protocol stack

Now that we have the IP address for the FBI's Web server, let us reconfigure our TCP/IP protocol stack. Specifically, go to Start>Settings>Control Panel>Network and double click on either the TCP/IP entry located on the tab labeled Configuration under Windows 95 and 98. For other versions of Windows select the tab labeled Protocols, click on Properties and then select the tab labeled IP Address. Figure 3.2 illustrates how this author configured his NT workstation with the IP address of the FBI Web server.

Now that we have configured the IP address of a computer with that of the FBI's Web server, a few words about the future use of the

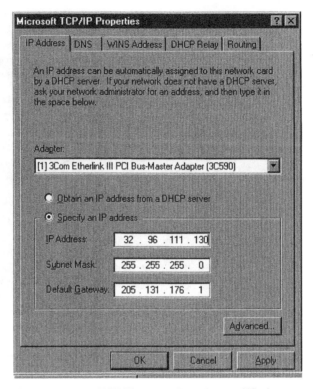

Figure 3.2 Configuring the TCP/IP protocol stack on a Windows computer with the IP address of the FBI's Web server

computer are in order. Because routers do not normally check source IP addresses we can use the computer to perform any type of network activity. However, because the IP address was changed responses will be directed to the IP address we are using. If our computer is connected to a network other than the network associated with the network address used in the IP address assigned to the computer, responses will never flow back to that machine. In effect, we will create a simplex or unidirectional transmission method with respect to the use of the TCP/IP protocol suite.

3.1.4 Spoofing example

To illustrate a relatively simple example of a spoofing attack, let us return to the use of the Ping utility program. If you enter the name of the program without any options the result is a display of the syntax or format of the program and a list of the program options. Figure 3.3 illustrates the resulting display obtained by entering the Ping command by itself. Note that the first option, −t, can be used

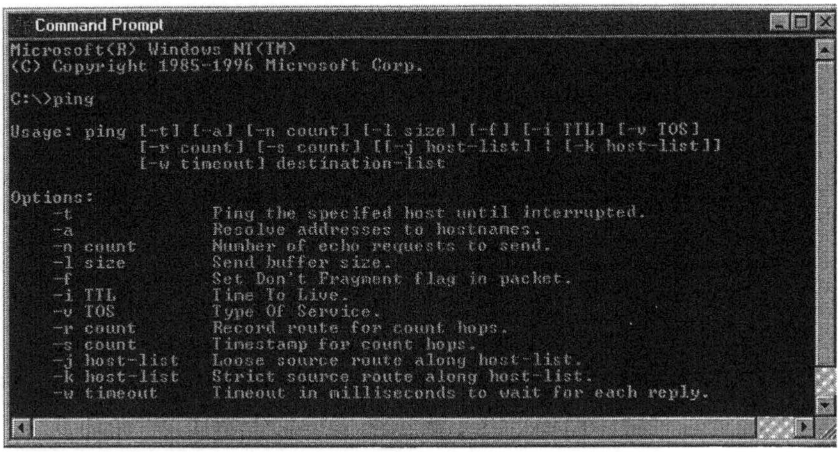

Figure 3.3 Entering the command Ping by itself results in a display of the command format and a description of its options

to generate a continuous series of pings and in fact often represents an unsophisticated attack method since the target device must answer each ping.

To continue our examination of IP spoofing and the use of the Ping utility program, let us point our 'pinger' toward the White House Web site. That is, we will use the Ping command with the −t option and the host address of www.whitehouse.gov.

Figure 3.4 illustrates the initiation of three 'ping attacks' against the White House Web server. Although we used the −t option in each attack, Microsoft's implementation of Ping is similar to many other implementations in that it requires a response. Thus, by default it issues four pings and waits 5 seconds for a response to each ping. If the response is not received the program will terminate. Because we spoofed the IP address of the FBI's Web server we will obviously not receive a response. Thus, this represents a minor predicament for a hacker. The hacker can sit in front of his or her computer and press the F3 key to redisplay the previously entered Ping command and then press the enter key to have the command executed again. Or, with a little bit of effort the hacker can create a batch file that continuously executes another batch file containing the Ping command line shown at the top of Figure 3.4, which pipes the resulting error message onto a file. Regardless of the method used, a stream of pings will flow towards the White House Web server, each containing an IP source address of the FBI's Web server. While the preceding action might result in an interesting conversation in the technical control center of the White House, the important point to note is the fact that IP address

Figure 3.4 Attempting to continuously ping the White House Web server with a spoofed IP address

spoofing represents a powerful technique that is relatively easy to use. Thus, it is important to note the fact that unless we are under attack from a dumb hacker, they will more than likely attempt to hide their identity via IP spoofing.

3.1.5 Why address hiding is difficult to locate

The address hiding method can become more difficult to trace if the hacker uses a random number generator to create spoofed IP addresses instead of using a fixed IP address. This is because although it will take time to trace the use of a fixed spoofed IP address towards its source, it will be relatively impossible to trace changing source addresses. Concerning address tracing, this becomes possible by examining one or more major nodes in a network to determine the port into a router from which the packets with a fixed spoofed IP address are flowing. Working backwards, it becomes possible to trace the source of the packets. However, this tracing takes time since several ISPs could be involved and the actual examination of packet flow requires technicians to program a sniffer to check for the fixed IP source address in packets or the modification of router access lists to log packets that have the source IP address under investigation.

When IP source addresses are randomly changed, it is much more difficult to attempt to locate the source of the attack. This is because each packet has a different source address, which makes it virtually impossible to trace the source of the attack by focusing on the source IP address at different nodes. If the target being attacked is a popular site your logical inclination to backtrack based upon the packet flow to the target destination address would result in a web of locations from which packets originate. This explains why some well-publicized attacks on company Web sites during the late 1990s and during the first year of the new millennium were slow in the identification and arrest of the hacker or hackers whose malicious efforts essentially shut down the target's ability to respond to legitimate requests, an attack referred to as a Denial of Service (DoS) attack (which is covered later in this chapter).

3.1.6 Address selection

While anyone with a bit of knowledge about IP addressing has a virtually unlimited number of addresses to use for spoofing, for some unknown reason (and a few good ones) there are four blocks of favorites. Three of those blocks represent RFC 1918 addresses. As noted in Chapter 2, RFC 1918, titled 'Address Allocation for Private Internets', reserved the following three blocks of IP address space for private internets:

10.0.0.0 to 10.255.255.255 (10/8 prefix)

172.16.0.0 to 172.31.255.255 (172.16/12 prefix)

192.168.0.0 to 192.168.255.255 (192.168/16 prefix)

The key rationale for the selection of an address within one of the above three blocks results from the fact that they cannot be legitimately used on the Internet. Therefore if a host responds to the spoofed address the response will wander the Internet until the datagram's time-to-live (TTL) value decrements to zero and a router throws the datagram into the bit bucket. Thus, nobody is the wiser that the target is busy sending responses to an address that cannot say, 'Help! I'm under attack'.

The fourth block of IP addresses from which a spoofed IP address is commonly selected is the network address of the target to be attacked. For example, assume a hacker is considering attacking the host whose IP address is 205.131.176.11. Because the 205.131.176.0 network is a Class C network, the hacker might consider any source IP address in the range 205.131.176.1 to 205.131.176.254 in an inbound datagram as their spoofed IP address. In Chapter 6 we will describe the use of a router's access list to block packets that have RFC 1918 source addresses, along with other commonly spoofed addresses.

Now that we have an appreciation for IP address spoofing, let us turn our attention to the primary focus of this chapter, network attack methods. In doing so you will note that this author attempted to group related types of network attack method into several common categories. The first general category of network attack methods was classified by this author as general software-based attacks.

3.2 GENERAL SOFTWARE-BASED ATTACKS

Because we have illustrated the effect of IP spoofing via the Ping utility, it represents a good starting point to describe and discuss several attack methods that can be placed under the category of general software-based attacks. Other types of attack that can be considered as general software-based attacks include bogus Java applets, CGI script exploitation, and dictionary attacks. Because each of these attacks is primarily used against hosts, we would normally discuss each method in detail in Chapter 7 when we discuss host attack methods. However, because bogus Java applets can be controlled by a router's access list and dictionary attacks are applicable to breaking into both routers and hosts, we will primarily discuss these two methods in this chapter.

3.2.1 Ping of death

The 'ping of death' is a special term for the use of the Ping application to generate a continuous stream of ICMP echo-request messages to a target. Because most implementations of Ping will terminate when the application detects the absence of a reply, a common method employed by hackers is to use a batch file to continuously run a file containing an appropriate command line entry in another batch file.

The actual generation of a continuous stream of echo-requests can be easily responded to by a host or router. Thus, to generate additional traffic that will further occupy the target in responding to the echo-requests one of three methods is typically used. Those methods include using multiple batch files to generate more traffic, running multiple command prompt windows with each window running the previously described batch file or performing one or more the preceding actions on multiple computers. Concerning the latter, one of the favorite techniques of an unsophisticated hacker is to go into the computer laboratory on a Friday evening and move from computer to computer, creating the previously mentioned batch file and minimizing the window.

The name 'ping of death' associated with this attack method results from the fact that if a sufficient amount of echo-requests flow to a target it will become so busy responding to those requests that it will not have sufficient time available for responding to legitimate service requests. Another common name for this type of attack is a denial of service to other users. Later in this chapter we will describe several types of more sophisticated denial of service attack.

It should be noted that another type of ping of death attack results in the use of a ping utility to create an oversized IP datagram. The length of this datagram exceeds the maximum of 65,536 supported by IP, and when transmitted to some devices causes the target's operating system to crash, hang or reboot. Fortunately, most vendors have correctly modified their TCP/IP protocol stacks and now correctly respond to oversized packets without crashing, hanging or rebooting.

The primary method used to defend against a ping of death attack is to stop echo-request packets from entering your network. Because the router represents the first line of network defense it is quite common to program a router access list to block echo-request packets. In Chapter 4 when we discuss the role of the router we will also discuss and describe how we can program a router's access list to send ICMP echo-request packets to the great bit bucket in the sky.

3.2.2 Bogus Java applets

An applet is a Java program that is executed from within a Web browser. By default, a downloaded applet is considered to be distrusted. This means that a Java-enabled browser will not allow the applet to read or write files nor can the applet start programs on the client system. While these restrictions preclude the ability of an applet from transferring your files to an undesired destination or wiping out your hard drive, it is still within the realm of possibility that a bogus applet can perform a rogue process on a person's computer.

Some applets have been developed that consume resources in a malicious manner, using either all the CPU or memory resources of a computer or tricking the computer user into thinking that a dangerous attack occurred. Concerning the latter, one applet attack paints a large black window on a screen and then displays a fake name, password, or some other information in a dialog box, instructing the user to enter the required information to restart their browser securely. Obviously, any entered information is transmitted to an undesirable location where it can be exploited.

There are two methods commonly used to counter the effect of bogus applets. One method is to prevent applets from reaching a network. This can be accomplished through the use of either a router or firewall. Techniques to block applets will be described later in this book. A second method is to simply educate your user population to kill the browser running on their computer if they encounter an apparent awkward situation. Because many persons surf the Web and select links that can result in a random walk through the Web jungle, education can be an important tool in countering the effect of bogus applets.

3.2.3 Dictionary attacks

A dictionary attack, as its name implies, involves the use of an electronic dictionary to break into a password protected device. That device can be a router, firewall or a host computer. The rationale for the use of an electronic dictionary is the fact that many persons use common names for their passwords. Thus, using the contents of a dictionary will normally ensure success.

Although a 'good' password from the standpoint of protection is one that does not include common names, places, nouns and similar words found in a dictionary, one popular name creation method can be easily compromised and deserves mention. That method involves the placement of numerics as a prefix, suffix, or between concatenated words. For example, consider the potential use of the words 'dog' and 'cat'. A person might be using a computer that requires a minimum of five or six characters for a password. Thus, they might believe that using 'dog4me', 'cat4dog', '29catdog' and similar creative passwords would represent good choices against a dictionary attack. Unfortunately, sophisticated hackers have been known to write scripts that instead of using a dictionary simply try every combination of characters beginning with the smallest size (in characters) password permitted by the target operating system. This type of attack is referred to as a brute force attack.

There are three general preventive measures you can consider against dictionary and brute force attacks. First, if the operating system includes a lockout feature, ensure it is enabled. The lockout feature disables all future login attempts after a defined number of erroneous logins occurs. While many network managers and LAN administrators automatically turn to the use of a lockout feature, it is important to note that it is also a two-edged sword. The reason for this is due to the fact that if a person finds out the user IDs of employees, it is very easy to clock them out of their access to organizational servers over a weekend and observe the fireworks on Monday morning when the LAN administrator has to manually remove lockouts from hundreds or thousands of accounts. The reason for this results from the fact that most organizations use a standard naming convention for user IDs. That convention is the prefix of an employee's initials for their first, middle and last names. If an employee does not have a middle name the letter 'X' is commonly used. For example, John Robert Smith would have the user ID JRSMITH, while John Smith would have the user ID JXSMITH.

While it is necessary to have a lockout facility, it should be employed with other security techniques. Two of those techniques are filtering packets as they flow through a router into the network, and using a firewall to block repetitious actions, such as a sequence of login attempts. If you configure router access lists to only permit packets from trusted networks you may minimize the potential for persons to attempt to break in to the hosts on your network. However, if you operate hosts that permit public access it would be extremely difficult, if not impossible, to block access into your organization's network. In such situations you need a communications device that can examine the contents of packets and compare the contents of preceding and succeeding packets flowing to a common destination to look for suspect activities, such as repeated login attempts. That device is a firewall. In Chapters 4 and 5 we will examine the use of routers and firewalls to enhance network security.

3.3 APPLICATION-BASED ATTACKS

Another grouping of network based attacks can be categorized as application-based attacks. Such attacks use TCP/IP applications, such as electronic mail and the file transfer protocol (FTP) in an attempt to do harm to an organization.

3.3.1 Email-based attacks

Although most readers are more than likely familiar with the term 'spam', used to identify unsolicited junk email, this problem is minor in comparison to the potential effect of a person obtaining the email broadcast address of an organization. To illustrate the adverse potential of the latter, consider Figure 3.5, which illustrates the use of the address 'all.xyz.gov' to protect the guilty at many government agencies. Many times either a location such as 'DC', 'Atlanta' or 'Macon' is used as a prefix to an email address to generate a distribution list to employees within a geographical area, or the term 'all' or 'allemployees' is used as a distribution list name to send an email message to all employees in an organization. In Figure 3.5 we are sending an email to all employees at a government agency. If the agency did not configure their internal email system to preclude access to distribution lists from external mail, the special notice shown in Figure 3.5 would be sent to all employees. Just imagine the effect of this email being sent at 4:00 p.m. on a Tuesday, Wednesday or Thursday! If the person that composed the email visited a public library that was connected to the Internet and did not restrict outbound email, it might be very difficult, if not impossible, to determine the originator of the email, especially if it is a busy library.

Another source of email-related problems is the attachment of a virus to email. During 1998 and 1999 there were a number of well-publicized real and imaginary virus attacks. Concerning the real attacks, some persons simply attached an executable program virus, while the other main attack method was to use a macro so that clicking on the message automatically opened a word processing or spread-sheet program which would in turn automatically execute the macro.

There are several countermeasures you can consider using against email-based attacks. First, you can consider the use of many commercial-based products to filer span. In addition, if your organization only wants to receive email from a defined population, such as another company location, you can use the capability of router access lists or firewalls to filter email originating from other locations.

The ability to disrupt an organization via email to one or more distribution lists can be countered by restricting access to such

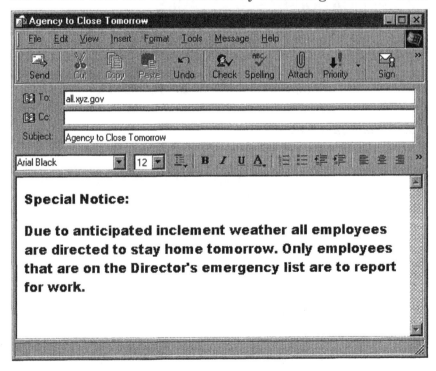

Figure 3.5 Creating a bogus email directed to the distribution list of a government agency

lists. Concerning viruses via email, the solution to this type of attack is twofold. First, a virus scanner should be used. The use of a scanner will be covered in Chapter 6. Secondly, because it is highly possible that a virus scanner may not recognize all types of virus, you need to education your employee population not to open email from unknown sources. Another solution to this problem is to instruct your user population to disable macros so that if they open an email by mistake that they would be better off trashing, it will not have its attached macro automatically executed.

Now that we have a general appreciation for email attacks, let us turn our attention to another popular type of application-based attack: the use of the file transfer protocol (FTP).

3.3.2 FTP attacks

There are several popular FTP types of attack. One attack method recognizes the fact that many Web servers also operate as an FTP server. Thus, if you can break into the computer via FTP you can change Web pages, add or delete files, and perform other malicious acts.

Figure 3.6 illustrates the use of the Windows Command Prompt dialog box for accessing a government operated Web server. Note that FTP transmits passwords in the clear, which results in the ability of many hackers to determine the applicable password to use to break into a computer. Even if an FTP server only provides anonymous access, it is entirely possible to severely impact the ability of the server to perform productive work, as we will shortly note.

In returning our attention to Figure 3.6, it should be noted that this author accessed the FTP server via one of several 'free' Internet accounts he obtained by surfing the Internet. If you examine the last line shown in Figure 3.6, this author was in the process of issuing an mput command that can be very disruptive and will be shortly described.

Figure 3.7 illustrates the use of Windows to obtain access to an FTP server. By experimenting with URLs it is quite possible to determine if a Web server supports FTP and whether or not support is for anonymous FTP or if FTP is password-protected. For example, a popular Web site is http://www.opm.gov. By changing the URL to ftp://www.opm.gov you would be informed that that FTP server does not support anonymous connections; however, because a 'Login as' dialog box was displayed, this informs you that the location supports password-protected FTP.

Once a person is able to log into an FTP password-protected server, they will have the ability to perform several types of disruptive operation. To illustrate this, consider Figure 3.8, which provides a Windows view of the FTP server to include the folders and files on the host. Just imagine the effect of changing a few cgi files, altering the contents of a Web page, or deleting all of the files and folders! Although the preceding may appear to represent the exception rather than the rule for hacker operations, without adequate protection it is possible for this situation to occur.

To protect FTP access you should consider two methods. First, you can configure your access list to support FTP access from approved locations. However, because access via the Internet typically results in the temporary assignment of an IP address, it is difficult to configure a conventional access list to permit authorized users to access FTP. Instead, you will more than likely have to consider the use of a dynamic access list, which is described in Chapter 5.

3.3.3 mget and mput

One of the problems associated with FTP is the fact that you cannot control individual commands. This means that a person that is able to access your organization's server, either via an anonymous or user ID connection, can disrupt network transmission facilities as well as server storage via the use of mget and mput FTP commands. As a refresher, mget permits the reception of multiple files, while mput supports the transmission of multiple files.

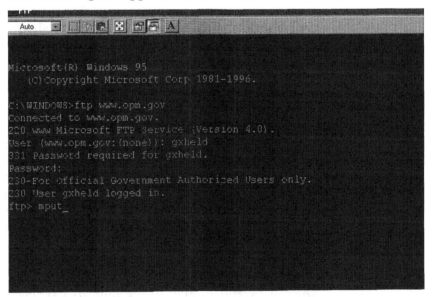

Figure 3.6 Accessing an FTP server via the Command Prompt dialog box

If a hacker accesses an FTP server the simple command mget *.* will result in the retrieval of all files in the current directory. Thus, even if the directory is restricted to read only, the use of a batch file to continuously perform mget *.* operations would adversely effect the ability of legitimate users to receive responses to queries directed to your organization's server. If a spoofed IP address is used your server will be literally pumping out information into the Internet bit bucket!

The use of mput can provide a similar tie-up of your organizations transmission facilities. In addition, if the hacker has a sufficient database to place onto your server, you might return to work on a Monday morning and determine that all available storage is used. Fortunately, Windows 2000 now includes the ability to control the allocation of storage. Concerning the use of mget and mput, the best method to control their use is to preclude their use via a firewall. In Chapter 6 we will examine this topic. However, it should be noted that a batch file that contains a loop can be used to continuously issue get and put commands. Thus, to paraphrase a famous general, 'there is no substitute for several methods of FTP control'. This means that in addition to the use of a firewall you should also consider the use of an access list as well as host FTP configuration controls.

Although the use of mget and mput commands results in an attempt to deny service to a target's legitimate user population, there are several network attack methods that were developed to consume server resources and more accurately represent denial of service attack methods. Thus, let us turn our attention to another

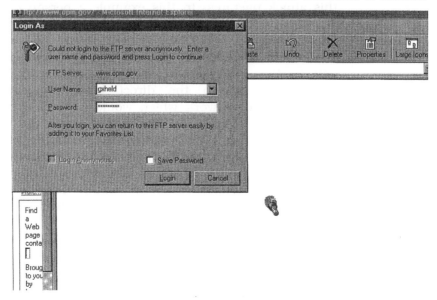

Figure 3.7   Logging onto a password-protected FTP server via Windows

group of network-based attacks that we will classify as denial of service attacks.

3.4 DENIAL OF SERVICE

A true denial of service (DoS) attack is one that attempts to flood a device with so many bogus service requests that its resources are consumed to the point that the target device has little or no capability available to respond to legitimate requests. In this section we will examine the operation of several DoS attack methods, as well as describing appropriate countermeasures and referring to subsequent chapters where detailed countermeasures are described.

3.4.1 Directed broadcasts

One of the favorite methods of some hackers exploits the mapping of an IP broadcast address to a MAC broadcast address. In doing so one IP packet can be converted into hundreds or thousands of frames. It is also possible for this attack method to generate hundreds or thousands of IP packets that attack a third party. Although this attack method represents a directed broadcast attack, it is also popularly referred to as a Smurf attack (named after the cartoon).

To illustrate the potential effect of a directed broadcast, consider Figure 3.9, which illustrates an example of the manner by which this attack operates. In this example a person configures their TCP/IP protocol stack with a spoofed IP address, such as the FBI Web server address. Next, the malicious person generates a continuous sequence of pings to the broadcast address of the network they are attacking. In the example shown in Figure 3.9 pings are sent to the direct broadcast address of the 205.131.175.0 network which would be 205.131.175.255. The router then converts one ping to 254 Ethernet frames that are sent to stations with MAC addresses associated with IP addresses 205.131.175.1 through 205.131.175.254. Depending upon what stations are powered on, up to 254 echo-response packets could be generated. Those responses would flow to the source IP address in the ping. Since the IP address was spoofed to that of the FBI's Web server, each ping generated by the hacker results in 254 packets flowing towards the FBI's Web server. Note how insidious this attack is. Not only does it generate a lot of traffic onto the target network, but it also adversely affects outbound traffic as well as the third party network, in this example, the FBI. Fortunately, the solution to this attack is relatively simple. If

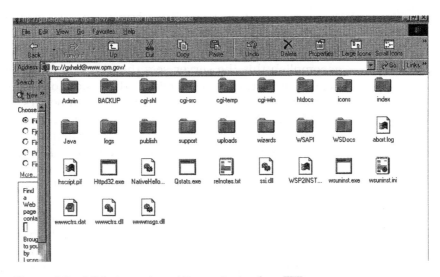

Figure 3.8 A Windows view of the contents of an FTP server

you do not need to support directed broadcasts you can simply stop this capability. To do so in a Cisco router environment you would use the following command:

no ip directed–broadcasts

If you need to support multicast transmissions you should then consider blocking echo-request packets. To do so you would add a deny statement to your router's access list. We will discuss this topic in Chapter 5.

3.4.2 SYN attack

Another popular DoS attack takes advantage of the manner by which TCP operates. This attack method, referred to as a SYN attack, specifically takes advantage of the TCP 3-way handshake that occurs when a host attempts to establish a connection with another computer. To illustrate how this attack occurs let us review the manner by which the 3-way handshake occurs.

Figure 3.10 illustrates the 3-way handshake process that occurs between a client program wishing to connect to a server. This connection could represent a Telenet initial handshake via TCP on port 23, a Web server initial handshake via HTTP on port 80, or another TCP application beginning its operation.

Under the 3-way handshake the client sets its SYN flag bit to tell the server it is requesting a connection. The client also sets the sequence number field in the TCP header to its initial sequence number (ISN). Upon receipt of the SYN segment the server responds with its own ISN and acknowledges the client's first segment. To accomplish this the server sets the SYN and ACK flags in the TCP header it returns. The client then acknowledges the server response and the actual data transfer then occurs.

Under a SYN attack a hacker generates a series of TCP SYN packets. Each packet causes the target system to issue a SYN-ACK response. When the target issues the SYN-ACK response it queues the response into a backlog queue, a temporary holding area to store pending connections. At the same time the target sets a timer, which will cause the entry in the queue to be removed if no response is received and the timer value expires.

Because the backlog queue is of finite length the flooding of TCP SYN packets can rapidly fill the queue and keep it full. Once the queue is full the target will ignore incoming SYN requests. Because any intelligent hacker will use spoofed IP addresses that do not exist, the system being attacked will never receive a response to its SYN-ACK responses. Since the timer is relatively long, it is easy to keep the target's backlog queue full and make it very difficult, if not impossible, for legitimate TCP SYN requests to be accepted by the target.

Both new router features and firewalls provide you with the ability to stop SYN attacks in their tracks. In fact, Cisco's Firewall Feature Set (FFS) is now supported as an extended access list capability referred to as Context Based Access Control (CBAC) and its operation will be described in Chapter 5.

3.5 UDP FLOODING

A UDP flood is also referred to as a chargen (character generator) attack as it takes advantage of the chargen service on a host. When simple TCP/IP Services are installed on a host a UDP datagram sent to the subnet broadcast address of a network with a destination port value of 19 results in each host on the network responding with a packet of 0 to 512 characters chosen randomly for testing purposes. If the hacker generating a sequence of UDP datagrams spoofs the IP address for another host with simple TCP/IP services, the result will be one host, the target, generating a series of characters to the spoofed IP address for each packet it receives. The third party will echo those characters in an attempt to facilitate network testing. Unfortunately, the result of this action is a virtually non-stop flood of useless data passed between the direct target and the third party.

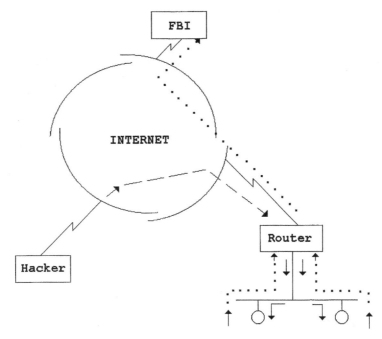

Figure 3.9 A directed broadcast attack using a spoofed IP address associated with the FBI. → ping sent to 205.131.175.0 network; ←· · · responses send to spoofed IP address

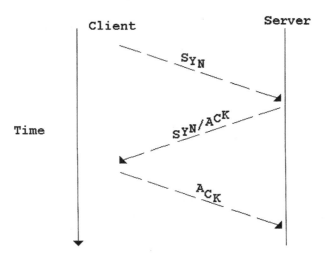

Figure 3.10 The TCP 3-way handshake

There are several methods that can be used to stop the UDP flood. Obviously you could examine all UDP traffic and send UDP datagrams with a destination port 19 to the bit bucket. This could be done via a firewall or a router's access list. In addition, because this malicious attack is most effective by sending datagrams to the subnet broadcast address, turning off directed broadcasts is highly recommended.

In a Windows environment UDP flooding was a serious problem in the past. However, Microsoft issued a hot fix to this problem for both Windows NT Version 4.0 Servers and Workstations. The hot fix results in a default of OFF for receiving and responding to broadcast datagrams on UDP port 19. However, it is still possible to adversely use other hosts or have two routers send a sequence of chargen packets between each device. To prevent the latter you should turn off the router's small server features. Because this is a mechanism to prevent router disturbance we will discuss this technique in the next section in this chapter.

3.6 ROUTER DISTURBANCE

The previously mentioned transmission of a series of UDP datagrams with the destination IP address of a router and a destination port value of 19 represents one method that can adversely effect a router. In addition to causing a sequence of packets to flow to a spoofed address the generation of packets can easily bump up a router's level of utilization. In a Cisco router environment the generic term TCP and UDP small servers is used to refer to echo, chargen and discard used by TCP and UDP. Discard simply ignores whatever is sent to the TCP or UDP port. Because this dynamic troika does not provide any critical service, it is a good idea to turn it off. To do so you would enter the following commands in a Cisco router environment:

no service tcp–small–servers

no service udp–small–servers

A second method that can cause router disturbance will occur when an unauthorized person gains access to the router. This was briefly mentioned when we discussed dictionary attacks, and we will cover this topic in detail in the first portion of Chapter 4 when we discuss the security role of routers.

THE SECURITY ROLE OF THE ROUTER

Because the router functions as a gateway between networks it also represents your first line of network defense. In this chapter we will turn our attention to the security role of this vital communications device. In the first portion of this chapter we will focus our attention upon router access control. The rationale for this coverage is based upon the fact that most routers are remotely administered. Thus, they can be remotely accessed by persons with evil intentions as well as by authorized employees.

In the second portion of this chapter we will turn our attention to router access lists, examining how they are created, their use, and limitations. Because Cisco Systems has approximately 70 percent of the market for routers, we will primarily describe and discuss access control and access lists with respect to Cisco routers. However, the principles to be covered in this chapter are also applicable to other vendor products.

4.1 ACCESS CONTROL

Cisco's Internetworking Operating System (IOS) controls the operation of that vendor's communications devices, including routers and switches. IOS support a command line interface that can be accessed via the router console port, a modem connection, or via a Telnet connection. Of the three methods only the first can offer the possibility of being truly secure as it requires a directly connected terminal device which can be co-located with the router in a secure locked area. Because the other two methods support remote access, they theoretically permit a virtually unlimited number of persons to attempt to access a router's operating system and represent potential vulnerabilities that you need to consider. However, prior to doing so a brief discussion of one of the reasons it is relatively simple to attack a router is in order.

4.1.1 Address and message identity

Many organizations employ an IP addressing scheme which results in the assignment of a .1 (dot one) network address to a router's interface. Thus, if you can use ping or nslookup to determine the IP address of a host, it is then relatively easy to replace the host address with a 'dot 1' address to determine if the device at that address is a router.

A second technique that enables the location of a router to be known is to ping a host for which pings onto the host network are blocked. As previously discussed in Chapter 3, this results in a router returning a 'destination net unreachable' message. If the previous methods do not yield results another popular method is to develop a Telnet scanner to search for the prompt 'User Access Verification' which is returned by Cisco routers when you 'Telnet' to a router's IP address that supports remote access. You can note this by examining Figure 4.1, which indicates an attempted access to a router whose IP address is 205.131.176.1. Note the prompt "User Access Verification".

Cisco routers provide you with three tries to enter a password. If you do not enter a correct password the router displays the message '% bad passwords' and terminates the Telnet session. This results in the display of the dialog box shown in the middle of the display that informs the user 'connection to host lost'. At this time you can manually reconnect and try another series of passwords.

Although we did not break into the router in Figure 4.1, we had three tries to do so. If we write a program to continuously try different combinations of characters over a long weekend it may be possible to gain access to the router. Thus, let us examine router access in detail.

4.1.2 Cisco EXEC sessions

Access to a Cisco router results in a command line session that is referred to as an EXEC session. For those familiar with Unix, an EXEC session is similar to a Unix shell process.

There are two different types of EXEC session supported by Cisco routers: user EXEC and privileged EXEC. A user EXEC session allows a person to perform a limited number of functions, such as

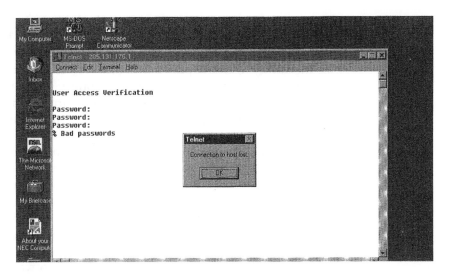

Figure 4.1 Attempting to use Telnet to gain access to a Cisco router

displaying interface information, but does not allow the user to change the router's configuration. In a privileged EXEC session you obtain the ability to perform router configuration operations as well as all of the functions available to the user EXEC session mode of operation.

All logins to a Cisco router first result in an entry into the router's user EXEC mode. When this occurs you will encounter a greater than sign (>) prompt. That prompt follows the name configured for the router or, if no name was assigned, the default 'Router' is displayed. To enter the privilege EXEC mode a person first enters the command 'enable'. This action results in the prompt 'Password': which, when a password is successfully entered, places the user in the privileged EXEC mode. When this occurs, the prompt changes to a pound (#) sign as illustrated by the following sequence for a router named Macon.

        Macon>enable
        Password:
        Macon#

4.1.3 Password protection

If you have initial access to a Cisco router you can assign a password for initial access to the router with the password line command. The format of this commands is:

Password text

where 'text' can contain any string of alphanumeric characters, including spaces up to 80 characters in length. The alphabetic characters are case sensitive, which provides a router administrator with the ability to create passwords that would be extremely difficult and time-consuming to guess via a dictionary or brute force attack method. Unfortunately, in a haste to configure a router for remote access and to keep things simple, many administrators use such classic passwords as 'bingo', 'tiger', 'router', and even 'Cisco'.

To assign a password for the privileged command level you would use a router's enable password global configuration command. This means you must first enter the privileged command level via the enable command. If a password for the privileged mode was not previously set, you will not be prompted for one. Unfortunately, this is a common omission when some organizations receive their first few routers and rush to establish an Internet connection. The absence of router passwords can be equated to walking barefoot. While you might reach your destination unharmed, there is also a distinct chance for a serious reversal of fortune! Once you enter the privileged mode you could use the enable password command as shown below to set the password to supersecret.

    enable-password supersecret

4.1.4 Telnet access

Each Telnet port on a router is referred to as a virtual terminal (vty). Cisco routers support a maximum of five vty ports that are numbered 0 through 4. You can configure nonprivileged passwords for Telnet access via the use of the password command. The following example illustrates the assignment of the password 4hard2guess to vty ports 0 through 4.

    line vty 0 4
    login
    password 4hard2guess

When a user Telnets to the router's IP address, the router will prompt the user to enter a password. The user-router interaction will be similar to that shown below:

    %telnet 198.78.46.1
    Trying. . . .
    Connected to 198.78.46.1
    Escape character is '^]'

User Access Verification
Password:

Once the user has entered the correct nonprivileged password, the following prompt is displayed:

Router>

At this point the remote user can use the enable command in an attempt to access the router's EXEC privileged mode.

4.1.5 Password encryption

By default anyone that has privileged access to a router can view all of the passwords set on the router. For example, suppose you assigned usernames techman and investor the passwords good4me and notgood4u as shown below.

username techman good4me
username investor notgood4u

Without encrypting passwords anyone with privileged access to the router can view each user's password as well as the general user and enable passwords. This means that it becomes possible for one user to access the router as another user. If you configured your router to log activity to a server you might be tempted to blame the wrong party for the mess he or she creates, either on purpose or inadvertently.

Prior to discussing password encryption a few words about usernames are in order. The use of the username command allows you to assign separate, unique, personalized login names for each administrator. By assigning usernames to virtual terminal (vty) lines you can require persons attempting to gain remote access to a router to know both a username and associated password which makes it more difficult for an uninvited user to gain access to a router.

To encrypt router passwords you would use the service password-encryption global configuration command. The format of that command is:

service password-encryption

It should be noted that Cisco's password encryption scheme produces what is referred to as a type 7 password due to this digit being used as a prefix to the encrypted password scheme. It should also be noted that a search of the Web using 'type 7 passwords' or 'Cisco router password encryption' will provide several references to the fact that the encryption scheme used is more accurately a simple scrambling method and that the resulting scrambled passwords can be decoded quite easily. Due to this it is suggested that the enable secret command should be used to better protect the enable password.

4.1.6 Using the enable secret command

The enable secret command uses Message Digest 5 (MD5), a one-way cryptographic hash function to encrypt the password. This means simple re-scrambling will not suffice to obtain the source of the password. Instead, someone must use a password generation program against the algorithm and compare the result against the MD5 result to determine the clear value of the password. This is obviously much more difficult than simply viewing stored passwords. The following example illustrates the use of the enable secret global configuration command:

```
Macon(config)#enable secret bingo7
Macon(config)#exit
Macon#show running-config
Building configuration. . .

enable secret 5 $e$K3ghM$4X. . .
```

Note that a prefix of '5' is used to identify the use of MD5. Because of this, the resulting encrypted password is also referred to as a type 5 password. You should also note that because MD5 is a one-way hash algorithm, it cannot be used to encrypt all passwords, such as those used by the Network Time Protocol (NTP) and similar protocols that require access to clear text strings.

You can considerably preclude dictionary and brute force attacks by selecting applicable length passwords with an appropriate mix of characters. By encrypting passwords you make it more difficult for one person to use the access privileges of another. While these techniques are recommended to provide a barrier to unauthorized persons gaining access to your organizational routers, you can also limit access via the use of an applicable access list.

4.1.7 Access list restrictions

Although we will discuss the use of Cisco access lists in considerable detail in the second portion of this chapter, we note that you can limit access or even block all Telnet access. To do so you would use several IOS commands. For example, you can use the transport command in conjunction with a line command to disable the Telnet listener on your router. The following example turns off the Telnet listener on all vty lines.

```
line vty 0 4
transport input none
```

You can also use the access-list and access-class commands to limit access from specific IP addresses. For example, assume you want to restrict vty access to your router to users on the 198.78.46.0 network. To do so you would use the following IOS statements:

```
access-list 1 permit 198.78.46.0 0.0.0.255
!
line vty 0 4
access-class 1 in
```

In the preceding example, the access list statement permits packets with a source address on the 198.78.46.0 network. As we will note when we examine access lists in detail in the second portion of this chapter, 0.0.0.255 represents a wildcard-mask that functions in a reverse manner to a subnet mask, requiring matches for '0' bit positions and not caring for '1' bit positions.

The access-class statement provides you with the capability to define the access checks made in a particular direction. The format of this command is shown below:

```
access-class list number {in|out}
```

where the list number is an integer between 1 and 99 and refers to the direction in which an access list is applied. Because the list number is between 1 and 99 this also means that the access-class statement is only applicable to a standard access list. The keyword 'in' applies to incoming connections, such as virtual terminals. In comparison, the keyword 'out' applies to outgoing Telnet connections, such as a person who gains access to your router's EXEC mode and attempts to initiate a Telnet connection to another host. Thus, the preceding series of three IOS commands restricts the ability to connect to the virtual terminals on the router (terminal lines 0 through 4) to hosts on the 198.78.46.0 network.

4.1.8 Protecting the hardwired connection

Because a connection to the console is accomplished by directly cabling a terminal device to the port, it is assumed that the person operating the terminal is authorized. Due to this, this type of connection is by default provided EXEC mode access without a password. Because it is quite possible for an unauthorized person to experiment with gaining full router access, it is a good idea to set a user EXEC password on those ports. To do so you would enter the following statements:

```
line console 0
login
password hard2guess4
exec-timeout 5 0
```

When you log onto the router its login prompt would be as follows:

```
User Access Verification
Password:
```

At this point you would have to enter the password to gain access to the router. Because the default timeout for an unattended console is 10 minutes you may wish to lower this value. To do so you would use the exec-timeout command whose format is shown below:

```
exec-timeout m s
```

where m is the time in minutes and s is the time in seconds of an activity that forces a session timeout. In the above example we lowered the timeout to 5 minutes.

Table 4.1 provides a summary of Cisco security management related commands that we previously examined. While the exec-timeout command can technically be applicable to supporting a policy to prevent persons from connecting and hogging access to

Table 4.1 Cisco security management commands.

Command	Operational effect
line console 0	Establish a password on the console terminal.
line vty 0 4	Establish a password for Telnet connections.
enable-password	Establish a password for access to the privileged EXEC mode.
enable secret	Establish an enable secret password using MD5 encryption.
exec-timeout m s	Establish an idle timeout period in minutes and seconds which when reached terminates the connection.
password text	Establish a password for access to user EXEC mode.
service password-encryption	Scramble the display of passwords to protect them from view by the use of the show running-config command.

the router throughout the day, this author also considers the command to enhance security management. Thus, this command is included in the referenced table.

4.1.9 Considering SNMP

The Simple Network Management Protocol (SNMP) represents a potential vulnerability because it uses community names for access control that are test strings. All too often the default community name of 'public' is used and it provides a mechanism for persons to attempt to exploit an opening in your router's defense.

You can use the snmp-server community command to assign a community name as well as restrict SNMP operations to read only. The format of this command is shown below:

snmp-server community name {ro|rw} list number

where 'name' represents a community name, 'ro' represents read only, and 'rw' represents read/write capability so certain Management Information Base (MIB) objects can be changed. 'List number' represents an integer between 1 and 99 that refers to a standard access list.

To illustrate an example of the use of the snmp-server community statement, assume you want to restrict access to SNMP reads to one host on the 198.78.46.8. To do so you would code the following IOS commands:

snmp-sever community yo4mo52be ro 1
access-list 1 permit host 198.78.46.8

Note that in the first statement we changed the default community name to you4mo52be. Because you can configure the management station with the changed community name, you should always use a hard-to-guess name. In addition, note that we used the 'ro' option to restrict access to the MIB to read-only and used a list number of 1 to associate the first command with the access list which only permits access from the hosts we previously defined.

A second SNMP related area you need to consider is the transmission of traps. Although most SNMP commands are initiated by a management station to an agent, an agent can be configured to transmit unsolicited packets to the management station where certain predefined conditions occur. These unsolicited packets represent SNMP traps.

There are three snmp-related commands you can use to control traps. The first is snmp-server trap-authentication, which enables a router to transmit a trap message when it receives a packet with an incorrect community string. This is a highly recommended command to use as it will alert the management station to both mistaken access attempts as well as brute force and dictionary based attacks.

The second command is snmp-server trap-source, which indicates the interface where traps originate. The third command, snmp-server host, permits you to associate an IP address or host name with a community name. For example, assume you want to send traps to the host at 198.78.46.8 from interface Ethernet1 using the community name yo4mo52be. You would then code the following IOS statements:

```
snmp-server trap-authentication
snmp-server trap-source Ethernet1
snmp-server host 198.78.46.8 yo4mo52be
```

Now that we have an appreciation for router access control methods to include SNMP, let us turn our attention to a more formal and detailed examination of access lists.

4.2 ACCESS LISTS

An access list can be defined as 'an ordered set of statements that permit or deny the flow of packets across an interface'. As such, an access list represents a filtering mechanism since the list parameters are matched against applicable information in each packet.

4.2.1 Interface considerations

The creation of an access list represents the first part in a two-part process. The second step is to apply the access list to a specific direction on an interface. Concerning the direction, it is important to note that the flow of packets from a router is considered to represent an outbound direction while the flow of packets toward a router represents the inbound direction. This means you must carefully consider the direction of packet flow in conjunction with the devices whose packets you wish to filter. To better understand this concept, consider Figure 4.2 which illustrates the direction of inbound and outbound packet flow with respect to a router that has one serial and two Ethernet ports.

In examining Figure 4.2 note that if you want to stop certain types of packets arriving from the Internet you would apply an

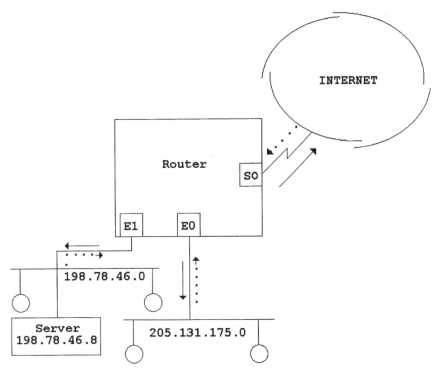

Figure 4.2 Inbound and outbound packet flow. → outbound packet flow; - - → inbound packet flow

access list to the s0 (serial^0) port in the inbound direction. In comparison, let us assume you want to block certain users on the Ethernet1 (e1) network from accessing the Internet. You could apply an access list to either the e1 or s0 interface. If you apply the access list to the e1 interface you would apply it in the inbound direction. In comparison, if you wanted to use the s0 interface you would apply the access list in the outbound direction.

Also note that if you want to block traffic from the 198.78.46.0 network from flowing to the 205.131.175.0 network, you could either filter packets inbound to interface e1 or outbound from interface e0. In comparison, if you wanted to block traffic on the 198.78.46.0 and 205.131.175.0 networks from flowing to the Internet you could apply an appropriate access list to interface s0. This illustrates an important concept concerning access lists. That is, you must carefully consider both the interface and the direction in which an access list is applied to an interface, topics which we will examine in additional detail as we expand our coverage of access lists in this chapter.

4.2.2 Types of access list

Cisco routers support two types of access list, standard and extended. In the first portion of this chapter we briefly looked at the use of a standard access list to control hosts that could gain vty access to a router. Now we will examine the format and use of access lists in much more detail. In doing so we will primarily focus our attention upon IP access lists since IP is the only protocol supported for use on the Internet.

4.2.3 Standard IP access lists

The format of a standard IP access list is shown below:

access-list [list #] [permit | deny] [source
address] [wild-card-mask] [log]

In examining the format of a standard IP access list a few items require a degree of elaboration. First, the term 'access-list' requires a dash between the two words. Secondly, the list number is a numeric between 1 and 99 for the IP protocol and is used to identify the access list statements belonging to a common access list. Because a standard IP access list number must be within the range 1 to 99, the list number also defines the protocol that the access list operates upon.

Keywords

The permit or deny keyword identifies whether filtering permits or prohibits packets that match the source address and wildcard mask from flowing through an interface. The keyword permit allows packets to flow through an interface that match the address criteria, while the keyword deny sends packets matching the specified source address into the bit bucket.

Source address

For a standard IP access list the source address represents the IP address of a host or group of hosts specified using dotted decimal notation. In actuality, the specification of a group of hosts is accomplished through the use of a wildcard-mask. Thus, let us turn our attention to this topic prior to examining several examples of the use of standard IP access list statements.

The wildcard-mask

As previously noted in this chapter, the wildcard-mask functions in a reverse manner to a subnet mask. That is, this mask uses a binary 0 to represent a match and a binary 1 to represent a 'not caring' condition.

To illustrate the use of a wildcard-mask, assume your organization has the Class C network address of 205.131.175.0. If no subnets were configured for that network, each station would have a subnet mask of 255.255.255.0. Here each binary 1 (255 is a byte of all 1's) represents a match, while a 0 bit represents a not caring condition. Thus, specifying 255 in each of the first three positions of the four position subnet mask field results in the TCP/IP protocol stack matching the network address in each packet and not caring about the host address. Because the Cisco wildcard-mask functions in an opposite manner with respect to binary 1's and 0's, the mask required to allow all packets with a source network address of 205.131.175.0 would be 0.0.0.255. Then, a standard access list statement that would enable all packets with a source network address of 205.131.175.0 would be coded as follows:

> access-list 1 permit 205.131.175.0 0.0.0.255

Because the wildcard-mask represents the complement of the subnet mask, you can determine the subnet mask and take its inverse. For example, a subnet mask of 255.255.0.0 results in a wildcard-mask of 0.0.255.255.

To illustrate another example of a standard access list suppose you wish to permit packets from hosts on the previously mentioned network as well as the 198.78.46.0 network but preclude hosts from the 198.78.22.0 network. Your access list would be as follows:

> access-list 1 permit 205.131.175.0 0.0.0.255
> access-list 1 permit 198.78.46.0 0.0.0.255

Wait! Where is the deny statement, you ask? While you could add the appropriate statement, each access list has an implicit deny everything at the end of the list. Because access lists are processed top down, we only need to permit what we want to permit, as all else is denied. For those of us that get tired of typing network addresses and wildcard-masks, Cisco access lists support two keywords that can simplify the address specification process. A third keyword provides a logging function. Although most access list keywords are only applicable to extended access lists, these three are also applicable to standard access lists, so let us examine them now.

The host keyword

Host is used to denote an exact match and represents a shorthand notation for a mask of 0.0.0.0. For example, assume you want to permit packets from the host address 205.131.175.1. To do so you could code the following access list statement:

access-list 1 permit 205.131.175.1 0.0.0.0

Because the keyword host signifies an exact match you can re-code the previous access list statement as follows:

access-list 1 permit host 205.131.175.1

The any keyword

A second keyword supported by a standard access list is any. This keyword is used as an abbreviation for a source address and wildcard-mask of 0.0.0.0 255.255.255.255. To illustrate the use of host and any keywords let us assume you want to deny packets from source address 205.131.175.1 and permit all other addresses. The standard access list statements to accomplish this would be as follows:

access-list 1 deny host 205.131.175.1
access-list 1 permit any

If you observe the order of the two statements, we first explicitly denied packets from the specified host. This is because processing occurs top down. If we reversed the order the effect would be to permit all packets, a condition we would not want to occur in this situation.

The log keyword

The keyword log represents an addition to access lists that occurred in IOS Version 11.3. When you include this keyword in an access list it results in the logging of packets that match permit and deny statements in the access list.

After you apply an access list with the log keyword to an interface the first packet that meets a condition in the list causes an immediate logging message to occur. Thereafter, packets matching the access list conditions are either displayed on the console or logged to memory every five minutes. Logged messages include the access list number, whether the packet was permitted or denied, the source IP address and the number of packets that were matched during the five minute interval succeeding the first match. For example, assume the following standard IP access list statement:

>   access-list 1 permit host 205.131.175.1 log
>   access-list 1 deny host 205.131.175.2 log

Assume that over a five minute period host 205.131.175.2 issued 10 packets. When the first match occurred the following would be displayed on the router console or logged to memory, with the actual logging controlled by the 'logging console' command.

>   list 1 deny 205.131.175.2 1 packet

Then, five minutes later the following display or logged message to memory would occur:

>   list 1 deny 205.131.175.2 9 packets

The ability to log access list matches provides you with both a testing and alert capability. You can use logging to test the development of different access lists by observing the resulting match of packets as different activities are attempted. When used as an alert facility, you would scan the display to locate repeated attempts to perform an activity you designed an access list to deny. In this situation, repeated attempts to perform an activity which the access list statement was developed to deny, would more than likely indicate a potential attack.

In examining the standard access list format, you will note it only provides a mechanism to filter based upon source address. In comparison, an extended access list, as its name implies, extends the packet filtering capability.

4.2.4 Extended IP access lists

Through the use of an extended IP access list you obtain the ability to filter based upon source and destination address, protocol, source and destination port, as well as other options that significantly enhance your ability to permit or deny packets flowing across an interface. The general format of an extended IP access list is shown below:

>   access-list[list#][permit | deny][protocol][source
>   address source-wildcard][source port][destination
>   address destination-wildcard][destination
>   port][log][options]

To obtain an appreciation of the operation of an extended IP access list, let us examine the use of each of the fields in the above format, including some of the options supported by this statement.

The list number field

The list number field identifies statements that make up an access list as well as the type of access list. An extended IP access list uses numbers 100 through 199 which enables 100 unique extended IP access lists to be defined.

The protocol field

The protocol field entry defines the protocol to be filtered. You can filter on IP, TCP and UDP, as well as on different routing protocols. When creating an extended IP access list statement, it is important to remember the relationship of protocols within the TCP/IP protocol suite that form IP datagrams. As indicated in Chapter 2, an IP header is used to transport ICMP, TCP, UDP and various routing protocols. This means that if you specify IP as the protocol to be filtered, all matches against other fields will cause the packet to be either permitted or denied regardless of whether the packet represents an application transported by TCP or UDP, an ICMP message, or a routing protocol. This also means that if you intend to filter based upon a specific protocol you need to specify that protocol. Thus, you need to specify more specific entries prior to less specific entries. For example, assume the following statements:

```
access-list 101 permit ip any any
access-list 101 deny tcp any host 198.78.46.8
```

Because the first statement permits IP from any host to any host, this means you could not block TCP from any shot to the host whose IP address is 198.78.46.8 as the second statement would never take effect. You would need to reverse the order of statements which is why more specific entries should be placed ahead of less specific entries.

Source address and wildcard-mask fields

The source address and wildcard-mask for an extended IP access list functions in the same manner as for a standard IP access list.

This means you can use the keywords 'host' and 'any' and avoid specifying a mask.

Source port number field

You can use either an integer or mnemonic to specify a port number. For example, to specify the Web's HyperText Transmission Protocol (HTTP) you can use either 80 or http. In addition, for TCP and UDP you can use the keyword operators lt (less than), gt (greater than), eq (equal), and neq (not equal).

Destination address and wildcard-mask fields

The destination address and wildcard-mask have the same structure as the source address and wildcard-mask. Thus, you can use the keywords 'host' and 'any' to specify a specific address or any destination address without having to specify a mask.

Destination port number

Similarly to the source port, you can specify the destination port as a numeric or mnemonic. You can also use an operator to specify a range. The following example illustrates the use of both a numeric and mnemonic to block Web surfing from any source to the 198.78.46.0 network.

```
access-list 101 deny tcp any 198.78.46.0 0.0.0.255 eq 80
access-list 101 deny tcp any 198.78.46.0 0.0.0.255 eq http
```

Options

Extended IP access lists support a wide range of options. One commonly used option is 'log' which was described when we examined standard IP access lists. Another commonly used option is 'established'. This option is only applicable to the TCP protocol and is employed to restrict TCP traffic in one direction as a response to sessions initiated in the opposite direction. To accomplish this, an access list statement that contains the word 'established' results in each packet being examined to determine if its ACK or RST bit is set. If so, this condition indicates that the packet is part of a previously established TCP connection.

To illustrate the use of the keyword 'established' in an extended IP access list statement, let us assume that the Ethernet network shown in Figure 4.2 has the IP address 205.131.175.0. To restrict TCP packets flowing from the Internet to those in response to packets originating on the Ethernet network you would use the following access list statement:

> access-list 101 permit tcp any 205.131.175.0 0.0.0.255 established

In examining the use of the keyword 'established' there are several points to note. First, although its use provides a mechanism to control access from a router's untrusted side based upon traffic originated from the trusted side, the method used is rather primitive. That is, packets are considered to be kosher if their ACK or RST bit is set, a condition easy for a hacker to overcome. Secondly, 'established' is only applicable to TCP as there is no field in a UDP header to indicate that a UDP segment is a response packet. As we will note later in this chapter, reflexive access lists and Context Based Access Control (CBAC) provide more powerful mechanisms for controlling access via the untrusted side of a router based upon the flow of packets from the trusted side of the router.

To facilitate the use of Cisco extended IP access lists, Table 4.2 provides a list of commonly used keywords and a brief description of their use. As we continue our examination of the use of IP access lists in this chapter, we will examine the use of most of the keywords listed in this table. However, one keyword deserves a brief mention now as it provides a mechanism to add comments to an access list. That keyword is remark, which is placed after an access list number and allows you to place a comment in an access list. The following example illustrates its use.

> access-list 101 remark allow TCP to our network
> access-list 101 permit tcp any any

4.2.5 Rules and guidelines

There are several general 'rules' and guidelines you should consider when creating and applying Cisco access lists. The rules we will examine represent factual information, while the guidelines represent informative suggestions. The factual information is based upon the manner by which access list processing occurs, while the information suggestions are based upon the experience of this author.

Table 4.2 Extended IP access list keywords.

Keyword	Utilization
any	an abbreviation for an address and wildcard-mask value of 0.0.0.0 255.255.255.255. This keyword is applicable to both source and destination address fields.
established	Causes a match if the ACK or RST bits are set in the TCP header.
host	An abbreviation for a wildcard-mask of 0.0.0.0. This keyword is applicable to both source and destination address fields.
icmp-type	Provides a mechanism for filtering ICMP messages by their message type. You can also specify the ICMP message code (0 to 255).
port	Provides a mechanism to define the decimal number or name of a TCP or UDP port.
protocol	Provides a mechanism to define a specific protocol for filtering. The specified protocol can include one of the keywords eigrp, gre, icmp, igmp, igrp, ip, ipinip, nos, ospf, tcp or udp, or an integer between 0 and 255 which represents an IP protocol.
precedence	Provides a mechanism for filtering by the precedence level name or precedence number (0 to 7) in the IP Type of Service field.
remark	Provides a mechanism for adding text comments for an access list.
TOS *tos*	Provides a mechanism for filtering based upon the name or service level in the IP Type of Service field.

Top down processing

The evaluation of an access list results in a sequential examination of statements commencing at the top of the list. This means you must carefully consider the order in which you place statements in an access list.

Access list additions

New entries are automatically placed at the bottom of an access list. This means it may be difficult or even impossible to change the functionality of an access list. If so, you will then have to consider creating a new list, deleting the existing list, and applying the new list to an interface.

Access list placement

You should consider placing extended access lists as close as possible to the source being filtered. This is because this minimizes the potential effect of filtering on the dataflow on other interfaces. In comparison, consider placing standard access lists as close as possible to the destination. This results from the fact that a standard access list is limited to filtering on source addresses. Thus, if you placed the list too close to the source it could block the flow of packets to other ports.

Statement placement

Because an IP datagram is used to transport ICMP, TCP, UDP and various routing protocols, you should place more specific entries in an access list before less specific entries. This ensures that the placement of one statement before another does not negate the effect of a statement appearing later in the list.

Access list application

An access list does not go into effect until it is applied to an interface via an access-group command. Remember, until the access list is applied to an interface the list has no effect upon the flow of packets.

Filtering direction

Use the filtering direction to define whether inbound or outbound packets are filtered. Remember that packets flowing away from a router's interface are outbound while packets flowing towards a router are inbound.

Router generated packets

Packets generated by a router, such as a 'destination net unreachable' message or a routing table update, cannot be filtered by an access list applied to outbound traffic. However, you can control such packets either by filtering their arrival via an access list applied in an inbound direction or turning their generation off via an applicable IOS command.

4.2.6 Creating and applying an access list

Cisco routers support the creation of an access list via several methods. You can create an access list directly from the console, via a vty connection, or via a word processor or text editor. If you use a word processor or text editor you would store the resulting file as

ASCII text and use the computer you stored the file on as a server. To accomplish this you need to install a trivial file transfer program (tftp) on your computer that operates as a server and you would then use the router as a client to upload or retrieve the previously created file. Figure 4.3 illustrates the Cisco TFTP Server screen with its option dialog box displayed. Note that this is a relatively simple program that allows you to specify the TFTP server root directory and the name and location of a log file as well as whether or not the progress of file transfers are displayed and logging is enabled.

To apply an access list to a router requires a three-step process. First, you need to create an access list. Then you need to apply it to an interface. Finally, you need a method to define the direction in which the access list will be applied to an interface.

4.2.7 Specifying an interface

You specify a router interface through the use of the 'interface' command. For example, to apply an access list to serial port 0 (previously shown in Figure 4.2), you would define the interface with the following command:

    interface serial0

Similarly, to apply an access list to a router port connected to a LAN you would use the interface command with the name and port identifier of the connection. For example, assuming the router port was e0 shown in Figure 4.2, you could enter the following:

    interface ethernet0

Because you can abbreviate most keywords in a command, you could also use e0 in the command as shown below.

    interface e0

4.2.8 Using the ip access-group command

The third step in the three-step process is to define the direction of the interface that the access list works on. To do so you would use the ip access-group command whose format is shown below:

    ip access-group [list number] [in | out]

Similarly to other commands, the list number identifies a particular access list. The keyword 'in' or 'out' identifies the direction in which the access list will be applied. That is, if packets are flowing towards

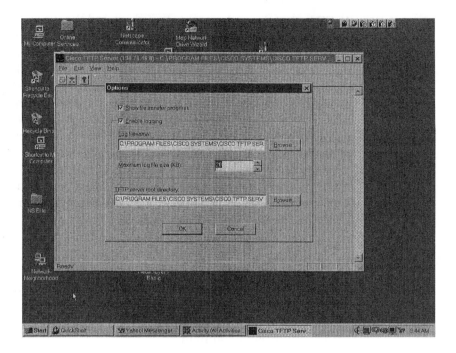

Figure 4.3 Cisco's TFTP server program permits you to create access lists that can be uploaded from a PC to a router

the router you would use the keyword 'in', while you would use the keyword 'out' if they are flowing out of a particular router interface.

To illustrate an example of the three-step process, let us create an access list. In doing so assume our network configuration is that shown in Figure 4.2. Let us further assume that we want to restrict data originating from the Internet to Web traffic bound for the host whose IP address is 198.78.46.8. In addition, we want to allow users on the 205 and 198 networks shown in Figure 4.2 to initiate Telnet and Web-based queries to hosts on the Internet and allow the results of those queries to return via the Internet. To do so our access list would be as follows:

```
interface serial0
ip access-group 110 in
access-list 110 remark allow TCP with ACK or RST bit set
access-list 110 permit TCP any any established
access-list 110 remark allow Web access to server
access-list 110 permit TCP any host 198.78.46.8 eq 80
```

access-list 110 remark block everything else
access-list 110 deny ip any any

In the preceding example the 'interface' command was first used to define serial port 0. Next, the 'ip access-group' command was used to apply the access list statements we will enter as access list number 110 in the inbound direction on the serial interface. This was followed by the entry of six access list statements that form the actual access list. Note that for internal documentation three statements include remarks. Thus, let us focus our attention upon the other three statements in the access list.

The first non-remark statement permits TCP traffic that responds to queries initiated from the internal Ethernet networks. This is due to the keyword 'established' in the statement. The second non-remark statement permits Web traffic (port 80) from any host on the Internet to the server whose IP address is 198.78.46.8. The third non-remark statement is not really necessary as an access list has a 'deny all' implicitly placed at the end of the list.

In examining the preceding access list it is important to note it could create a problem for Web surfers and other persons using the Internet. This is because, although TCP traffic is permitted, all other traffic is blocked. This means your internal network users cannot use DNS as it is carried via UDP, nor can they use ping as ICMP messages are not permitted.

To allow UDP we could add the following statement before the deny statement:

access-list 110 permit UDP any any eq 53

In the preceding statement port 53 represents DNS. Thus, instead of opening all UDP access we will just allow DNS.

To allow pings we can permit echo replies to echo requests. Thus, we could add either of the following statements to our access list:

access-list 110 permit icmp any any echo-reply
or   access-list 110 permit icmp any any eq 0

Here the value 0 represents the ICMP type number for echo reply. Table 4.3 provides a summary of ICMP message type codes and the corresponding name associated with the type code.

4.2.9 Limiting ICMP

To make your TCP connection more secure you should consider limiting the types of ICMP message allowed to flow through your router. As previously indicated in our short extended IP access

Table 4.3 ICMP type numbers.

Type number	Name
0	Echo Reply
1	Unassigned
2	Unassigned
3	Destination Unreachable
4	Source Quench
5	Redirect
6	Alternate Host Address
7	Unassigned
8	Echo
9	Router Advertisement
10	Router Selection
11	Time Exceeded
12	Parameter Problem
13	Timestamp
14	Timestamp Reply
15	Information Request
16	Information Reply
17	Address Mask Request
18	Address Mask Reply
19	Reserved (for Security)
20–29	Reserved (for Robustness Experiment)
30	Traceroute
31	Datagram Conversion Error
32	Mobile Host Redirect
33	IPv6 Where-Are-You
34	IPv6 I-Am-Here
35	Mobile Registration Request
36	Mobile Registration Reply
37	Domain Name Request
38	Domain Name Reply
39	SKIP
40	Photuris
41–255	Reserved

list example addendum, you can include a permit statement to allow a specific type of ICMP message. If you do not allow any ICMP and do not include a permit for the IP protocol, then all ICMP messages will be blocked. Before you block all ICMP messages there are certain ICMP messages you should consider permitting and others you may wish to block. Thus, let us focus our attention upon those messages. In doing so we will again assume the access list will be applied to the serial interface in Figure 4.2 in the inbound direction to the 205.131.175.0 network. You would obviously add an additional permit statement if you wish to allow applicable traffic to the other Ethernet network.

4.2.10 Permitting echo-reply

If you have no outbound restrictions then you are only filtering inbound packets. Thus, echo-requests transmitted from either Ethernet result in an echo-reply. To allow responses to those pings you could code the following statement into your access list:

> access-list 101 permit icmp any 198.78.46.0 0.0.0.255 echo-reply

4.2.11 Permitting pings

Although ping can be used as a discovery weapon to probe your network to discover information about your organization's resources, it can also be helpful for determining the status of certain devices. For example, if your organization administers a remote Web server you might wish to permit pings to that server from your IP address. Assuming your IP address is 192.36.25.11, to permit pings to the server at 198.78.46.8 you would enter the following statement:

> access-list 101 permit icmp host 192.36.25.11 host 198.78.46.8 echo

4.2.12 Considering destination unreachable

By default, when an access list sends a packet to the great bit bucket in the sky the router will return a type 3 ICMP message that has a code value of 13. This message, which is displayed as 'Destination net unreachable', informs the person issuing the packet that the router on the path to that target address is performing access list filtering. There is a special router statement you can use to prevent this information from being determined by a potential hacker. After all, why make their job easier? That statement is:

> no ip unreachables

which you would enter for each router interface providing an Internet connection. The reason you cannot use an access list statement is due to the fact that router generated packets are not checked by an access list applied in an outbound direction. Thus, to turn off the previously mentioned message you need to enter the no ip unreachables statement.

4.2.13 Anti-spoofing statements

Regardless of the type of access list employed, one of the first series of statements in your list should be anti-address spoofing statements. Because hackers like to use RFC 1918 addresses you should deny all packets with a source address in three address blocks in RFC 1918. In addition, you should block all packets with an IP address of all zeros, all ones, and the IP loopback address of 127.0.0.0. If your organization does not support multicast (Class D) nor any experimental access via Class E addresses, there is also no reason to allow packets with Class D or class E source addresses. Finally, because some hackers think it is funny to use a source address of the network they are attacking, you should block all packets with a source address associated with your network. If we assume the internal network to be protected has the network address 198.78.46.0, then the initial anti-spoofing statements at the beginning of your access list would be as follows:

```
!Anti-spoofing statements
!
!Deny RFC 1918 addresses
access-list 101 deny 10.0.0.0 0.255.255.255 any
access-list 101 deny 172.16.0.0 0.31.255.255 any
access-list 101 deny 192.168.0.0 0.0.255.255 any
!
!Deny address all zeros, all ones, loopback
access-list 101 deny 0.0.0.0 0.255.255.255 any
access-list 101 deny host 255.255.255.255 any
access-list 101 deny 127.0.0.0 0.0.255.255 any
!
!Deny Class D and Class E addresses
access-list 101 deny 224.0.0.0 15.255.255.255 any
access-list 101 deny 240.0.0.0 7.255.255.255 any
!
!Deny source address of your network
access-list 101 deny 198.78.46.0 0.0.0.255 any
```

Now that we have an appreciation for the operational capabilities of standard and extended IP access lists, let us turn our attention to new features that were added over the past few years that significantly enhance the capability of router packet filtering technology.

4.2.14 New capabilities in access lists

In tandem with several relatively recent updates to the Cisco Internetwork Operating System (IOS) were improvements to the functionality and capability of access lists. Six additions to access lists that warrant attention include named access lists, dynamic access lists, reflexive access lists, time-based access lists, TCP intercept and Context Based Access Control (CBAC). In actuality, these additions represent new capabilities added to access lists and do not literally represent new types of access list.

4.2.15 Named access lists

Because standard and extended access lists have a limited range of acceptable numbers, it is theoretically possible, although highly unlikely, that you could run out of numbers when configuring an enterprise router. Perhaps a more important reason for the use of named access lists is the fact that a name can be more meaningful than a number. In addition, as we will shortly note, you can delete statements in a named access list while a numbered list does not provide this capability.

4.2.16 Overview

Named access lists were introduced in IOS Version 11.2. As its name implies, a named access list is referred to by a name instead of a number.

4.2.17 Standard named IP access lists

Named access lists are applicable to both standard and extended lists. The format of a standard named IP access list is shown below.

ip access-list standard name

where 'name' represents the name you would assign to the standard named IP access list. The preceding statement is then followed by one or more permit or deny statements that define the filtering to take place. The following example illustrates the creation of a standard named access list to which we assigned the name 'inbound' to denote it will be applied in the inbound direction. In this access list we only permit traffic from two defined network addresses.

```
ip access-list standard inbound
permit 205.131.175.0 0.0.0.255
permit 198.78.46.0 0.0.0.255
```

To apply a named access list we use a modified version of the previously described ip access-group command. That modified version includes the name of a named access list and has the following format:

```
ip access-group name [in|out]
```

where 'name' represents the name of the named access list. Thus, to apply the previously created named access list to the serial0 interface to filter inbound packets, our IOS statements would appear as follows:

```
interface serial0
ip access-group inbound in
!
ip access-list standard inbound
permit 205.131.175.0 0.0.0.255
permit 198.78.46.0 0.0.0.255
```

Now that we have an appreciation for the creation of standard named IP access lists, let us turn our attention to extended named IP access lists.

4.2.18 Extended named IP access lists

An extended named IP access list is similar to a standard named IP access list. The format of the extended named IP access list command is shown below:

```
ip access-list extended <name>
```

where 'name' represents the name assigned to the access list.

You can use an extended named IP access list in the same manner as a standard named IP access list. However, because extended access lists provide considerably greater filtering capability you can perform more functions with this access list. To illustrate an example of the use of an extended named IP access list, assume you only want to allow http access to the server shown in Figure 4.2 whose IP address is 198.78.46.8. Let us further assume you will name the access list 'security'. Because you want to filter packets flowing from port 80, you would apply the access list in the outbound direction. Based upon the preceding, the extended named IP access list statements would be as follows:

```
interface ethernet1
ip access-group security out
!
ip access-list extended security
ip permit tcp any host 198.78.46.8 eq 80
```

In examining the preceding extended named access list, you might be puzzled as to the selection of the ethernet1 interface instead of the serial0 interface. The reason we applied the access list to the ethernet1 interface instead of the serial0 interface is due to the fact that selecting the latter would block all Internet traffic flowing into the router other than Web traffic flowing to the specified server. Also note that we specified the direction of the list as being applied to outbound (OUT) traffic. This is because packets leave the ethernet1 interface to flow to the specified network.

4.2.19 Editing capability

We previously mentioned that one advantage of a named access list is the fact that you can remove previously entered list statements. To do so you would reenter the configuration mode and enter a 'no' prefix for the statement you previously entered. It should be noted that you cannot delete specific entries in a numbered access list. One other point that deserves mentioning is the fact that you cannot selectively add statements to any type of access list other than to the bottom of the list. To add statements to a numbered or a named access list you must delete an existing list and reapply a new or modified list with appropriate entries. Now that we have an appreciation for the operation and utilization of named access lists let us continue our exploration of additional list features and turn our attention to dynamic access lists.

4.2.20 Dynamic access lists

As the name of this access list implies, dynamic access lists create dynamic entries in a list. Those dynamic entries represent temporary openings in an access list that occur in response to a user authentication process.

4.2.21 Rationale for use

The primary use of a dynamic access list is to obtain the ability to authenticate users attempting to access your network. To accomplish this you would first set up user accounts on your router. Next, you would create and apply a dynamic access list to the serial port of your router in the inbound direction, assuming you wish to authenticate users transmitting in that direction. Users then open a Telnet session to your router and authenticate themselves, normally by providing a user ID and password. Once the user has been authenticated, the router will close the Telnet session and place a dynamic entry in an access list, which permits packets with a source IP address of the authenticated user's workstation.

One of the key advantages associated with the use of a dynamic access list is that it can be used for certain situations where it is not possible to use a static access list. For example, many Internet Service Providers (ISPs) assign dynamic IP addresses to subscribers. This means that there is no way to create a static access list entry to allow authorized users accessing your network via an ISP connection that have dynamically assigned addresses other than allow all ISP network addresses. Because this would result in a potentially large security gap and is not recommended, you would more than likely turn to the use of a dynamic access list for this situation.

4.2.22 Utilization

The dynamic access list is very similar to an extended IP access list, with a key difference being the inclusion of the keyword 'dynamic' in an extended access list statement. The format of a dynamic access list entry is shown below:

access-list <list number> dynamic <name> [timeout
n][permit|deny] <protocol> any <destination address>
<destination mask>

The first variable field, 'list number', follows the same format as a traditional extended access list and represents a number between 100 and 199. The second variable field, 'name', represents the designated name of the dynamic access list. The optional timeout variable can be used to specify an absolute timeout for a particular dynamic entry. The 'protocol' parameters represent any one of the TCP/IP protocols, such as IP, TCP, UDP and ICMP. Because the source IP address is always replaced by the IP address of the authenticating host, the keyword 'any' should be used for the source IP address field. The last two variable fields, 'destination address' and 'destination mask', are used in the same manner as in an extended IP access list.

Prior to examining an example of the use of a dynamic access list a few additional details warrant discussion. First, you cannot specify more than one dynamic access list statement per access list. This means you need to carefully consider which protocols you want to create dynamic openings in an access list. Secondly, you need to permit users to Telnet to your router, or they will not be able to authenticate themselves and proceed to create dynamic openings in the access list. Third, to allow dynamic entries to be created, you must use the 'autocommand' parameter under the vty line configuration. An example of the use of this command parameter is shown below:

```
line vty 0 3
login local
autocommand access-enable host timeout 5
```

In the preceding example the 'host' parameter enables the source IP address of the authenticating host to be substituted into the dynamic entries that will be created. The 'timeout' parameter is optional and when included specifies an idle timeout. If you use both absolute and idle timers the idle timer value should be set to a value less than the absolute timer. As a minimum, at least one timer value should be configured. This is because without a timer the dynamic entries will remain until the router is reinitialized.

One additional point deserves mention prior to illustrating the utilization of a dynamic access list. This point is of key importance, for its omission can become a network administrator's nightmare if he or she is remotely administrating a router. Because a Telnet session is immediately closed after authentication this action will prevent you from managing a router via Telnet. If you configure your virtual terminal lines as previously described you would be up the creek without a paddle. The way around this problem is to specify the 'rotary 1' command beneath one or more vty ports as this command enables normal Telnet access to a router on port 3001. For example, to enable normal Telnet access on port 3001 for vty 4, you would enter the following commands:

```
line vty 4
login local
rotary 1
```

Once the preceding has occurred, you would set your Telnet application to use port 3001. For example, if your router's IP address is 205.131.176.1 you would enter the following command:

```
telnet 205.131.176.1 3001
```

Now that we have an appreciation for the details concerning a dynamic access list, let us focus our attention upon an example. In doing so, assume your router is connected to the Internet as shown in Figure 4.4. The serial port of your router has the IP address 205.131.175.1 and you only want to allow persons with predefined user IDs on the router to access your private network. In addition, we will assume you wish to permit remote administration of the router via Telnet. To accomplish the preceding you would enter the following IOS commands. Note that only the relevant portions of the configuration commands are listed.

```
username gxheld password gizmo87
!
interface serial0
  ip address 205.131.175.1 255.255.255.0
  ip access-group 101 in
!
access-list 101 permit tcp any host 205.131.175.1 eq 23
access-list 101 dynamic gxheld 10 permit ip any
      198.78.46.0 0.0.0.255
!
line vty 0 3
  login local
  autocommand access-enable host timeout 5
line vty 4
login local
rotary 1
```

In the preceding example note that we created the user name gxheld and referenced it in the second access list statement. This makes it harder for an attack since a person must specify both a user name and password to gain access. Also note that the first access list statement restricts access to the router to Telnet (port 23). The second access list statement contains the keyword 'dynamic'. This statement creates dynamic openings in the access list, substituting the source address of the authenticated Telnet

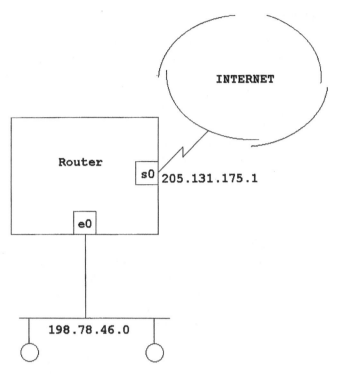

Figure 4.4 Configuration to reference for creating a dynamic access list which permits authenticated users access to the 198.78.46.0 network

user for all IP traffic with a destination address on the 198.78.46.0 network. Now that we have an understanding of the operation and utilization of dynamic access lists, let us turn our attention to reflexive access lists.

4.2.23 Reflexive access lists

When we previously discussed the use of the keyword 'established' in an extended IP access list, we noted that it is only applicable to TCP. If you wish to control other upper-layer protocols, such as UDP and ICMP, you would have to either permit all incoming traffic or define a large number of permissible source/destination host/ port addresses. In addition to representing a time-consuming and tedious task the resulting access list could conceivably require more memory than available on your router. Perhaps in recognition of this problem, Cisco introduced reflexive access lists in IOS Version 11.3.

4.2.24 Overview

A reflexive access list creates a dynamic and temporary opening in an access list based upon a mirror image of an IP traffic session originated from inside your network to an external network. The temporary opening is always a permit entry and specifies the same protocol as the original outbound packet. This opening also swaps source and destination IP addresses and upper layer port numbers and remains in existence until either the session initiated on the trusted network is closed or an idle timeout value is reached.

4.2.25 Rationale for use

The rationale behind the use of a reflexive access list is to enable employees on the trusted internal side of the router to control openings in the access list that occur from the untrusted side of the network. An example of the operation of a reflexive access list is shown in Figure 4.5. In examining Figure 4.5 note that the inbound opening reverses source and destination IP addresses and port numbers. Also note that the initial Telnet session uses a destination port of 23 and a random source port number greater than 1023. Thus, the opening results in a source port value of 23 and a destination port value greater than 1023.

4.2.26 Creation

There are four general tasks associated with the creation of a reflexive access list. The first task is to create an extended named access list. In an IP environment you would use the following command format:

ip access-list extended name

where 'name' represents the name of the access list.

The second task is to create one or more permit entries to establish reflected openings. Because you normally apply a reflexive access list to outbound traffic, it will result in an inbound access list. When defining permit statements for your outbound access list, you use a slightly modified format of the permit statement. This modified format is shown below:

permit protocol any any reflect name [timeout seconds]

Here the protocol represents the protocol for which you want reflexive openings created. Because you normally want any user behind the router to create dynamic openings the keyword 'any' is

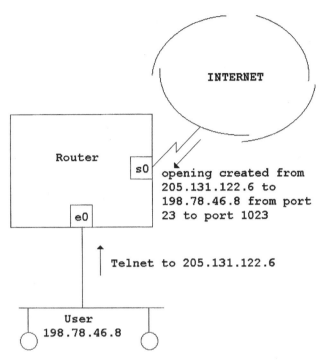

Figure 4.5 Examining the operation of a reflexive access list

used for the source address. Similarly, because reflexive results can represent any swapped addresses and port numbers you would also use the keyword 'any' for the destination address. The keyword 'reflect' identifies the statement as a reflexive statement, while 'name' represents the name of the access list. The optional keyword 'timeout' is used to assign a timeout period to each reflexive entry created in the inbound direction. If this option is omitted a default timeout value of 300 seconds is used.

You can also place a global timeout value that will be applicable to all reflexive statements. To do so you would use the ip reflexive-list timeout global command whose format is shown below:

     ip reflexive-list timeout value

where 'value' represents the global timeout value in seconds.

The third task associated with the creation of a reflexive access list is to create an access list for inbound filtering. This is required as dynamic reflexive entries will be added to this access list.

The last task in the reflexive list creation process is to conclude your list with the evaluate command whose format is shown below:

     evaluate name

where the variable 'name' represents the name of the access list and results in packets to be evaluated by reflexive entries.

To illustrate the use of a reflexive access list, let us assume we want to limit reflected openings to 240 seconds of idle time. Also assume your inbound access list will initially be coded to perform anti-spoofing operations by sending RFC 1918 addresses as well as 'all 0's', loopback and all 1's source addresses to the bit bucket. The following example illustrates the creation of the applicable statements for the previously described reflexive access list. In examining the statements note that the six deny statements in the extended access list named 'inbound' are conventional statements that are not reflected but where reflexive statements will be dynamically added.

```
ip reflexive-list timeout 240
!
ip access-list extended outbound
  permit tcp any any reflect my-session
  permit udp any any reflect my-session
  permit icmp any any reflect my-session
!
ip access list extended inbound
  deny ip 127.0.0.0 0.255.255.255 any
  deny ip host 255.255.255.255 any
  deny ip 0.0.0.0 255.255.255.255 any
  deny ip host 255.255.255.255 any
  deny ip 10.0.0.0 0.255.255.255 any
  deny ip 172.16.0.0 0.31.255.255 any
  deny ip 192.168.0.0 0.0.255.255 any
evaluate my_session
```

4.2.27 Limitations

Although the use of reflexive access lists considerably enhances the ability to secure the flow of packets from an untrusted side of a router, their key limitation is the fact that they are limited to supporting single channel connections. This means that applications such as file transfer protocol (FTP) that use multiple port numbers or channels cannot be supported by reflexive access lists. To obtain support for multi-channel applications Cisco initially provided a special release of IOS referred to as the Firewall Feature Set (FFS) that was limited with respect to the platforms it operated upon. During 1999 FFS was incorporated into IOS Release 12.0 under the name Context Based Access Control (CBAC). CBAC not only supports multi-channel applications but, in addition, adds a Java blocking capability as well as denial of service prevention and detection, real-time alerts, and audit trails. Due to CBAC representing the most sophisticated variation of access lists, we will defer an examination of this access list to the last section in this chapter. Thus, we will continue our examination of access lists by turning our attention to time-based access lists.

4.2.28 Time-based access lists

Until the release of IOS Version 12.0 there was no easy method to establish different security policies based upon the time of day or date. Although you could create multiple access lists and apply them at different times of the day, doing so could entail a work effort that might be less than desirable. For example, to implement a new security policy to enable Web surfing after 6:00 p.m., you would either have to stay in the office until that time or Telnet from home and revise your access list. If your organization decides that the policy should also revert back to blocking Web surfing at 5:00 a.m. it might not be very appealing to get up before your pet to go to work. With the introduction of IOS Version 12.0 you can now use time-based access lists to obtain the ability to implement different security policies based upon the time of day.

4.2.29 Creation

The creation of a time-based access list is a relatively straightforward two-step process. First, you define a time range. Once this has been accomplished you reference the time range in an access list entry.

The specification of a time range is accomplished through the use of a time-range statement whose format is shown below:

    time-range time-range-name

where the 'time-range-name' represents the name you assign to the time range. Once this task is accomplished you can specify a time range in one of two ways. You can use an 'absolute' statement or you can use a 'periodic' statement. The format of each statement is shown below:

absolute [**start** time date] [**end** time date]
periodic days-of-the-week hh:mm to [days-of-the-week]
hh:mm

The 'time' parameter in an absolute statement is entered in the format hh:mm, where hours (hh) is expressed in a 24-hour format. For the periodic statement you can list the days of the week separated by spaces or use the keywords 'daily' or 'weekend'. Once you have created a time range you can reference it through the optional keyword 'time-range' in a conventional access list entry.

4.2.30 Example

Since the old adage 'the proof of the pudding is in the eating' holds true today, let us focus our attention upon an example. The following example illustrates the creation of a time-based access list that restricts Web access to Saturday and Sunday from 9:00 a.m. until 5:00 p.m.

```
time range allow-http
!
periodic weekend 09:00 to 17:00
!
access-list 101 permit tcp any any eq 80 time-range
    allow-http
```

4.2.31 TCP intercept

TCP intercept represents a feature that was added in IOS Version 11.3 as a mechanism to minimize the effect of a special type of denial of service attack referred to as SYN flooding and which is also known as a Smurf attack, after the cartoon character. With the release of IOS Version 12.0, TCP intercept was incorporated into Context Based Access Control. Thus, we can literally cover two topics at the same time by deferring a discussion of TCP intercept and covering it in the next section of this chapter.

4.2.32 Context-based access control

Context-based access control (CBAC) represents the latest addition to Cisco router packet filtering capabilities. Introduced during

1999, CBAC provides a router administrator with the ability to create dynamic entries in a router's access list for both single and multi-channel applications. In addition, CBAC provides the ability to control the flow of Java applets as well as the ability to minimize the effect of certain types of denial of service attack.

4.2.33 Overview

Until 1999 CBAC was a special feature referred to as the firewall feature set (FFS) that was only available for use on the Cisco series 1600 and 2500 router platforms. During 1999 the release of Cisco's Internetwork Operating System (IOS) Release 12.0T expanded the availability of FFS, which is now referred to as CBAC, to Cisco 800, uBR900, 1600, 1700, 2500, 2600, 3600, 7100 and 7200 series platforms.

CBAC operates similar to reflexive access lists which were previously covered in this chapter. As we noted earlier, a reflexive access list is used to create dynamic openings in an inbound access list in response to an outbound data transmission. A key limit of a reflexive access list is its inability to support multi-channel applications, such as FTP, CU-SeeMe, H.323, and similar transmissions that use two or more TCP or UDP ports. CBAC overcomes this limitation, providing you with the ability to extend the capability of reflexive access lists to multi-channel applications.

Table 4.4 provides a list of representative applications that CBAC can securely support. Concerning that support, CBAC functions by examining packets that enter or exit a specified interface. Key

Table 4.4 Examples of applications supported by CBAC.

Single-channel TCP (i.e. Telnet)
Single-channel UDP (i.e. DNS)
CU-SeeMe (White Pine Software version)
FTP
H.323 (NetMeeting, ProShare)
IP Fragments
Java (Applets embedded in HTTP)
Unix r commands (rlogin, rexec, etc.)
RealAudio
RPC (Sun version)
SMTP
SQL*Net
TFTP

---

information contained in the packet, such as IP addresses and layer 4 port numbers, are placed in a state table. The contents of that table are then used by CBAC to create temporary openings in an access list for returned traffic. Although the previously described operating is similar to a reflexive access list, CBAC does this for both single- and multi-channel applications. In addition, CBAC tracks the sequence numbers used in a TCP conversation to ensure they are within the expected range which can prevent a sophisticated attack by someone monitoring a conversation and attempting to piggyback onto it to break into a network resource.

In addition to extending the ability of reflexive access lists, CBAC adds several new features that result in much more than an access-list enhancement. Those additional features include Java blocking, denial-of-service prevention and detection, and the ability to provide real-time alerts and audit trails. Thus, CBAC can be considered to represent a comprehensive set of security tools even though it is enabled in a manner similar to other types of Cisco access list.

4.2.34 Operation

As previously noted, CBAC extends the capability of reflexive access lists to multi-channel applications in addition to adding several new features. Because CBAC monitors outbound traffic to create applicable inbound access list entries, two access lists are required. One CBAC access list will define the packets that will be inspected by CBAC. The second access list will include the entries that CBAC dynamically creates, as it compares outbound packets against the statements you will code into an access list that will be applied to a particular interface in the outbound direction.

The actual CBAC configuration process is similar to the manner by which a reflexive access list is created. That is, you would first select an interface and then configure the applicable access lists on the interface. In doing so you will use one or more 'ip inspect' statements in the access list you are configuring which informs IOS that it should perform CBAC operations.

4.2.35 CBAC example

To illustrate the creation of an access list with CBAC capability, let us assume your organization has a branch office with a connection to the Internet as illustrated in Figure 4.6. In this example we will

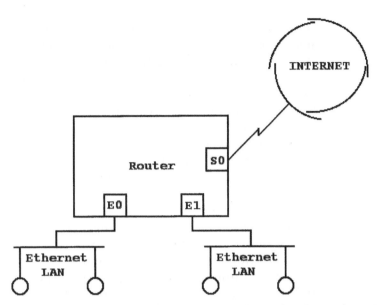

Figure 4.6 A sample network to be used for illustrating the configuration and operation of context-based access control (CBAC). ○ workstations

assume the branch office operates two Ethernet LANs, connected to ports #0 and E1 on the router, while port S0 provides a serial interface to the Internet.

4.2.36 Interselection

Because the first step in creating any type of access list is to select an appropriate interface, let us do so. Assuming we are attempting to protect internal users on the two Ethernet LANs from the virtually unlimited Internet user population, we would configure CBAC on the external interface, S0. This would result in any traffic attempting to reach either internal Ethernet networks being inspected by CBAC. Now that we have selected an interface, a few words are in order about the type and direction of the access lists to be applied to the interface.

Since we want to protect internal users from traffic flowing inbound from the Internet, we would create an outbound access list that specifies the traffic to be inspected by CBAC. This access list can be either a standard or extended IP access list. As CBAC examines outbound packets it will dynamically create openings in an inbound access list which governs the flow of traffic from the Internet that can reach either Ethernet network located behind the router. This access list must be an extended access list.

One aspect of CBAC that requires elaboration is the fact that it is important to remember that its use creates dynamic openings in an inbound access list based upon the IP address and layer 4 ports used in packets flowing in the outbound direction that match your defined criteria. This means that unless you supplement your CBAC related statements with permissions for different types of data originated from the Internet, your organization's Internet connection will block all inbound traffic originated on the distrusted side of the router. While this may represent your intention, suppose one of the Ethernet networks shown in Figure 4.6 is connected to a Web server you wish to allow the general Internet population to access. To do so you must include an applicable permission in the inbound access list to enable traffic to flow through the router to the Web server. Another aspect of CBAC that warrants attention is the fact that it does not protect your organization from certain types of HTTP application-layer attack, such as the exploitation of cgi scripts. Thus, it is important to note that CBAC is not a total barrier to security problems. Instead, it represents a sophisticated tool that adds to the capability of your organization's total security policy. That said, let us turn our attention to the statements that add CBAC capability to your access list.

4.2.37 The inspect statement

The ip inspect statement represents the key IOS command associated with configuring a monitored connection for inspection by CBAC. The format of this command for all protocols other than Java and RPC (remote procedure call) is shown below:

ip inspect name inspection-name protocol
[alert{on | off}] [audit-trail] [on | off] [timeout seconds]

In the preceding format, the ip inspect command's optional keyword 'alert' causes CBAC to generate messages to a syslog server or the router's buffer whenever it detects a violation in the monitored application. For example, if you configure CBAC to monitor TCP and an illegal TCP operation is detected when audit is enabled, the router will send an alert to the syslog server.

The keyword 'audit-trail' enables CBAC to track the connections for a protected application. When this keyword is used, the router will log information for each permitted application, including source and destination IP addresses, ports used, and the number of bytes transferred. Although the audit trail was probably developed to enable network managers to obtain information on the traffic characteristics of network applications, it also enables managers to determine the locations employees are accessing. Thus, it also provides a database that could be used to determine if employees are viewing the stock market, accessing Web auction locations, or performing other activities that management may not particularly support.

The keyword 'timeout' provides you with the ability to specify the duration of inactive sessions. In addition to being able to specify a general inactive timeout for specific protocols, CBAC also supports the capability to prevent denial-of-service (DOS) attacks by monitoring the number and frequency of half-open connections. For TCP a half-open connection represents a session that has not completed the initial three-way (syn-syn-ack) handshake. Because UDP has no handshake, a UDP half-open session is one for which CBAC has not detected return traffic.

You can control the number of TCP and UDP half-open connections through the use of ten ip inspect related statements that assign a timeout or threshold value. Table 4.5 lists those commands, their default values, and a brief description of each statement.

To obtain an appreciation for the entries in Table 4.5 a brief review of the operation of denial-of-service (DOS) is warranted. In a DOS attack a hacker floods a network with either TCP or UDP requests and does not five responses to those requests. This action rapidly consumes all available resources on the target host that is then forced to deny service to legitimate users. While using a router to intercept and control DOS attacks ensures that computer resources on the network are available for legitimate use, the router could easily have its resources consumed. To prevent this situation from occurring there are timeout and threshold defaults associated with CBAC as indicated in Table 4.5. You can either elect to accept those defaults and do nothing, or modify one or more of those defaults through the use of the ip inspect commands listed in Table 4.5.

To illustrate the use of the basic ip inspect command, let us assume you want to create dynamic openings in the inbound direction from the internet for TCP and UDP applications originating on the trusted side of the router. Let us further assume you want to assign a 60-second timeout for TCP connections and a 30-second timeout for UDP connections. To do so you would use the following ip inspect commands:

```
ip inspect name firewall tcp 60
ip inspect name firewall udp 30
```

Table 4.5 ip inspect commands used to configure time-out and threshold values used by CBAC.

Command	Default value	Description
ip inspect tcp synwait-time seconds	30s	length of time to wait for TCP session to be established.
ip inspect tcp finwait-time seconds	5s	length of time TCP is managed after FIN exchange.
ip inspect tcp idle-time seconds	3600s	TCP idle time-out
ip inspect udp idle-time seconds	30s	UDP idle time-out
ip inspect dns-timeout seconds	5s	DNS lookup idle timer
ip inspect max-incomplete high number	500 sessions	Maximum number of half-open connections permitted before CBAC begins closing connections.
ip inspect max-incomplete low number	400 sessions	Number of half-open connections causing CBAC to stop closing connections.
ip inspect one-minute high number	500 sessions	Rate of half-open sessions per minute before CBAC begins closing connections.
ip inspect one-minute low number	400 sessions	Rate of half-open sessions per minute causing CBAC to stop deleting connections.
ip inspect tcp max-incomplete host	50 sessions	Number of existing half-open sessions with the same destination address before CBAC begins closing sessions.

To complete our discussion of ip inspect command formats, let us turn our attention to the two previously mentioned variations in the command format for RPC and Java. For RPC the format of the command is slightly different, as illustrated below:

ip inspect name inspection-name rpc program-number number [wait-time minutes] [alert{on | off]] [audit-trail{on | off}] [timeout seconds]

To illustrate an example of a CBAC inspect statement for RPC, assume you want to allow RPC program number 14000 and effect a 60 second idle timeout. To do so you would use the following inspect command:

> ip inspect name firewall rpc program-number 14000
> timeout 60

To use CBAC for Java blocking you need to associate a list of permitted IP addresses via the use of a standard IP access list to a slightly modified inspect command. This modified inspect command format is shown below:

> ip inspect name inspection-name http[java-list access-list#] [alert{on | off}]] [audit-trail{on | off}] [timeout seconds]

In the preceding format the access-list# represents the standard IP access list number you wish to associate with Java blocking. If you should reference an undefined access list in the Java-list definition, the default behavior will result in all Java applets being denied since there are no permitted IP addresses associated with the ip inspect command.

To illustrate an example of the use of CBAC to block Java applets, let us assume the network address of a parent Ethernet network located on the other side of the Internet in Figure 4.6 is 198.78.46.0. Then, to block all Java applets other than those from the parent network, you would code the following commands:

> access-list 1 permit 198.78.46.0 0.0.0.255
> ip inspect name firewall http java-list 1

Although the preceding commands block all Java applets other than those originating from the 198.78.46.0 network, it should be noted that in its current incarnation CBAC does not block ActiveX. At the present time Cisco recommends the use of a dedicated content-filtering product if you need to perform an extensive amount of content filtering or if you need to filter one or more applications not presently supported by Cisco access list features to include CBAC.

4.2.38 Applying the inspection rules

Similarly to other types of access lists, once you have created your CBAC inspection rules you need to apply those rules to an interface. To do so you would use an ip inspect command that indicates the direction of inspection. The format used to apply an inspection rule is shown below:

ip inspect inspection-name {in | out}

Note that when applying the inspection you should apply it to the direction of outbound traffic to ensure CBAC checks inbound traffic. This means that if you are configuring inspection on an internal interface, the outbound traffic from the network is entering the interface. Thus, in this situation the inspection rules should be applied inbound. If you are configuring inspection on an external router interface, the outbound traffic is leaving the interface. In this situation the inspection rules should be applied in the outbound direction. While the preceding may appear a bit confusing, you can avoid potential confusion by remembering that you would apply the inspection rule to packets leaving the interface to be guarded to ensure that return packets are checked.

4.2.39 Using CBAC

Since the proof of the pudding is in the eating, let us illustrate the manner by which we can use CBAC. For our example, let us assume our organization has a two-port router with the serial port providing a connection to an Internet Service Provider while the Ethernet interface provides a connection to the internal Ethernet network. Let us further assume you want to allow the internal users on your Ethernet LAN to have access to the Internet for Web browsing, FTP and electronic mail. Let us also further assume that your parent organization whose network address is 205.131.175.0 should be the only network from which Java applets will be allowed to flow through your router onto your network. In addition, we will assume that you would like to use the alerting capability of CBAC to provide information concerning when Java applets are blocked or permitted and the auditing capability of CBAC to provide you with information concerning FTP traffic. Last but not least, you want to enable your internal Ethernet users to perform ping and traceroute operations to hosts on the Internet.

The specific coding we would use to implement the previously stated network requirements are listed below:

```
interface ethernet0
 ip address 198.78.46.1 255.255.255.0
 ip access-group 101 in
!
```

```
!
interface serial0
  ip address 198.78.40.5 255.255.255.0
  ip inspect firewall out
  ip access-group 102 in
!
!
ip inspect alert-off
ip inspect name firewall http java-list 1 alert on
ip inspect name firewall ftp audit-trail on
ip inspect name firewall smtp
ip inspect name firewall tcp
ip inspect name firewall udp
!
ip access-list 1 permit 205.131.175.0 0.0.0.255
!
ip access-list 101 permit ip any any
!
ip access-list 102 permit icmp any any echo-reply
ip access-list 102 permit icmp any any time-exceeded
ip access-list 102 permit icmp any any packet-too-big
ip access-list 102 permit icmp any any unreachable
ip access-list 102 permit icmp any any administratively-
    prohibited
```

In examining the coding note that the IOS commands are grouped into several areas. First, we configured the Ethernet interface by assigning an IP address to the interface and then associating access list number 101 in the inbound direction with the interface through the use of an ip access-group statement. This is followed by the configuration of the serial interface. Because we will apply CBAC inspection to the serial interface we included an ip inspect command under the serial interface. Note that the ip inspect command is set up to inspect packets flowing in the outbound direction as we want CBAC to create temporary openings in the inbound direction. Because we used the ip access-group command under the serial interface CBAC will create temporary openings at the bottom of access list 102 whose statements we will shortly review.

After the two interfaces are configured, you will note a block of six ip inspect commands. The first ip inspect command disables global alerting, permitting us to selectively enable this feature for http in the second ip inspect command. Note that the second ip inspect command specifies that CBAC should use access list number 1 to selectively permit Java applets. Also note that after the six ip inspect commands we defined a standard access list number 1 that only allows traffic from the 205.131.175.0 network. Because the second ip inspect statement is linked to access list number 1, this means that only Java applets from the 205.131.175.0 network will be permitted inbound through our router. Also note that because we previously mentioned we wanted to be alerted concerning the permission or blocking of Java applets, the second ip inspect command includes an 'alert on' option.

The third ip inspect command configures inspection for FTP while the fourth command provides inspection for sending email. Because we mentioned a requirement to audit FTP, the third ip inspect command contains an 'audit-track on' option. The fifth and sixth ip inspect commands provide generic TCP and UDP inspection to allow return traffic for queries using different protocols form your internal network. For example, by specifying generic TCP permissions your employees could use call control protocols required for voice over IP (VoIP) session setup. TCP also allows the use of the post office protocol (POP) which enables your internal users to retrieve their email from an ISP's mail server. In comparison, we explicitly specified smtp in an ip inspect command since it is used for sending email and without specifying a generic TCP our employees would be limited to sending but not receiving email. This obviously would not be particularly useful. The use of a generic UDP permits the actual transfer of VoIP packets which applications transfer using the connectionless operation of UDP. In addition, the generic UDP command permits employees to use DNS and SNMP as both are transported as UDP datagrams.

After the block of six ip inspect commands we entered two access list statements. The first is a standard access list statement which, as previously noted, is linked with our Java applet blocking. The second access list, list 101, permits all IP traffic to flow in the inbound direction to the router from the Ethernet network. This access list is not required but was included as a reference point in the event we later expanded the router and wished to block certain types of traffic from the Ethernet network into the router. Because the access list permits all IP traffic from any source address to any destination address, its current effect is the same as if we did not associate an access list to the Ethernet port in the inbound direction.

The last four statements in our router configuration listing consist of four access-list statements. Those statements make up an IP extended access list numbered 102 which is applied in the inbound direction on the serial interface. Because CBAC only inspects TCP and UDP traffic we must explicitly permit other types of IP traffic through the serial port in the inbound direction. Since part of our previously defined requirement was to permit employees to perform ping and traceroute operations we need to explicitly enable IP traffic required to allow these operations. Thus, we coded several ICMP permissions. The permission of echo-reply allows internal users to ping hosts on the Internet and receive a reply. The permission of the time-exceeded and unreachable ICMP statements allow traceroute to function. Although not part of our requirement, we added permissions for packet-too-big and administratively prohibited ICMP messages. These messages enable MTU (maximum transmission unit) discovery and messages indicating possible access lists on Internet sites our users may attempt to reach. If we did not include these ICMP permissions, it is possible that our internal users might experience significant delays when attempting to access some locations and may be prevented from reaching other locations. Because CBAC will ensure that TCP and UDP entries are automatically created for return traffic, once traffic from the internal Ethernet network flows toward the Internet we do not have to explicitly enable other protocols. Thus, in addition to creating dynamic openings CBAC permits us to simplify our access list creation process.

4.2.40 Summary

Although there is no typical organization and each reader can be expected to have different security requirements, the material presented in this chapter can be viewed as similar to a package of Leggo blocks. That is, this information about the operation and utilization of different types of access list provides you with a foundation to construct a defensive packet filtering capability to meet your organization's network infrastructure and your networking requirements.

THE ROLE OF THE FIREWALL

In Chapter 4 we noted that the router represents the first line of defense of an organization's private network when that network is connected to the Internet. The key method of defense is the creation of applicable access lists that perform packet filtering. While there are several types of access list and access list feature you can employ by themselves, they are not sufficient to prevent many types of undesirable operation against hosts residing behind a router. One solution to this security gap is to use another communications device that provides additional capability beyond packet filtering. That device is the firewall, which is the focus of this chapter.

In this chapter we will first review the basic operation of router access lists and some of their limitations. Using this information as a base, we will then describe and discuss the operation of different types of firewall feature and how they can be used to provide an enhanced level of network protection.

5.1 ACCESS LIST LIMITATIONS

In Chapter 4 we noted that Cisco routers support two types of access lists, standard and extended. A standard access list supports packet filtering based upon the source address within a packet. In comparison, an extended access list supports packet filtering based upon source and destination addresses, source and destination upper layer ports, protocol, and even the status of the ACK and RST bits in a TCP header within an IP datagram.

Although Cisco routers support many new access list features, including dynamic lists that provide an authentication capability and reflexive and context-based access control that create dynamic openings in an inbound access list based upon outbound activity from the trusted side of a network, they all have one serious limitation. That limitation is the fact that all access lists are relatively blind with respect to the operation being performed. This results from the inability of router access lists to look further into the contents of a packet as a mechanism to determine whether or not an apparently harmful operation is occurring, and if so, to either stop the operation or generate an appropriate alert message to one or more persons in the form of an audio signal, email message, pager alert, or a combination of such mechanics.

5.1.1 Repeated logon attempts

To illustrate a potential limitation of router access lists, consider the network configuration illustrated in Figure 5.1. In this example the private network with the IP address 198.78.46.0 is shown connected to the Internet. Let us also assume that your organization has 100 hosts on the 198.78.46.0 network.

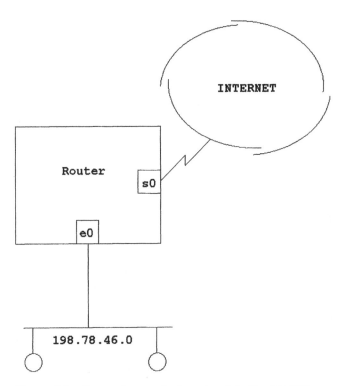

Figure 5.1 Connecting a private network to the Internet.
e0, Ethernet0 port; s0, serial0 port

Assume that you permit employees to use FTP, email, Web surfing and to perform other Internet activities. Thus, it is possible for a hacker to attempt to gain access to your hosts, have some fun, and lock out legitimate users from accessing one or more servers. The hacker could also perform a combination of activities harmful to the health of your employees' ability to use organizational computational equipment. For example, by transmitting repeated logins a person may either be able to break in to a host or lock out a legitimate user. For either situation the hacker repeats a sequence of login actions. Because an access list does not check the contents of packets, it is possible that the repeated actions continue until a break in occurs or the lock out value for a particular valid user ID on a server is reached. One solution to this problem is to examine the contents of each packet and note repeating patterns which are then blocked. Because this action requires a considerable amount of processing power, it is normally performed by a firewall. In performing this function the firewall maintains a state table of operations between a particular source and destination address, with the examination of packets occurring in an attempt to both determine and prohibit certain activities, with the process referred to as stateful inspection.

5.1.2 Application harm

A second example of an activity that illustrates a limitation of access lists can be obtained by discussing certain operations associated with the file transfer protocol (FTP). Although we will focus our attention upon the manner by which the FTP application can be hazardous to the health of a remote computer, it should be noted that other TCP and UDP applications can at times be harmful when used in certain manners.

When using a router's access-list, you can enable or deny FTP sessions based upon the source IP address and/or destination IP address contained in each packet transporting FTP information. Suppose that your organization operates an FTP server supporting anonymous access, allowing any person connected to the Internet to access and retrieve information from the FTP server, a relatively common occurrence on the Internet. Let us further assume your organization has a large number of files on the server available for downloading. This means that a person could either intentionally or non-intentionally use the FTP mget (multiple get) command to retrieve a large number of files with one FTP command line entry. In fact, if the person accessing your organization's FTP server issued the mget command using the wildcard operator of an asterisk (*) in the filename and file extension position to form the command line entry mget *.* then this command would result in your organization's FTP server downloading every file in the directory, one after another, to the remote user. If your organization has a large number of files whose aggregate data storage represents several gigabytes of data and a low speed connection to the Internet, such as a 56 Kbps, 64 Kbps or fractional T1 connection, the use of an mget *.* command could tie up the outbound use of the Internet connection for many hours and possibly days. If your organization operated a World Wide Web (WWW) server as well as an FTP server and provides Internet access to employees over a common access line the use of mget on an intentional basis can be considered to represent an unsophisticated but effective denial of service (DOS) attack method. This type of attack is perfectly legal as the person employing the mget command is performing a perfectly valid operation even though the result of the operation could tie up your organization's connection to the Internet for hours or even days. Similarly, letting someone have the ability to download data to your organization's FTP server means they could consider using the reverse of mget, which is the mput command. Through the use of mput with wildcards they could set up an antiquated 286 machine and pump gigabytes of data to your ftp server, clogging the inbound portion of your organization's Internet access line. Recognizing the need to examine application layer operations and provide organizations with the ability to control applications resulted in the development of a proxy services capability which is included in many firewalls.

5.2 PROXY SERVICES

Proxy services represents a generic term associated with the use of a proxy server. The proxy server is normally implemented as a software coding module on a firewall and supports one or more applications for which the server acts as an intermediary or proxy between the requestor and the actual server that provides the requested service. When implemented in this manner all requests for a specific application are first examined by the proxy service operating on the proxy server. If the proxy service was previously configured to enable or disable one or more application features for a specific TCP/IP application then the proxy service examines the contents of each packet and possibly a sequence of packets and compares the contents against the proxy service configuration. If the contents of the packet or sequence of packets that denote a specific operation are permitted by the configuration of the proxy service then the service permits the packet to flow to the appropriate server. Otherwise the packet is either directly sent to the great bit bucket in the sky, or possibly permitted with the server generating a warning message and an alert or alarm message to the firewall administrator or other designated personnel.

5.2.1 Operation

To illustrate the use of a proxy service let us return to our FTP server access example. A common FTP proxy service permits a firewall administrator to enable or disable different FTP commands. Using this feature the firewall administrator can control the ability of FTP users to issue different types of FTP commands, such as mget and mput.

In a Microsoft Windows environment you can use mget in either a streaming or an interactive mode. Concerning the latter, FTP will prompt you through the use of a question mark (?) whether or not the next file should be transferred. An example of the use of mget is illustrated in Figure 5.2. Note that by simply entering a carriage return in response to the ? prompt the next file is transferred. Thus,

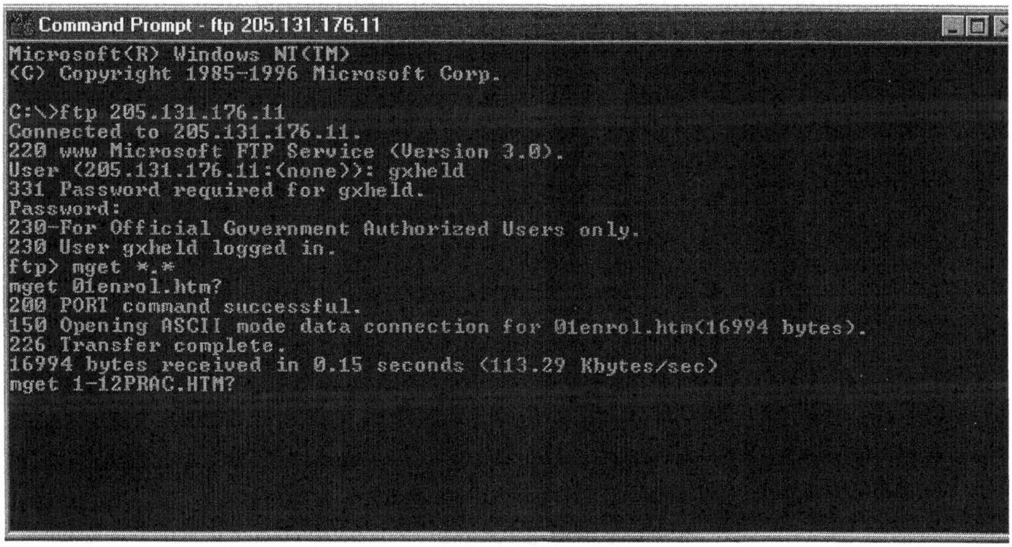

```
Command Prompt - ftp 205.131.176.11

Microsoft(R) Windows NT(TM)
(C) Copyright 1985-1996 Microsoft Corp.

C:\>ftp 205.131.176.11
Connected to 205.131.176.11.
220 www Microsoft FTP Service (Version 3.0).
User (205.131.176.11:(none)): gxheld
331 Password required for gxheld.
Password:
230-For Official Government Authorized Users only.
230 User gxheld logged in.
ftp> mget *.*
mget 01enrol.htm?
200 PORT command successful.
150 Opening ASCII mode data connection for 01enrol.htm(16994 bytes).
226 Transfer complete.
16994 bytes received in 0.15 seconds (113.29 Kbytes/sec)
mget 1-12PRAC.HTM?
```

Figure 5.2 Using mget under Windows NT requires a response to each file prompt, which can be simply a carriage return

it is relatively easy for a hacker to write a script to stream files when using mget under Windows' interactive mode and a no-brainer under its streaming mode.

If you are familiar with the manner by which an FTP server is configured you probably realize that the FTP server administrator is limited to assigning read and/or write permissions to directories and possibly, depending upon the operating system used, to files within a directory for either anonymous or non-anonymous users, with the latter a term used to denote persons that have an account on the server. However, there is no mechanism that this author is aware of that enables an FTP server administrator or a router administrator to selectively enable or disable individual FTP commands. Thus, an FTP proxy service provides the FTP server administrator with a significantly enhanced capability that can be used to configure the capability and features of FTP services that other users can access.

5.2.2 Firewall location

The capability for employing proxy services is based on the use of a firewall located between a router and network servers connected to a LAN behind the router.

To illustrate the common placement of a firewall as well as a term associated with its use, let us assume we wish to add protection to the network configuration illustrated in Figure 5.1. One common method used to protect an internal private network from packets flowing from the Internet is to place a firewall between the router and the network to be protected. In doing so you would install an essentially non-populated hub whose only connections would be to the router and firewall as illustrated in Figure 5.3. Because there are no workstations nor servers nor any other device except the router and firewall connections on this hub, it is referred to as a DMZ LAN. Here the term DMZ is an acronym for 'demilitarized' and originated from a strip of land where no military activity occurred. If you examine Figure 5.3 you will note that this network configuration ensures that the flow of packets to and from the Internet have to pass through the firewall before they can effect a host located either on the public Internet or private network.

The firewall illustrated in Figure 5.3 represents a generic device whose functionality is highly dependent upon the product selected. Just about all firewalls support packet filtering similar to the filtering performed by router access lists as a basic capability.

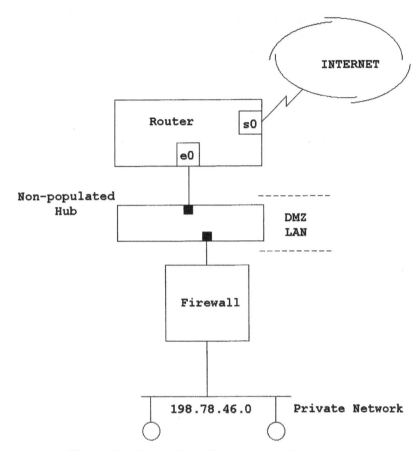

Figure 5.3 Using a firewall to protect a private network

Thereafter, the functionality of firewalls can vary based upon functions and features incorporated into different vendor products. Those functions and features can include proxy services, for different applications that allow administrators to control different application commands, limiting the rate of pending connections to counter different types of denial of service attacks, provide network address translation to hide internal host addresses from direct attack via the Internet, perform authentication, virus scanning, and even encryption of data which is a necessity when creating a virtual private network (VPN). It should again be noted that the specific features and functions performed by a firewall considerably vary between vendor products, a situation we will note when we turn our attention to two vendor products later in this chapter.

For organizations that support public access to a Web server, a second common network configuration method is to separate the public and private network and limit firewall protection to the private network. An example of this network configuration is illustrated in Figure 5.4. In this example a public Web server is located on the 205.131.175.0 network while the firewall is used to protect organizational hosts on the 198.78.46.0 network. If the Web server is the only network device on the 205.131.175.0 network you would more than likely create a router access list to limit inbound traffic to the HTTP protocol to the address of the Web server. You should also consider programming TCP intercept to minimize the effect of SYN flooding to the Web server and block commonly used spoofed addresses in your access list.

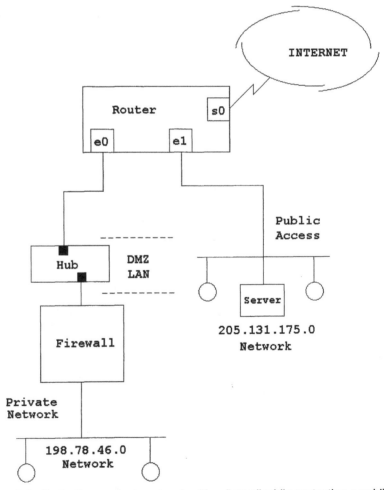

Figure 5.4 Protecting a private network with a firewall while protecting a public network with a router access list

Another popular alternative configuration used with firewalls is to connect both public and private access organizational networks behind the firewall as illustrated in Figure 5.5. In this configuration the firewall is used to protect both network segments. This action permits you to reduce or eliminate the access list processing activity on the router as well as a router port. Because many firewalls use PC-based platforms, it is normally much less expensive to add an additional firewall in the form of a LAN adapter card than to add a port to a router.

While it is possible to protect the public access server by connecting the network it is located on to another firewall port,

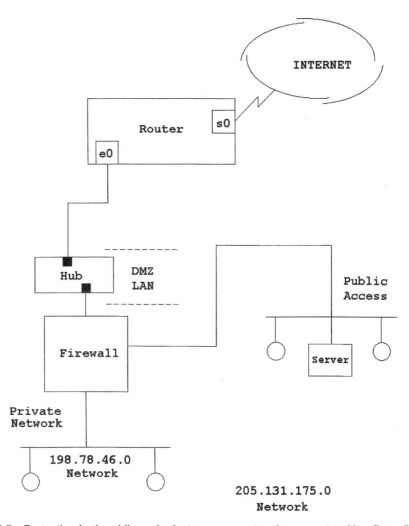

Figure 5.5 Protecting both public and private access network segments with a firewall

the decision to do so is usually based upon the operations supported by the public access host or hosts. If the server only provides HTTP support, usually protection via a router's access list should be sufficient. If your organization supports public access for HTTP, FTP, Telnet and other applications, you would then probably elect to connect the public access network to the firewall as shown in Figure 5.5.

5.2.3 Types of proxy service

The type of proxy service that can be provided is only limited by the requirements of an organization and the programming capability of firewall programmers. Some of the more popular types of proxy service include remote terminal Telnet and TN3720 proxy services, Simple Mail Transport Protocol (SMTP) proxy service, HyperText Transport Protocol (HTTP) proxy service, the previously discussed FTP proxy service and ICMP proxy service. The later represents a special type of proxy service which deserves a degree of elaboration due to the enhanced security capability it provides against certain types of hacker attack.

The Internet Control Message Protocol (ICMP) represents a layer 3 protocol within the TCP/IP protocol suite. ICMP is used to transmit error messages as well as status queries and responses to those queries. ICMP packets are formed by the use of an Internet Protocol (IP) header which contains an appropriate numeric in its Type field which identifies the packet as an ICMP packet. Although the use of ICMP is primarily oriented towards transporting error messages between devices operating a TCP/IP protocol stack and are transparent to users of a network, the protocol is also popularly used by many individuals who are probably unaware that they are using transmitting ICMP packets.

Two of the more popular types of ICMP packet are echo request and echo reply, which are better known to most persons as a ping operation or application. Depending upon the manner by which the ping application is implemented on a specific TCP/IP protocol suite a user typically enters the application command name ping followed by the host name or host IP address and one or more optional parameters which governs how ping will operate.

The use of ping is primarily designed as a mechanism to allow a user to determine if a remote host is operational and using a TCP/IP protocol stack. Pinging a distant host with an ICMP Echo Request packet results in the distant host returning an ICMP echo reply packet if the distant host is reachable, operational and its

TCP/IP stack is functioning. The reason the use of ping also notes if a distant host is reachable and a ping timeout does not necessarily mean the distant host is not operational is due to the fact that one or more communications devices in the path to the distant host could be down while the distant host is operational. However, in most cases ping represents the first troubleshooting method to use when it appears that a host is not responding to a query.

In addition to indicating that a host is potentially reachable and operational, the use of ping provides information concerning the round-trip delay to a remote host. This information results from the ping application on the originator setting a clock and noting the time until a response is received or a timeout period occurs and no response is received. The time between the transmission of the ping and the receipt of a response represents the packet round trip delay and can provide valuable information about why time-dependent operations, such as Voice over IP (VoIP), produce reproduced voice that sounds like a famous mouse instead of a person.

Because the first time you ping a destination using a host name your protocol stack may have to perform an address resolution operation to determine the IP address needed for routers to correctly direct the packet to its destination, an additional delay can affect most implementations of ping by default issue between three and five consecutive echo request packets. However, some implementations of ping permit the user to set an option which results in the host continuously issuing pings, one after another until the person operating the computer generating the pings issues a CTRL-BREAK to terminate the application.

Although continuous pinging may appear innocent, in actuality it represents a method for a hacker to initiate a denial of service attack. This is because the pinged host must stop what it is doing, even if its only for a few milliseconds, and respond to the ping with an echo reply ICMP packet. If the person that sets the ping application to continuous pinging also sets the packet size beyond its default size of 32 or 64 bytes, depending upon implementation, that person forces the destination to respond with increased length responses which requires the use of additional network resources. Thus, although the use of the ping application may not bring the destination host to its knees, it can be configured to operate in a manner that can significantly interfere with the ability of the destination to perform its intended operations.

Another problem associated with the unrestricted use of ping is that it can be used as a mechanism to discover hosts on a distant network as a prelude for attacking those hosts. For example, a hacker could write a script to cycle though all 254 possible addresses on a Class C IP network as a mechanism to discover which addresses are currently operational.

Based upon the preceding, many organizations may wish to control the operation of ping and other types of ICMP messages. While many router access-lists provide administrators with the ability to filter ICMP packets based upon source and/or destination IP address and the type of ICMP message, such access-list filtering is an all-or-nothing operation. That is, a router access-list cannot selectively examine and note that a sequence of ICMP echo requests from the same source address occurred after a predefined number of requests flowed through the router and subsequent requests should be prohibited. In comparison, on some firewalls an ICMP proxy service feature can be configured to differentiate between a single sequence of echo request packets and the intentional or unintentional setting of a ping application to continuously ping a host. Similarly, an ICMP proxy service capability can be employed to distinguish between a person that may have difficulty accessing a server and another person that is using the ping application in an attempt to discover all hosts on your organization's network. Thus, ICMP proxy service represents an important type of proxy service whose use can enhance the security of a network.

5.2.4 Limitations

Although proxy services can provide a considerable degree of security enhancement to networks there are certain limitations associated with their use that warrant discussion. First and foremost, a proxy service requires a detailed examination of the contents of individual and sequences of individual but related packets, forcing the application to look deeper into each packet. This results in an additional degree of processing occurring on each packet which introduces a degree of delay. Secondly, a sequence of packets may have to be examined to determine if it is acceptable to enable those packets to flow to their destination. This means that one or more packets in each sequence may have to be buffered or temporarily stored until the proxy service can determine if the packets can proceed to their destination or should be sent to the great bit bucket in the sky. This also means additional buffer storage in the proxy server or firewall will be required and the temporary storage of packets adds to the latency of remote requests flowing to servers operated by your organization. In fact, according to test performed by several communications testing laboratories, using proxy services from different vendor firewalls resulted in between 20 and 40 percent of the bandwidth of an Internet connection at the proxy server side being unused during the full utilization on the other side due to proxy server delays. This also resulted in a packet loss between 20 and 40 percent, resulting in additional remote transmissions to the desired site. Thus, you must consider the effect of proxy service delays and the potential need to upgrade your Internet access line against the potential enhancements to the security of your organization's network.

5.3 OPERATIONAL EXAMPLES

Now that we have an appreciation for the capabilities of a proxy firewall we will turn our attention to an examination of the capabilities of two firewalls. First, we will examine several configuration screens generated by the Interceptor firewall, a product of Technologic of Atlanta, GA. Once this has been accomplished, we will turn our attention to the FireWall-1, a product of Check Point Software Technologies Ltd. of Ramat Gan, Israel and Redwood City, CA.

5.3.1 The Technologic Interceptor

Similarly to most modern firewalls, the Technologic Interceptor supports its configuration via a Web browser. Figure 5.6 illustrates the Interceptor's Advanced Policy Options screen in which the cursor is shown pointed to the toggled check associated with the FTP Put command to block FTP uploads. In examining Figure 5.6 and subsequent Interceptor screen displays, you will note they represent HTML screens displayed using a Netscape browser. The Technologic Interceptor firewall generates HTML forms to enable network managers to view, add and modify firewall configuration data. To secure such operations the firewall uses encryption and authentication by supporting the Secure Sockets Layer (SSL) protocol for encrypting all traffic between the firewall and a Web browser used to configure the firewall while passwords are used for authentication. This means network managers can safely configure the firewall via the World Wide Web.

Using classes

The Technologic Interceptor firewall includes a class definition facility which provides users with a mechanism to replace address

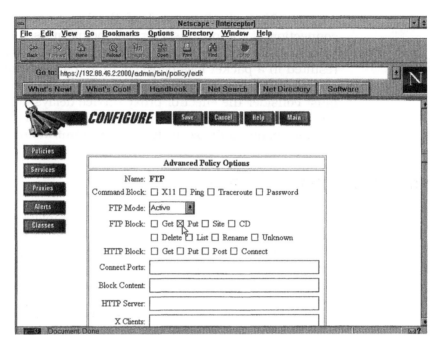

Figure 5.6 Using the Technologic Interceptor firewall configuration screen to block all FTP PUT commands

patterns, times of day or URLs by symbolic names. Classes are initiated by selecting the Classes button on the left portion of the configuration screen. By using an equal sign (=) as a prefix, they are distinguished from literal patterns.

Through the use of classes you can considerably facilitate the configuration of the Technologic Interceptor firewall. For example, suppose you want to control access from users behind the firewall to Internet services. To do so you would first enter the IP addresses of computers that will be given permission to access common services you wish them to use. Then you would define a class name that would be associated with the group of IP addresses and create a policy that defines the services the members of the class are authorized to use.

Figure 5.7 illustrates the use of the Technologic Interceptor Edit Policy configuration screen to enable inbound traffic for FTP, HTTP, Telnet and SNMP. Note that this policy uses the classname '=ALL-Internal-Hosts' in the box labeled 'From'. Although not shown, you would have first used the class configuration to enter that class name and the IP addresses you want associated with that class. Then, this new edit policy would allow those IP

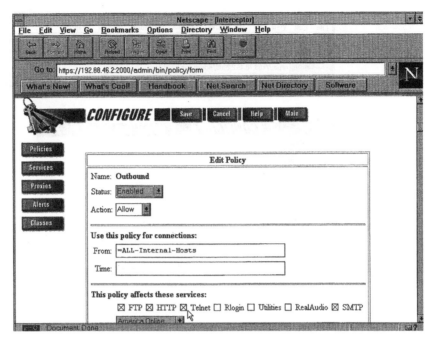

Figure 5.7 Using the Technologic Interceptor firewall to create a policy allowing outbound FTP, HTTP, Telnet and SMTP traffic from all users in the previously defined class 'All_Internal-Hosts'

addresses in the predefined class =ALL-Internal-Hosts to use FTP, HTTP, Telnet and SMTP applications.

Alert generation

The capability of a firewall is significantly enhanced by an alert generation capability, enabling a firewall to alert a network manager or administrator to a possible attack on their network. Figure 5.8 illustrates the Technologic Interceptor Add Alert screen display with the IP-spoof pattern shown selected.

In the example shown in Figure 5.8 the IP Spoof alert is used as a mechanism to denote a connection request occurring from a host claiming to have an IP address which does not belong to it. In actuality, it can be very difficult to note the occurrence of IP spoofing. Although it is relatively easy to consider such source IP addresses as those in RFC 1918, all zeros, all ones, loopback and your network as spoofed IP addresses, others are difficult, if not impossible, to detect. This is because unless the firewall previously

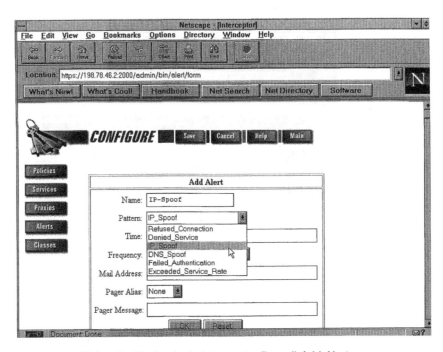

Figure 5.8 Using the Technologic Interceptor firewall Add Alert configuration screen

obtained information about IP addresses, such as their locations on segments whose access is obtained via different firewall ports, or notes restrictions on service by IP address, it will assume an IP address is valid. In comparison, other patterns such as refused connections or failed authentication are much easier to note. For each alert you would first specify a name for the alert definition, such as IP-spoof for that pattern. After selecting the pattern, you can specify the days and times of day and the frequency of occurrence that, when matched, should generate an alert. The Interceptor supports two methods of alert generation, either via email or pager. If you select the use of a pager to transmit an alert you can include a message, such as a numeric alert code, to inform the recipient of the type of alert.

Packet filtering

In concluding our brief examination of the operation of the Interceptor firewall, we will examine the initiation of packet filtering. Although the packet filtering capability of firewalls functions in a manner similar to that router feature, the firewall is usually easier to configure and provides more flexibility in enabling or disabling access based upon the set of rules that can be developed.

Figure 5.9 illustrates the Technologic Interceptor Network Services display which lists the protocols for which this firewall accepts connections. Note that the HTTP protocol is shown selected as we will edit that service. Also note the columns labeled 'Max' and 'Rate'. The column labeled 'Max' indicates the maximum number of simultaneous connections allowed for each service, while the column labeled 'Rate' indicates the maximum rate of new connections for each service on a per minute basis. By specifying entries for one or both columns you can significantly control access to the network services you provide as well as balancing the loads on heavily used services.

Figure 5.10 illustrates the Technologic Interceptor Edit Service display configuration screen. In this example, HTTP service is enabled for up to 256 connections, and a queue size of 64 was entered, limiting TCP HTTP pending connections to that value. The Max Rate entry of 300 represents the maximum rate of new connections that will be allowed to an HTTP service. Once this rate

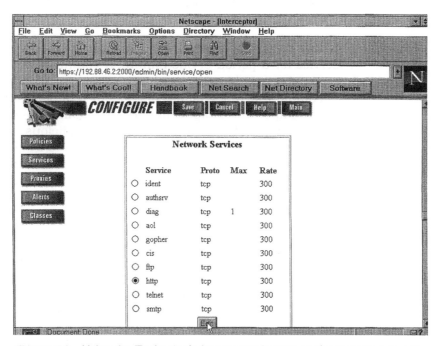

Figure 5.9 Using the Technologic Interceptor firewall configure screen to edit HTTP network services

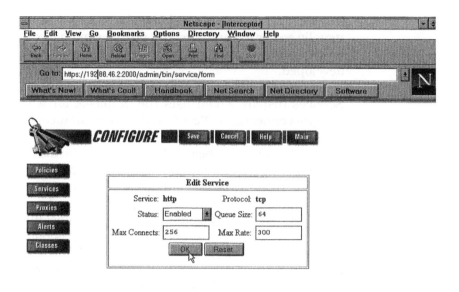

Figure 5.10 Using the Technologic Interceptor firewall Edit Service configuration display to set a series of rules to govern access to HTTP

is exceeded, the firewall will temporarily disable access to that service for a period of one minute. If you allow both internal and external access to an internal Web server, the ability to control the maximum rate of incoming connections to a particular service can be an important weapon in the war against so-called denial of service attacks. Under this technique, a malicious person or group of hackers program one or more computers to issue bogus service initiation requests using RFC 1918, loopback addresses or random IP addresses that more than likely do not exist. Since each access request results in a server initiating a handshake response, the response is directed to a bogus address that does not respond. The server will typically keep the connection open for 60 or 120 seconds which represents a period of time during which a valid user may not be able to access the server when its connection capability is at the maximum. If you compare this method of limiting HTTP requests to the TCP intercept capability of Cisco routers presented in Chapter 4, you will note that the latter represents a better weapon against SYN flooding when compared to earlier versions of Cisco's IOS. This illustrates an important concept. That is, there are certain security features that a firewall provides that may not be available from routers and vice versa. Thus, it is important to carefully consider the capabilities of each device.

5.3.2 CheckPoint FireWall-1

The FireWall-1 is a scaleable modular product from CheckPoint Systems that runs on a variety of platforms ranging from Microsoft's Windows NT to Sun's Solaris, HP-UX and IBM's AIX version of UMX. The FireWall-1, which was in Version 4 when examined by this author, consists of a troika of components that include a Graphical User Interface client that operates on the previously mentioned platforms as well as Windows 95 and Windows 98, a management server onto which security policies created via the GUI are saved, and a FireWall module. The latter represents software that operates on a device that performs actual packet examination. The device that operates the FireWall module is normally considered as a firewall and is located at network choke points where it can examine all packets flowing between a public and private network or another network access location.

The Graphic User Interface

The Graphic User Interface provides the mechanism for defining an organization's security policy. To accomplish this, you would first review your network configuration and devise a security policy that corresponds to your organization's security requirements and its network configuration. For example, let us assume your organization plans to place public access devices, such as mail servers and Web servers, on a separate LAN behind a firewall while placing your organization's private network resources onto a separate connection behind the firewall. Figure 5.11 illustrates this network configuration. Note that in this example the public network resources placed on a segment located behind the firewall is referred to as a DMZ.

For the configuration illustrated in Figure 5.11 the security policy that could be developed can vary considerably from organization to organization. One possible policy for illustrative purposes would be to allow external users to access the local network facilities only to surf the organization's public Web server or to send mail. In the outbound direction let us assume internal users will be provided with the ability to access all network resources, including the servers on the DMZ LAN as well as the

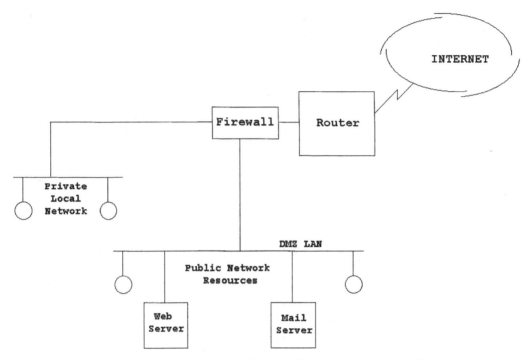

Figure 5.11 Protecting both private and public accessible network segments through the use of a firewall

Internet. Note that this policy protects private network resources from the untrusted side of the network represented by the Internet but does not place any restriction on local users on the private network segment.

Network objects

Once you have developed a proposed security policy you would use the FireWall-1's object manager to define one or more network objects that are used by the program's rule base. Network objects can represent any device that has an IP address, such as a router interface, a Web server or the hosts on an internal or external network.

From the Rule Base Editor you can invoke the program's Network Properties and Router Properties dialog boxes to define various types of network object. Figure 5.12 illustrates the entry of configuration information into the two previously mentioned dialog boxes during the network object definition process. The box on the

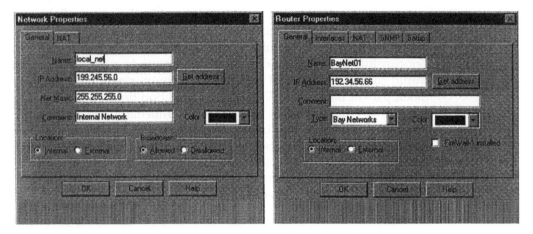

Figure 5.12 Assigning network object definitions for a local network and a router

left illustrates the entry of general network properties, including the name assigned to a local network, its IP address, network mask and applicable comment. Note that you can define the location as either internal or external and either permit or deny broadcasts by a simple cursor click. The right dialog box provides a similar network object definition process for a router.

For our previously described example the firewall, Web server, mail server and the private local network would represent network objects to be defined. Once this action has been accomplished you would define the services to be used to implement your organization's security policy. In doing so you would create individual rules that form a rule base.

FireWall-1 rules

The individual rules supported by the FireWall-1 includes seven field and follows this format:

Source	Destination	Service	Action	Track	Install On	Time

In the preceding rule format both source and destination fields can be set to represent a specific object or any device. For example, let us assume you previously used the program's object manager to assign the label Web server to that server. If you want to provide any internal or external user with the ability to access the Web server you would develop a rule with 'any' in the source field and Web server in the destination field. Because the Web server supports HTTP you would configure the rule for that service. Concerning the action field, since you want to allow traffic you would configure that field to 'accept'. In comparison, if you wish to block packet flow to the Web server the action field would be set to 'drop'. The track field can be used to log information or to generate alerts. The field labeled 'Install On' denotes the platform the rule being developed will operate upon. Finally, the field labeled 'Time' provides you with the ability to control when the rule remains in effect. The following two rules permit external users to send requests to the Web server and mail to the mail server at any time.

Source	Destination	Service	Action	Track	Install On	Time
Any	Web server	http	Accept	Log	Gateways	Any
Any	Mail server	smtp	Accept	Log	Gateways	Any

Because we also want to allow users on the internal private network to access both the Internet and the organization's public accessible network, we need a third rule. That rule would be as follows:

Source	Destination	Service	Action	Track	Install On	Time
Localnet	Any	Any	Accept	Log	Gateways	Any

Similarly to router access lists, the FireWall-1 will drop all packets that are not explicitly permitted by a security policy. Also similarly to our discussion of access lists in Chapter 4, rules like access list statements are examined sequentially and the first rule that matches a connection is applied. Although the implicit rule at the end of the FireWall-1 rule base is to drop all connections that do not match the previous rules, on occasion you may wish to log such connection attempts. To do so you could enter the following rule to terminate your rule base:

Source	Destination	Service	Action	Track	Install On	Time
Any	Any	Any	Reject	Long Log	Gateways	Any

One of the more interesting aspects of FireWall-1 is that it can convert your general rules into a series of access list statements that can be installed on any router that supports the Open Security Extension (OSE). This means that you can install your policy on a pure firewall as well as on certain router products.

Figure 5.13 illustrates an example of the use of the CheckPoint Software policy editor to create a series of six rules. Note that the last rule in effect represents an implicit deny all; however, instead of simply sending such traffic to the bit bucket, its occurrence will be used to generate alert messages.

Management functions

Although the previous rule creation example reminds us of access lists, in actuality you can assign a sophisticated series of properties to one or more rules. Properties are assigned through the use of a

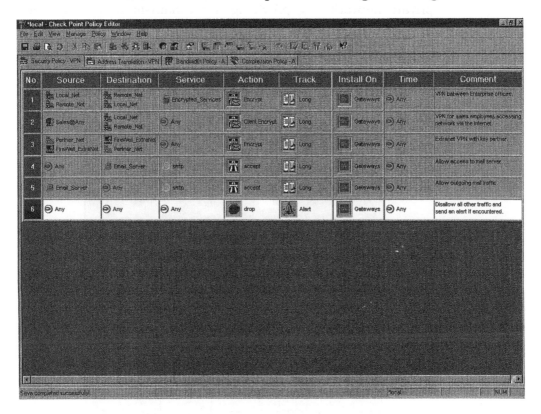

Figure 5.13 The CheckPoint policy editor uses six fields to define rules that are evaluated top to bottom similar to an access list

Properties Setup dialog box and specify both general and specific aspects associated with the flow of information. For example, through the Properties Setup dialog box you can define the direction by which gateway rules will be applied as well as the length of TCP session timeouts, encryption, authentication and whether or not to allow RIP, DNS and ICMP packets.

Figure 5.14 illustrates the Properties Setup dialog box. Note that at the top of the box are a series of tabs that enable you to perform the indicated functions labeled on each tab. In the foreground the Security Policy tab was activated. As you can note from the display you can use a drop down menu to select the direction of packet filtering as well as a simple click to enable numerous functions similar to an applicable router access list permit statement.

Concerning authentication, the FireWall-1 supports eight authentication schemes which range from password to S/Key, SecurID Tokens, RADIUS server and digital certificates. In addition, the FireWall-1 also supports the creation of virtual private networks by providing a mechanism to encrypt communications destined to other networks attached to the Internet, while passing packets flowing to non-VPN locations in the clear. While many of the functions performed by this firewall are similar to the capabilities performed by a router's access list, it is important to note two key differences between the two. First, as a stand-alone

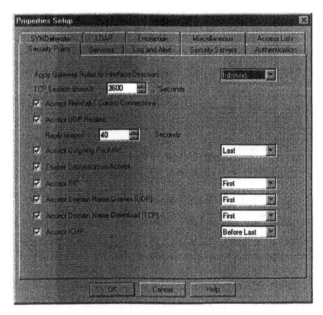

Figure 5.14 Examining the CheckPoint FireWall-1 Properties Setup dialog box

device a firewall provides more security-related functions than commonly available through router access lists. For example, the FireWall-1 can provide content checking for HTTP, SNMP and FTP, including anti-virus checking. Secondly, by off-loading communications security checking to a firewall you should obtain a higher level of router performance.

5.4 THE GAP TO CONSIDER

While routers and firewalls can be used to prevent unauthorized access to network hosts, they do not normally guarantee the security of the communications connection between client and server nor the security of the data being transported. The exception to this is when a router or firewall is used to create a virtual private network by encrypting data between two routers or firewalls. However, even when you use a VPN this does not necessarily provide encryption from client to server. To ensure you obtain full client to server encryption requires the use of a security protocol.

In concluding this chapter we will turn our attention to a security related function performed by both routers and firewalls that may not only hide the addresses of hosts from potential attacker, but also allows you to economize on the use of scarce addresses. This function is network address translation. For example, when using Web browsers you should consider the use of two related Internet protocols, Secure Sockets Layer (SSL) which was developed by Netscape, or the Secure Hypertext Transfer Protocol (S-HTTP) which was developed by Enterprise Integration Technologies as well as digital certificates available from several organizations. The former support several cryptographic algorithms that use public key encryption for which digital certificates provide authentication.

5.5 NETWORK ADDRESS TRANSLATION

We will conclude this chapter with a discussion of a feature that can be performed by both routers and firewalls. That feature is network address translation (NAT). Network address translation has its origin in the growing scarcity of IPv4 address space. As the use of the Internet expanded, the ability of organizations to obtain registered IP addresses from their service providers became more difficult. Recognizing the fact that only a small portion of local network users would be accessing the Internet at any particular point in time, it became possible for organizations to assign each station a private IP address, typically from one of the blocks of addresses reserved in RFC 1918 which was covered in Chapter 4. Then, an address translator could be used to map or translate unregistered private IP addresses into registered addresses on the other side of the device. If an organization has 1000 stations the mapping of 1000 private unregistered IP addresses to the 254 addresses in a Class C network enables one Class C network address to be used instead of four. However, if more than 254 users simultaneously require Internet access, some user requests must be queued until a previously used registered address becomes available. Although NAT was primarily developed as a technique to conserve difficult-to-obtain IPv4 addresses, a side benefit of its use is the fact that it hides the addresses of stations behind the translator. This means that a direct attack upon organizational hosts is no longer possible, and result in NAT functionality being incorporated into firewalls in addition to its use in routers.

Regardless of the device used to perform network address translation, its operation is similar. That is, as packets arrive at the device performing network address translation, the private source address is translated into a public address for transmission onto the Internet. In comparison, inbound packets have their public IP address translated into their equivalent private IP address based upon the state of an IP address mapping table maintained by the device.

5.5.1 Types of address translation

There are three types of network address translation that devices can employ. Those types or methods of address translation include static NAT, pooled NAT and port-level NAT, with the latter also referred to as Port Address Translation (PAT).

Static NAT

Static network address translation results in the permanent mapping of each host on an internal network to an address on an external network. Although static mapping does not provide a reduction in the number of IP addresses needed by an organization, after it is configured no further action is necessary and its simple table lookup minimizes delay.

Pooled NAT

When a pooled NAT technique is used, a pool of addresses on the external network is used for the dynamic assignment of IP addresses in place of private addresses on the internal network. Although pooled NAT enables users to conserve upon the use of public IP addresses, its use can adversely affect certain types of application. For example, SNMP managers track devices based upon the device IP address and an object identifier. Because a pooled NAT means that network addresses will more than likely change over time, this means that devices in front of the translating device cannot be configured to reliably transmit traps to devices behind the translating device. One possible solution to this problem is to permanently map an SNMP manager to an IP address while all other devices share the remaining addresses in the address pool. Of course, the device that supports pooled NAT must also be capable of permitting support for static mapping.

Port address translation

A third type of address translation results in the mapping of internal addresses to a single IP address on the external network. To accomplish this the address translator assigns different port numbers to TCP and UDP source port fields. The port numbers used for mapping are those above 1023, providing 64512 (65535 − 1023) simultaneous TCP/IP or UDP/IP connections on a single IP address. Because mapping occurs to a single IP address through the use of different port numbers, this technique is referred to as port address translation (PAT). The use of PAT results in all traffic transmitted onto the public network appearing to come from a single IP address.

Regardless of the method of NAT used, its use hides an organization's actual IP addresses. When incorporated into a firewall NAT represents a technique that forces direct IP address attacks to the firewall, which is hopefully hardened to withstand such attacks.

6

THE ROLE OF THE VIRUS SCANNER AND ENCRYPTION

The goal of this chapter is to become acquainted with two key network security-related areas: virus scanners and encryption. In the first section of this chapter we will briefly review some of the methods by which malicious code can adversely effect the operation of a computer. Once this has been accomplished we will describe and discuss the use of virus scanners to protect hosts on a network from receiving malicious code. In the second portion of this chapter we will turn our attention to the role of encryption in securing different types of communication. In doing so we will describe and discuss both private and public key encryption methods as well as their utilization for different types of communication-based applications.

6.1 VIRUS OVERVIEW

A virus is a program that reproduces its own code, placing its code in other programs so that when those programs are executed the infection spreads. Although not technically a virus, there are three additional types of malicious software that a good virus scanner will check for and which we should note. Those include logic bombs, worms and Trojan horses.

6.1.1 Logic bombs

A logic bomb is a program that lies dormant until it is triggered by a specific event. The trigger can range in scope from a specific date and time encoded in the software to the receipt of a command to initiate its predefined operation. Once activated, the logic bomb will normally perform some type of insidious operation, such as changing the value of data previously stored on disk, altering the value of a RAM memory location, or attacking a third party. Concerning the latter, the distributed denial of service (DDoS) attack employed against such popular Internet sites as Yahoo and EBay resulted from code placed on third party hosts that were activated by command.

6.1.2 Worms

A worm is a program that reproduces itself. Unlike a virus that both adversely infects and reproduces, the worm is relatively benign as it does not alter nor destroy data. However, each copy of the worm creates additional copies, which can rapidly consume all available computer resources.

Worms are usually planted on networks and in multi-processing operating systems where they can do the most harm. In fact, the well-known 'Internet virus' that brought several thousand computers connected to that network to a halt during the early 1990s was actually a worm.

6.1.3 Trojan horse

A Trojan horse represents a program that functions as a delivery vehicle for destructive code that will adversely affect the operation of a computer. Named after the Trojan horse that hid soldiers, a Trojan program will appear useful but when executed can function as a logic bomb, worm or virus.

6.1.4 Virus effect

According to several virus-scanning programs with a built-in database describing different malicious software, there are thousands of identified code which perform different types of malicious function. Thus, it is a bit difficult to attempt to categorize the effect of a virus. However, we note that their actual effect can vary from humorous to catastrophic. Some viruses may simply display the message 'X Shopping Days till Christmas', while other viruses can alter your hard drive's boot sector, resulting in the apparent inability to access information previously stored on your hard drive.

One of the most popular methods used by virus developers to replicate their code is to name their program as an external command file with the extension .COM when the real command program has the same name but the extension .EXE. The reason for doing so is that the entry of a command name results in the operating system executing the file with the extension .COM if it encounters both .COM and .EXE file extensions with the same file name. A smartly constructed virus using the .COM extension will also execute the actual .EXE command as it spreads its infection. Thus, for a period of time until the cumulative effect of the virus becomes noticeable, it will be hidden, for the command entered by the user will execute as expected. The previously described virus is referred to as a .COM infection.

6.1.5 Types of virus

The types of virus you can encounter depend upon the ingenuity of the hackers and pranksters that typically develop these programs. Although the types of virus are virtually unlimited, they can be categorized by the most common areas they attempt to infect. Those areas are the boot sector and file allocation table (FAT), system files and operating system commands.

Boot and FAT infectors

There are two locations that many viruses commonly attack due to the harm their alterations can cause. Those locations are the boot sector and the file allocation table. By changing information in the boot sector a virus can make your hard disk appear to be unusable. By changing data in the FAT a virus can make portions of your disk literally 'disappear' simply by marking good sectors as bad or changing a pointer to the next cluster used by a file to an end-of-file cluster value. A few viruses have been known to swap the starting FAT entry address in the root directory, which when performed on a database file can result in the subsequent execution of a database processing program using an output file as an input file and vice versa, a truly insidious trick!

System file infectors

> A system file virus infector changes one of the operating system files. Since system files are always executed upon power-on, their modification functions as an easy mechanism to replicate a virus. The most popular method to develop a system file infector is for the virus developer to attach their program code to a system file. A virus scanner can easily note the occurrence of this type of file by comparing its size to the size of the legitimate system file. Far more difficult to detect is the virus which rearranges system file code so it can insert itself into the file without altering the size of the file. Fortunately, very few persons have the knowledge and are willing to devote the time required to develop this type of virus. Even if someone does, many virus scanners can be configured to prevent any executable system file from being sent over a corporate network.

Command infectors

> As previously noted, a command (.COM) infector virus either attaches itself to an external command file or hides itself by naming itself after an .EXE file using the extension .COM. Since operating system commands are frequently executed many times during the day by many computer users, a command infector achieves the ability to frequently replicate itself by pretending to be a command. Now that we have a basic knowledge of the types of software attack we can encounter and the manner in which most viruses designed to cause harm operate, let us focus our attention upon methods we can consider to prevent a software attack and, if unsuccessful in our prevention methods, recover from the effect of an attack.

6.1.6 Infection prevention

> According to an article published in a recent edition of a national magazine, over 5000 types of worms, logic bomb and virus have been identified. This means that it is highly probable that no one prevention and detection strategy or virus scanning program can be expected to represent an absolute guarantee against infection. However, such programs do represent a good starting point to protect your computer.
>
> Infection prevention software functions as a filter, examining computer operations susceptible to modification by different types

of attack software. Most infection prevention software monitors all I/O operations and disallows any attempt by code to modify critical disk areas, such as the boot sector, FAT and areas where executable programs that are part of the operating system reside.

Typically, you load the infection prevention software on your hard drive and either modify your AUTOEXEC.BAT file to load the program each time you use the computer or place the program for automatic startup under Windows. For either method the infection program functions as a barrier to most of the commonly used attack software techniques known to result in destructive operations.

Since infection prevention software is designed to detect attack software once it begins to operate, such methods are normally used to locate dormant infections. To identify previously stored attack software commonly requires the use of detection software.

6.1.7 Detection software

A detection program, now commonly referred to as a virus scanner, searches your disk looking for identifying attributes associated with different types of attach software. Such software may examine the names and size of files to determine if they are disguised executable files, look for replication code, and search system files and the contents of memory looking for any suspicious alterations.

6.1.8 Virus scanning

Today both infection prevention and detection of malicious code is commonly performed by one program referred to as a virus scanner. To obtain an appreciation for the role of a virus scanner we will turn our attention to two types of product. One type of product operates as a stand-alone program on a desktop, while the second type of program guards the hosts on a network from malicious email, typically by examining inbound email.

6.1.9 Desktop program example

To illustrate the operation of a desktop virus scanner this author will use Command Software System's Command AntiVirus program. Figure 6.1 illustrates the main window of this program. Note that this program is installed with five predefined tasks, which are

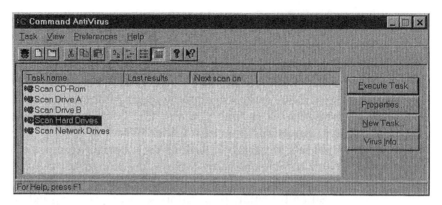

Figure 6.1 The main window of Command Software's Command AntiVirus program includes predefined tasks and allows the user to create new tasks

listed within the window. To illustrate the operation of this program this author will use it to scan his computer's hard drives. However, note that the program is also capable of scanning network drives. In addition, you can also create new tasks by clicking on the button with that label. Once you have done so you can enter a name for the task and use a resulting dialog box labeled properties to specify the type of scanning to be performed by the task. Later in this section we will examine the dialog box labeled properties and the properties that can be configured for a new task.

General features

One of the key features of the Command AntiVirus program is its ability to schedule a virus scan and send a message when an infection is found. Through the use of the program's Preferences menu you can send a message. Figure 6.2 illustrates the program's Network dialog box, which is selected from the Preferences menu. In examining Figure 6.2, note that it provides you with the ability to display a message when an infection is found as well as to send an email. This program integrates very well with Microsoft's Outlook, allowing a user to email a report as well as, if desired, the infected files discovered by the scanning process. Thus, you can configure the program to execute at predefined times and transmit via email any encountered infections to a help desk or another central location.

When you use the program dynamically, you can control both the scanning process and action when an infection is noted. To do so you would return to the Preferences menu and select the entry

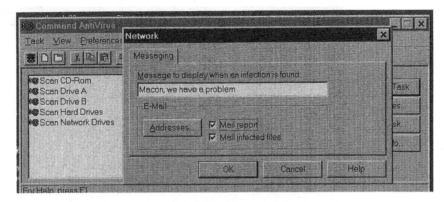

Figure 6.2 The Command AntiVirus program supports a messaging option which enables other members of an organization to be alerted when a scan indicates the discovery of the infection of a computer

labeled Active Protection. This action will result in the display of a dialog box labeled Active Protection, which contains two tabs labeled Dynamic Virus Protection and Memory Scanning. Figure 6.3 illustrate this dialog box with the tab labeled Dynamic Virus Protection in the foreground.

In examining Figure 6.3 note that the checkbox next to DVP must be selected to enable Dynamic Virus Protection. When enabled, the

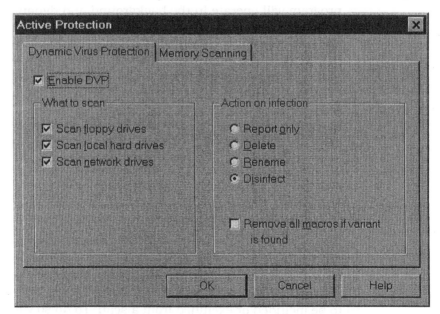

Figure 6.3 The Dynamic Virus Protection tab in the Active Protection dialog box provides users with the ability to specify what computer resources will be scanned and the action to be performed if an infection is determined

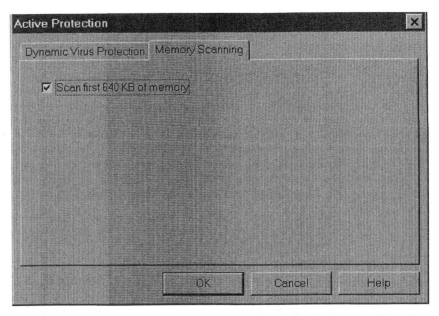

Figure 6.4 The Memory Scanning tab in the Active Protection dialog box provides users with the ability to control the scanning of the first 640 KB of computer RAM

program will operate in the background and dynamically scan the computer resources selected as well as perform the selected action when an infection is encountered. Concerning the latter, note that the right column provides you with five options concerning the action to be performed in the event an infection is encountered.

The second tab in the Active Protection dialog box is labeled Memory Scanning. Figure 6.4 illustrates the tab, which is now located in the foreground of the dialog box. Note that the version of the Command AntiVirus program used by this author was limited to allowing a scan of the first 640 KB of memory.

File scanning control

If you are scanning a large capacity hard drive or many network drives, the scanning process can require a considerable amount of time. Perhaps recognizing this fact, the Command AntiVirus program provides users with the ability to specify the types of file to be included or excluded from a scan. To do so you would return to the program's Preferences menu and select the Files to Include/ Exclude option. Figure 6.5 illustrates the dialog box labeled Files to

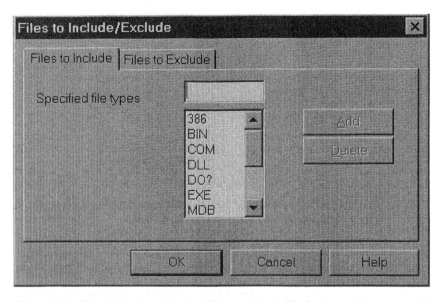

Figure 6.5 The dialog box labeled Files to Include/Exclude provides users with the ability to specify files via predefined or entered extensions for inclusion or exclusion in a subsequent scan

Include/Exclude. Note that in addition to predefining file extension you can add new file extensions for inclusion or exclusion in a scan.

The scanning process

Since the old adage 'the proof of the pudding is in the eating' holds true today, this author decided to run a scan. To do so the task labeled 'Scan Hard Drives, previously shown in Figure 6.1, was first selected. The box in the right portion of the display labeled 'Execute Task' was then clicked. Figure 6.6 illustrates the initial execution of the Command AntiVirus program at a point in time where 856 files were scanned. As the program scans your hard drive it displays a running progress of the scanning activity as a horizontal bar chart as well as by informing you of the path to the file being scanned. Note that at the particular point in time when the screen was captured no viruses had been found.

Virus information

One of the more interesting tutorial aspects of the Command AntiVirus program is its database of virus information. This

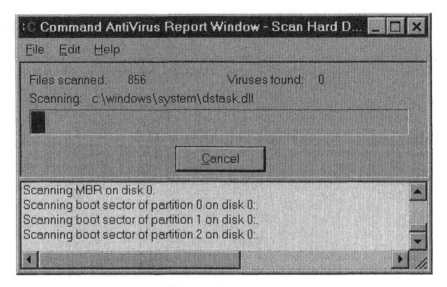

Figure 6.6 Viewing the progress of a virus scan

database is arranged alphabetically by virus name, as is illustrated in Figure 6.7. As you select a virus in the left portion of the screen, the right portion of the screen will display information about the selected virus. This information can be very helpful in allowing one to sleep at night. For example, assume a virus scan performed once a week located the 3Tunes virus, which you then deleted. You

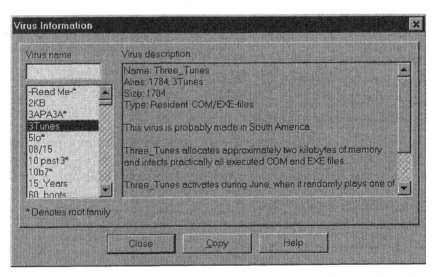

Figure 6.7 Using the Command AntiVirus program to display information about a virus

would now more than likely want to know the potential effect of the virus. Although you could more than likely guess its action from the name of the virus in this example, this is not always the case. Thus, the ability to view a description of encountered viruses can be an important consideration when selecting a virus scanner in addition to the number of viruses in its scanning database and other program features.

Controlling the virus scan

In concluding our examination of the Command AntiVirus program we will turn our attention to its Properties dialog box, which represents the key to controlling program scans. Figure 6.8 illustrates the Properties dialog box after the Scan Hard Drives task was selected.

In examining Figure 6.8 note you can specify the action to be taken if an infected file is encountered. You can also specify the drive and paths to be scanned, the types of file to be scanned, and other information you can note by examining the screen. The Properties dialog box also includes a button labeled Schedule. As you might expect, you can select that button to have scans automatically performed at predefined times. Now that we have an appreciation for the operation of a typical virus scanning program, let us turn our attention to the scanning of email.

6.1.10 Email scanning

According to several surveys of Internet users one of the highest ranking reasons for the use of the 'mother of all networks' is email. While email is certainly a key productivity enhancement method for both residential and business oriented persons it also represents a mechanism for the introduction of viruses. To facilitate the checking of email for attached files that could cause harm you can consider several options. Those options include placing a virus scanner on each desktop, precluding inbound email or attachments to email, adding virus scanning capability to your firewall, or installing a separate virus scanner. The first solution, providing client-based email scanning, can be relatively expensive to deploy due to the need to install and configure software on each desktop. Precluding inbound email or inbound email with attachments defeats the purpose of providing employees with this productivity tool. Thus, if your organization requires protection from email-based attacks your

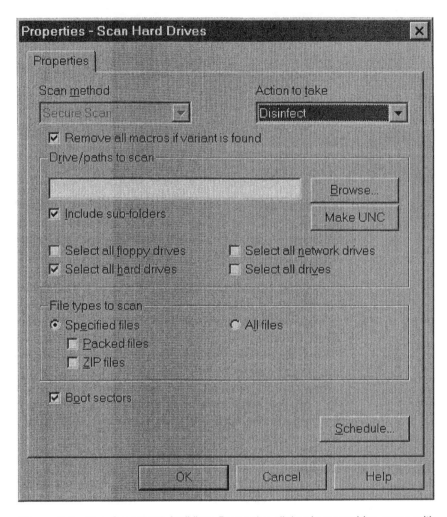

Figure 6.8 The Command AntiVirus Properties dialog box provides users with the ability to control both when and how a virus scan is performed as well as the actions to occur if infected files are discovered

realistic choice is between a software module on a router that will scan inbound email or a separate server that operates scanning software.

6.1.11 Protecting the enterprise

Figure 6.9 illustrates the relationship of an enterprise email scanner server to other network components. In examining Figure

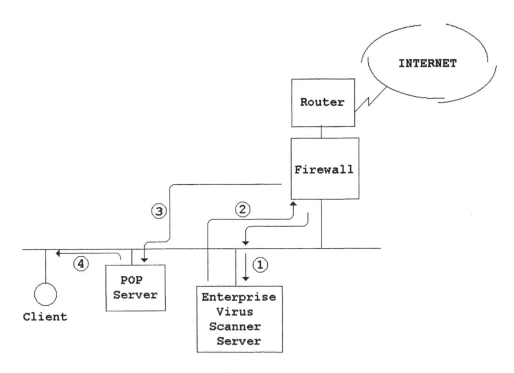

Figure 6.9 Using an enterprise virus scanner server

6.9 note that an email destined for any client on the local area network will first flow through the router and firewall (1), assuming the datagram(s) transporting the email and any attachments satisfy any constraints imposed by the router's access list or firewall configuration. The firewall can be configured to function as a proxy for the Post Office Protocol (POP) server and send the email and attachments directly to the enterprise virus scanner server, where it is scanned and returned (2) to the firewall. The firewall then forwards the email to the POP server (3). The POP server then forwards the message to the applicable client (4). Note that as an alternative to the dataflow previously described, it is possible to direct emails to the virus scanner and the scanner can then direct scanned email to the POP server.

Figure 6.10 illustrates the receipt of an email message that was scanned for viruses. If you examine the lower portion of the email dialog box you will note that the scanner used informs the recipient that the email was scanned. Although many scanners only scan inbound email, other products support a bi-directional scan. The use of a bi-directional scan may assist your organization in stopping the inadvertent infection of another organization from a

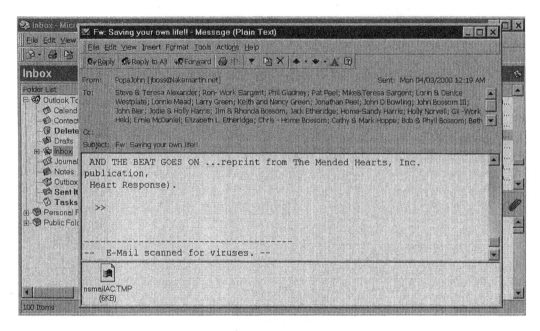

Figure 6.10 Many enterprise virus scanners denote that they operated upon an inbound email by placing an appropriate message at the bottom of the email

file downloaded at home by an employee who took the file to work and decided to share it with a friend at another organization.

6.1.12 Optional features

During the past two years several vendors have introduced virus scanning software oriented towards the enterprise that includes several features within and beyond virus scanning. Concerning additional virus scanning, some programs add scanning for FTP and HTTP in addition to the scanning of SMTP and mail attachments. Concerning features beyond virus scanning, some enterprise software programs now support span blocking as well as the ability to look inside the contents of email messages. In doing so some programs provide the administrator with the ability to define inappropriate words, such as obscenities, racist hate words, or other terms that should trigger alarms or block messages. Other programs have a database of terms the administrator can use as is or modify. For either method, the ability to stop inappropriate messages from flowing to their destination could save an organization a legal problem, possible embarrassment, along with bad feelings among employees.

Because the best plans and efforts taken to prevent a virus infection could be overridden by the development of a new strain, it is important to be prepared for the worst. Thus, in concluding the first portion of this chapter, which was focused on viruses, we will describe and discuss the common symptoms of attack software and the steps you can perform to minimize the effect of an attack.

6.1.13 Infection symptoms

A number of symptoms serve as a warning that your computer is under attack. Some are quite obvious, such as the display of a message that may contain profanity, attack a politician, or display a similar unexpected and unwarranted message. Other symptoms, such as the activation of a disk drive for no apparent reason and the illumination of the drive's light emitting diode, may be much more difficult to note as an indication that your computer is under attack.

Table 6.1 lists nine of the more common indicators that your computer has an unexpected visitor. If one or more of these symptoms should occur there are several actions you should perform and other actions you may wish you had performed unless you were fortunate enough to prepare yourself to recover from different types of disaster.

6.1.14 Recovery operations

One of the most important things to understand when you observe an indication that unwanted software is operating on your computer is that whatever harm that can happen has already occurred and your actions from this point onward can prevent further harm from

Table 6.1 Common infection indicators.

---
*Programs that take longer to load or execute than before.
*Disk accesses appear to be excessive for normal tasks.
*Disk drives are activated for no apparent reason.
*Programs that worked before do not work.
*Programs or data files appear to disappear mysteriously.
*The use of a utility program shows the presence of mysterious hidden files.
*You notice an unexpected reduction in available disk space.
*You notice the appearance of an inappropriate message on your screen or
 strange sounds come from your speaker.
*Less memory appears to be available for program execution than normal.

---

occurring. Unless the unwanted program has taken control of your computer and is writing continuously to disk, do not power off your computer. If you were not using a virus scanner and have a program available for use, run it. The chances are high that if you have a virus or another type of attack program its techniques may be recognized and the scanner can locate the program. If a scanner is not available or fails to locate any abnormal software, reboot your system using an original system diskette, which loads a good write-protected copy of the operating system, since the original system diskette is permanently write-protected.

Using the newly loaded operating system, attempt to examine the files you used during the operation that resulted in an infection indicator. For example, did you previously execute a command stored as an .EXE file and a directory listing shows both .COM and .EXE files? If so, the obvious cause of the problem is now apparent. However, what happens if you cannot access your hard drive owing to the modification of your boot sector, FAT or directory structure?

Although it is probably preferable to have used a disk recover program which keeps an image of your key hard drive sectors on another area of your drive to facilitate data recovery, you can also attempt to use an operating system command, such as the DOS command SYS C:, which will rewrite your DOS boot sector on your hard drive if that area was modified.

If this still does not fix the problem and persons you consult shrug their shoulders when asked what you should do next, you may be faced with having to reformat your drive and reload your software that was hopefully backed up on a regular basis. Although this represents a situation most of us will rarely have to encounter, if you have to reload previously backed up software it is important to recognize that the cause of your problem may also have been placed on your backup tape during your last backup operation. However, since you were able to notice an infection symptom you also noted an operation you performed which caused the symptom. Thus, after you reload your software, reboot from a write-protected copy of the operating system and attempt to locate and eliminate the cause of your problem.

6.2 ENCRYPTION

Both hardware and software solutions to the encryption of data are readily available on the commercial marketplace. The majority of software solutions are designed to encrypt or encipher files, protecting their contents both when stored on a system as well as when transferred on a communications facility. In comparison, hardware encryption devices are primarily designed to protect data being communicated and the encryption procedure is immediately reversed at the destination of the communications path.

6.2.1 Private key DES

Until recently, the most commonly used method to encrypt data was based upon US Federal Information Processing Standard (FIPS) 46, which was released by the National Bureau of Standards (now the National Institute of Standards and Technology) in 1977 to provide for the cryptographic protection of federal sensitive unclassified computer information. Referred to as the Data Encryption Standard or DES, FIPS 46 specifies the use of an algorithm which converts plaintext to ciphertext using a 6-bit key. The algorithm used to encipher data is also used with the same key to convert ciphertext back to plaintext.

DES represents a private key encryption method. Under private key encryption a single key is shared by the originator and recipient of a message. That key must be kept secret and controlled only by the parties that have access to the key for the cryptographic process to remain secure. Otherwise, if another person has access to the key, that person can use the key to decrypt the contents of a previously encrypted message or file.

The DES key is 56 bits long, and while its use as a private key can effectively prevent the disclosure of information, it has several limitations. First, a private key system limits the number of persons that can communicate, unless you are willing to have many persons share the same key. This widens the potential com-promise of data if a person discloses his or her key or if the equipment they use to encrypt and decrypt data is lost or stolen.

Another problem associated with private key systems is the fact that they do not verify the originator of a message or document. For example, an unauthorized person could sit down at a workstation that is connected to a network by a hardware product that automatically encrypts and decrypts data flowing on the network. Although the person's message will be protected by the hardware encryption process from observation by another person using diagnostic monitoring equipment, the encryption process does not authenticate the user or the document they created and transmitted. To do so requires a mechanism to provide or append digital signatures to documents.

In an electronic era where millions of Web surfers need encryption to make secure online purchases using credit cards, it would be impractical to use private key encryption due to the necessity to issue perhaps billions of keys. This is because each surfer would require a unique key to securely access each site where they wish to purchase an item. Needless to say, this would represent a significant key distribution problem. Thus, the primary role of DES is to secure leased line communications and the technology is not applicable for large-scale client-server operations. Since DES still represents a popular encryption method, let us examine its operation.

The DES algorithm consists of 16 'rounds' of operations that mix data and they key together in a prescribed manner based upon a series of permutations and substitutions. The goal of the DES algorithm is to scramble the data and key completely so that every bit of the ciphertext depends upon every bit of data plus every bit of the 56-bit key.

To break an encrypted message using DES would require testing approximately 72.059 quadrillion key combinations. Using a computer capable of performing 10 million key tests per second would require approximately 228 years until the message was decrypted. While this suggests that DES should provide sufficient strength to obscure the meaning of data until the data in the message is obsolete, recent advances in microprocessor technology makes it possible to use a brute force method in an economical manner to break the encryption technique. For example, the latest Intel microprocessor operates at a clock speed of 1 GHz, providing the capability to execute approximately 400 million instructions per second (MIPS). The use of a PC with a 1 GHz microprocessor can be expected to result in an average time of 5.7 years until a DES encrypted message is broken. Because the cost of a 1 GHz PC is only a few thousand dollars, it is possible for a government agency or large corporation to program a hundred or a thousand modern PCs to break a DES encoded message within a few days. Due to this, many organizations now use 'triple-DES' on their leased lines, which significantly enhances the ability to withstand a brute force attack. This is because each extra bit in the key doubles the number of possible combinations that must be searched.

The key to the enciphering process used by DES and other cryptographic techniques is modulo 2 addition and modulo 2 subtraction. The top portion of Figure 6.11 illustrates the use of modulo 2 addition to form an enciphered bit stream, while the lower portion of that illustration shows how the original plaintext bit stream is reconstructed by using the same key but now performing a modulo 2 subtraction upon the data.

A. *Encryption*

Plaintext Data	1010
⊕ Key	<u>0111</u>
Enciphered Data	1101

B. *Decryption*

Encrypted Data	1101
⊖ Key	<u>0111</u>
Reconstructed Plaintext Data	1010

Figure 6.11 Modulo 2 operations form the basis of enciphering and deciphering operations

A number of vendors, including Racal-Milgo, Technical Communications Corporation and Western Datacom, market DES-compatible products. In evaluating the potential use of such products you must differentiate between leased line and switched network connections.

6.2.2 Leased line versus switched network operations

On a leased line transmission facility, such as a circuit connecting two remote bridges or routers, you will only require two physical encryption devices. An example of this type of network configuration is illustrated in Figure 6.12a.

If you intend to use encryptors on dial-in lines, you can consider several options. First, you can install one dial-in line, modem and datacryptor to service each remote datacryptor user, providing a one-to-one correspondence between the key used by each remote user and the key used by each datacryptor at the dial-in site. A second method you can consider is to provide two or more remote datacryptor users with the same key, having them dial either a specific telephone number or a main rotary telephone number and contend for access to datacryptors programmed with the same key at the dial-in site.

An example of the latter is illustrated in Figure 6.12b. However, in this situation the loss of a datacryptor compromises all of the dial-in lines that use encryption devices that operate with the same key. In comparison, if each remote user had a datacryptor with a unique key to use with a specific dial-in port, the loss of a datacryptor only compromises one dial-in line. Then, if the loss is reported, the network manager only has to disconnect the line

a.   Leased line use.

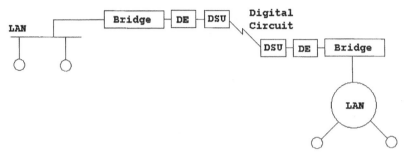

b.   Switched network use.

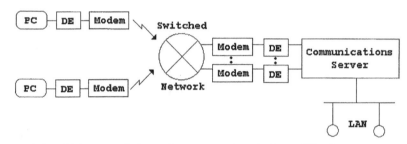

Figure 6.12   Using stand-alone data encryption devices. DE, data encrypter; DSU, digital service unit

serving the lost or stolen datacryptor to resolve the potential compromise.

6.2.3 Public key encryption

In concluding our discussion of encryption we will turn our attention to public key encryption. Public key encryption dates to 1976 when Whitfield Duffy and Martin Hellman published a paper covering the mathematics behind a cryptographic technique that used a public and private key pair. The private key is known only to the user and is not distributed. In comparison, the public key can be published or distributed at will. The public key is used to encrypt a message that is then transmitted to the party that developed the public-private key pair. The destination party uses the private key to decrypt the enciphered message back into its original form.

6.2.4 Advantage of use

The key advantage associated with the use of public key encryption is the fact that complete knowledge of the public key and the encrypting algorithm does not endanger the private key. In fact, the public key can be transmitted in the 'open' and published on a bulletin board or even at a person's business. Therefore, a secure communications line is not required to transport a public key. This means that when a browser is used to access a Web site and secure communications are required, the Web site can transmit its public key to the browser. The browser will then transmit information to the Web server using the public key to encrypt the data, with the server using its private key for decryption. Note that each user accessing the Web site can be sent the same public key, eliminating the distribution problem associated with the use of a private key system.

6.2.5 RSA

One of the most popular public key cryptographic systems is based upon the RSA algorithm, which was developed in 1977 by three MIT graduate students. The RSA algorithm obtains its name from the first letters of the names of the students: Rivest, Shamir and Aldeman. RSA employs modular exponentiation to encrypt and decrypt text messages. Text is first converted to numbers. Next, two large prime numbers, P and Q, are randomly generated. The product of these two numbers (N) is then computed.

One fundamental theorem of numbers is that each non-prime number is actually the product of a unique set of prime numbers. For example, 18 is $2 \times 3 \times 3$, all of which are primes. Under RSA, P and Q are the unique set of prime numbers that yield the product N.

Next, M is defined as the product of $(P-1)(Q-1)$. This is followed by the selection of the public encryption key (E) as a number between 3 and M which has no factors in common with M except the number 1. This means that E must be relatively prime with M and cannot be P or Q. Once E is selected, the private decryption (D) key is determined. There is only one unique D that forms a pair with E such that $E \times D \bmod M = 1$ with $D > 3$ and $D < M$. If T is a portion of text converted to a numeric value for encryption, the formula for the encrypted message (X) version of T becomes:

$$X = T^E \bmod N$$

This algorithm is used to encrypt messages. The party holding the private key (D) converts the ciphertext X back to its original text T using the following formula:

$$T = X^D \bmod N$$

6.2.6 Example

The following seven steps illustrate a simple example of public key encryption. Note that P and Q are randomly generated and should normally be very large in value and not small numbers as shown in the following example.

1. Select $P = 5$, $Q = 11$
2. $N = P \times Q = 55$
3. $M = (P - 1)(Q - 1) = 4 \times 10 = 40$
4. E must be greater than 3 and less than 40 with no common factors with 40 other than 1. Several choices are available. For this example $E = 23$ will be used as it satisfies the required conditions.
5. $E \times D \bmod N = 1$. Thus, $D = 7$ because $(23 \times 7) \bmod 55 = 1$.
6. The Encryption Process
   T always has a given value. For simplicity, let us assume $T = 2$. Then, to encrypt T using the public key into ciphertext X:

   $$X = T^E \bmod N = X23 \bmod 55 = 8388608 \bmod 55 = 8$$

   Thus, 8 is transmitted instead of 2.
7. The Decryption Process
   Given $T = X^D \bmod N$ we obtain:

   $$T = 8^7 \bmod 55 = 2$$

Because N is normally a number hundreds of digits in length it can be extremely time-consuming, if not impossible, to factor N back into P and Q. Because a 128-bit key provides an integer space in which 4.28×10^36 primes are available, the time required to attack RSA is prohibitive. Although public key systems are popularly used to encrypt transmission in a client-server environment, the computations required for public key encryption are extensive. This explains why the display of secure Web pages requires more time than when you surf the same server but are accessing pages that are not secure.

HOST ATTACK METHODS

The purpose of this chapter is to become acquainted with various methods used by persons to interrupt, disable or modify the operation or contents of a computer. Because the orientation of this book is upon the TCP/IP protocol suite and the Windows NT/2000 operating system, the examples discussed in this chapter will be focused upon this area. It is important to note that there is no limit to the number of different host attack methods that can be developed and used against an organization. This results from the fact that man is very ingenious and some persons will look at different applications, protocols and equipment configurations for loopholes they can exploit. Other people, being curious, may simply try different operations with no harmful intent and discover a new attack method, similar to the script-form attack method discovered by this author which was discussed in detail in the first chapter of this book. Thus, before we begin our coverage of host attack methods, it is important to note that any networked computer may never be totally secure from attack. This means that in addition to attempting as best as possible to guard our host from attack by using router access lists and firewalls, it is also important to log unnatural events and periodically examine those logs, an area that will be discussed in the next chapter in this book.

In this chapter we will first subdivide host attack methods into four specific areas or categories. Those areas are physical security, password security, user security and network security. Because many hackers are quite ingenious and frequently develop new techniques to harm our hosts, break into them, or simply deny access to our computational facilities, we will also examine several recent attack methods in this chapter.

In doing so we will primarily refer to the use of hot fixes, service packs, and a few specific techniques as solutions to most host attack methods covered in this chapter, waiting until the next chapter to cover general techniques such as the use of rights and privileges we can employ to harden our hosts against attack. However, prior to focusing our attention on different attack methods it is important to note that security is a continuous effort. Because new attack methods, such as a new virus or a corrupted type of IP datagram, may result in an unexpected security hazard, it is important to keep abreast of security-related information. In addition to the Computer Emergency Response Team (CERT) Web site that provides information about hacker attacks covering all types of platform, you can obtain specific security-related information about Microsoft applications and operating systems from the Microsoft Web site. Thus, let us turn our attention to the Microsoft Security Advisor prior to examining different categories of host attack methods.

7.1 THE MICROSOFT SECURITY ADVISOR

The Microsoft Web site includes a considerable amount of security-related information. The Microsoft Security Advisor, which has the URL of

http://www.microsoft.com/security/default.asp

provides a very useful location to periodically visit. When this book was written the Microsoft Security Advisor commenced with a series of headlines that provides a summary of security-related items and links to specific information for each headline. Because denial of service attacks were in the news when this book was written, as you might surmise, one headline on the Microsoft Security Advisor was focused on this topic.

Another valuable feature of the Microsoft Security Advisor is the fact that it provides links to valuable security-related topics from one central location. For example, another headline on the Microsoft Security Advisor when this book was prepared was a link to a checklist of security-related tasks for the Internet Information Server (IIS). Another headline informs visitors of a security planning tool for IIS, which covers authentication methods, how they differ and different techniques users can employ to control access to areas on a Web server.

While valuable information can be obtained by periodically checking the contents of the Microsoft Security Advisor, being human means we may periodically forget to check this site. To keep informed of security-related issues concerning different Microsoft products, it is highly recommended that you should subscribe to the Microsoft Security Notification listserv service. A subscription to this service will provide you with Microsoft security-related bulletins via email that will give background information on security issues, how they may affect your organization, how to protect your host against the issue and what Microsoft plans to do to fix any Microsoft problems.

7.2 HOST ATTACK CATEGORIES

As mentioned earlier in this chapter, we can subdivide host attack methods into four general security categories. Those categories include physical security, password security, user security and network security. In this section we will turn our attention to each of these host attack categories. However, before we do it should be noted that these are not distinct categories and threats can easily cross category boundaries.

7.2.1 Physical security

Physical security involves placing your organization's network servers in a controlled access, secure room or building. In addition to locating your servers in a controlled access environment it is important to control access to all networking equipment. Such equipment can include routers, hubs, switches, cables and client systems that can be located within the same building as the servers or in a building on a different continent.

There are several types of hacker attack that fall into the physical security category. One of the most common attack methods is for a visitor to an organization to observe user IDs and passwords posted on sticky notes attached to PCs as they walk through a cubical area. In this situation the initial hacker attack involves information gathering that will be used later in an attempt to gain access to a host. Another popular attack method that falls into the violation of physical security is the ability of many persons to easily obtain organizational phone directories. Such directories represent a very good starting point for many types of electronic attack against hosts. For example, many organizations assign user IDs based upon a naming convention. One popular naming convention is to prefix the last name of a person with their initials, using X as a middle initial if a person does not have one. Another popular attack technique that can be exploited through the use of a telephone directory is an email attack. By carefully studying an organization's telephone directory, it may become possible to note different departments and groups within an organization. From this information it becomes possible to make an educated guess concerning the name of different email groups. Then, a hacker could visit a public library and compose and transmit messages to different email groups whose contents could be quite disruptive to the organization.

When considering physical security it is important to consider your computer infrastructure, organizational standard operating procedures and personal information. As pointed out in this section, the simple availability of an organizational telephone directory can provide a convenient tool for hackers to begin several types of host attack.

7.2.2 Password security

The category of password security overlaps to a degree some aspects of the previously described category of physical security. That is, password security involves measures and techniques used to make it difficult, if not impossible, for a hacker to obtain account passwords.

One of the favorite techniques of hackers is to attempt to break into the administrator account. Because one predefined account with maximum rights and permissions is the administrator account, it is similar to a magnet, drawing hacker attempts to break into the account. Other predefined accounts that are commonly attacked include backup operator and guest, although due to the rights and permissions associated with them the administrator account is the preferred account for attack.

Once a user ID has been learned, it is a relatively simple process to locate a script on the Internet to run a dictionary or brute force attack against the password associated with the user ID. Learning the user ID makes the attack easier, since the hacker does not have to first search for a valid user ID to attack. In Chapter 8 we will turn our attention to several methods that can be used to minimize attacks focused upon gaining password access to user accounts.

7.2.3 User security

User security means providing users with certain rights and privileges commensurate with their operational requirements. If care is not taken with respect to the setup and maintenance of user accounts it may become possible for a hacker to gain access to one account which provides him or her with a lever to gain access to other accounts. In addition, they may obtain the capability to modify or delete folders and files which could have a most profound effect upon the operation of the host. In Chapter 8 we will focus our attention upon user security with respect to user rights and permissions.

7.2.4 Network security

The fourth category of hacker attack can be classified as falling into the network security area. Although just about all hacker attacks other than those occurring via a directly connected host console are network-based attacks, we can classify certain types of attack as belonging to this category. Those types of attack include Denial of Service (DoS), Distributed Denial of Service (DDoS), malformed packet attacks and virus and macro attacks. Because we examined both virus and macro attacks in Chapter 6 we will only briefly discuss them in this chapter in an attempt to hold to brevity, a trait this author is usually not known as possessing.

DoS/DDoS attacks

The goal of DoS and DDoS attacks is to attempt to flood a network with such volume of requests that those requests interfere with legitimate network traffic. The actual flood of packets or datagrams can be directed to any network device or a specific network device. Concerning the former, imagine your network consists of a router, firewall and a network segment that contains a Web server, as illustrated in Figure 7.1. If a person floods traffic to the router with sufficient volume, the router may be forced to drop legitimate packets. Because most routers can process packets far faster than that offered to it on T1 and T3 links, this represents a bad location for a hacker DoS or DDoS attack. This is the reason why TCP intercept on a Cisco router is able to stop a half-open connection method of attack as previously described in this book.

However, if a hacker has a connection to the Internet that is greater in bandwidth than the target's connection, the hacker has the ability to overwhelm the target's access line. This means that the hacker can generate packets or datagrams in sufficient volume that could overload the target's access line. Since routers will drop packets whenever their buffers are full, this also means that the ISP router that services the target will drop packets. Since some of

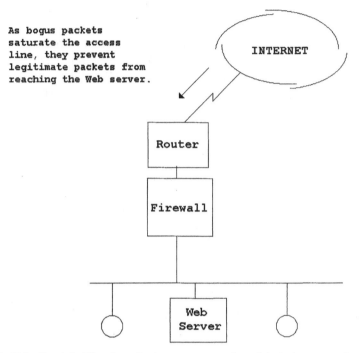

As bogus packets
saturate the access
line, they prevent
legitimate packets from
reaching the Web server.

Figure 7.1 Denial of Service attacks are commonly pointed at a server; however, they can also be directed at a router

those packets will be requests from legitimate users, this action, as the name implies, results in a denial of service.

If a hacker launches an attack on a Web server by constructing a table of legitimate URLs on the target and cycling through those URLs to request graphic intensive pages to be sent to different spoofed addresses, TCP intercept can place a cap on the number of open connections allowed. However, if the attack is distributed and occurs via several sites, it is quite possible that this action will prevent legitimate requests from flowing through the router. Thus, in this situation, bogus datagrams with legitimate URL requests flowing to the Web server will disrupt the ability of legitimate datagrams to reach their destination.

In examining Figure 7.1 note that up to now we have avoided mentioning the use of the firewall for preventing DoS and DDoS attacks. Although the firewall can prevent certain types of denial of service attack, its capability is mostly limited to two areas. One is to block the use of certain application commands, such as FTP's mget and mput commands. A second area that most firewalls support with respect to limiting DoS and DDoS attacks is to control the number of open connections. While both methods certainly make it easier for a targeted server to respond to legitimate requests, the firewall is similar to a router in that it cannot differentiate a 'good spoofed' address from a legitimate address. That is, if a hacker is smart enough to use non-RFC 1918 addresses, and does not use the target network address or a loopback address, the router or firewall cannot discriminate one attacking packet from a legitimate packet. Thus, the goal of the hacker to consume resources to prevent the legitimate use of the target can be met.

There are currently numerous attack methods that can be classified as denial of service attack methods. Probably one of the better locations to obtain up-to-date detailed information about DoS and DDoS attacks is the Computer Emergency Response Team (CERT) Web site. Specifically, readers may wish to access the following URL:

http://www.cert.org/tech_tips/denial_of_service/html

In addition, at the time this book was being prepared the FBI was offering a program called 'find Distributed Denial of Service (find_ddos)', which was available for locating suspicious files that could be used in a DDoS attack. Unfortunately, the program was only available for use on a Solaris 2.X or later system; however, readers may wish to check

http://foia.fbi.gov/mipc/README

to see if a Windows version becomes available.

Malformed packet attacks

In the past hackers have discovered that modifying certain types of packet beyond their normal boundaries would result in a Windows-based computer burping, closing down or freezing. In the past Microsoft has performed very responsively to such attacks, once it could obtain specific information about the attack, issuing a hot fix that was later incorporated into a Service Pack.

Because of the complexity of Windows and the TCP/IP protocol suite, it is quite possible that a hacker may discover the ability of a previously unknown malformed packet to adversely affect a Windows platform. Thus, it is quite possible that while writing this book a hacker could be well on his or her way to discovering a new type of malformed packet attack that can bring your Windows platform to its knees, freeze it, or cause some other type of harmful activity to occur.

7.3 PREVENTIVE MEASURES

While it may be difficult, if not impossible, to prevent some types of DoS, DDoS or malformed packet attack, there are certain things you can do to better secure your site against such attacks. Table 7.1 lists some of the prevention measures you can consider to make the life of a hacker more difficult, although there is no known method to fully secure a network-attached host against the ingenuity of hackers.

7.4 SECURITY CHECKLIST

The entries in Table 7.1 are general in nature and can also be considered as a checklist of functions and features of routers, firewalls and hosts you may consider implementing.

Although most of the entries in Table 7.1 have been discussed previously in this book a few require a bit of elaboration. First, under Windows 2000 it is now possible to place disk storage quotas on accounts. Thus, you should consider doing so to limit the effect of a person breaking into an account to use an inordinate amount of storage. The second measure that requires a bit of elaboration is the next to last item in Table 7.1, the use of Performance Monitor.

Under Windows you can configure Performance Monitor to track disk, CPU and network traffic. By setting reasonable thresholds for being alerted via pager or email you will let the operating system function as an alert mechanism if your other barriers are not comprehensive enough to prevent an attack or a new attack method is developed that attacks disk space, gobbles CPU usage or floods your network.

A third area that warrants attention is the last entry in Table 7.1, checking the registry setting on the host computer. Under both Windows NT and Windows 2000 there are certain registry settings that can increase the ability of a Windows host to operate under a network denial of service attack. Table 7.2 summarizes nine registry settings that can be used to enhance the ability of a Windows host to withstand a DoS or DDoS attack.

7.5 REGISTRY SETTINGS

Prior to discussing the entries in Table 7.2 a few words about registry settings are in order. First, be extremely careful when you change a registry setting as a slight error can make you into the

Table 7.1   General attack prevention measures to consider.

- ☐ Implement router filtering
  - Block RFC 1918 addresses as a source address
  - Block loopback address as source address
  - Block your network address as a source address
  - Permit only access to operational ports/addresses on specific hosts
  - Deny all else
- ☐ Implement TCP intercept
  - On router if supported
  - On firewall if supported
- ☐ Implement controls on open connections
  - On router if supported
  - On firewall if supported
- ☐ Block conversion of layer 3 broadcasts into layer 2 broadcasts
  - On Cisco router command ip directed-broadcast
- ☐ Configure proxy service on firewall
  - Block use of mget, mput for FTP
  - Block other commands as necessary
- ☐ Configure virus scanner
  - Block macro or provide warning
- ☐ Disable/block unused or not requires network services
  - Turn off file shares
  - Unbind NetBIOS over TCP/IP if needed
- ☐ Scan ports and turn off any not required
- ☐ Enable quotas via your operating system
  - Verify permissions and rights of accounts
  - Put limits on disk space per account
- ☐ Change name of Administrator account
- ☐ Select applicable Web sites for latest security information
- ☐ Subscribe to Microsoft Security Notification list service
- ☐ Restrict access to internal publications
- ☐ Use non-conventional user ID assignment
- ☐ Apply latest Service Pack and hot-fixes
- ☐ Use NTFS and not FAT
- ☐ Display a legal notice before logon
- ☐ Remove OS/2 and POSIX subsystems
- ☐ Remove all Net Shares
- ☐ Remove the Shutdown button from the logon dialog box
- ☐ Allow network-only lockout for the Administrator account
- ☐ Restrict anonymous network access
- ☐ Block external email access to internal group lists
- ☐ Use Performance Monitor to send alerts
  - Track disk, CPU, network traffic
- ☐ Check registry settings on host

Table 7.2 Windows registry settings to harden a host against a DoS or DDoS attack.

---

1. SynAttackProtect
    SKey: Tcpip\Parameters
    Value Type: REG_DWORD
    Value Range: 0.1, 2
    Default: 0
    Recommendation: 2

2. TcpMaxHalfOpen
    Key: Tcpip\Parameters
    Value Type: REG_DWORD-Number
    Value Range: 19909x/ffff
    Default:100 (Professional, Server), 500 (advanced server)
    Recommendation: Default

3. TcpMaxHalfOpenRetried
    Key: Tcpip\Parameters
    Value Type: REG_DWORD-Number
    Value Range: 80-0xFFFF
    Default: 80 (Professional, Server), 400 (Advanced Server)
    Recommendation: Default

4. EnablePMTUDiscovery
    Key: Tcpip\Parameters
    Value Type: REG_DWORD-Boolean
    Value Range: 0, 1 (False, True)
    Default: 1
    Recommendation: 0

5. NoNameReleaseOnDemand
    Key: Tcpip\Parameters
    Value Type: REG_DWORD-Boolean
    Value Range: 0, 1 (False, True)
    Default: (False)
    Recommendation: 1

6. EnableDeadGWDetect
    Key: Tcpip\Parameters
    Value Type: REG_DWORD-Boolean
    Value Range: 0, 1 (False, True)
    Default: 1 (True)
    Recommendation: 0

7. KeepAliveTime
    Key: Tcpip\Parameters
    Value Type: REG_DWORD-Time in milliseconds
    Value Range: 1-0xFFFFFFFF
    Default: 7,200,000 (two hours)
    Recommendation: 300,000

Continued

Table 7.2 *Continued*

8. Performance Discovery
    Key: Tcpip\Parameters\Interfaces
    Value Type: REG_DWORD
    Value Range: 0, 1, 2
    Default: 2
    Recommendation: 0

9. EnableICMPRedirects
    Key: Tcpip\Parameters
    Value Type: REG_DWORD
    Value Range: 0, 1 (False, True)
    Default: 1 (True)
    Recommendation: 0 (False)

'Grinch that stole Christmas'. Secondly, always back up your registry settings prior to changing a setting. Third, you would use Regedt32 to navigate to the following location:

HKEY_LOAL_MACHINE\System\Currentcontrolset\Services\
Tcpip\Parameters

which is abbreviated as Tcpip\Parameters in Table 7.2. Once you are on the Edit menu, you would use Add Value to select the applicable key, select its type and set the value to its applicable or recommended setting. With these points in mind, let us turn our attention to the nine keys listed in Table 7.2.

7.5.1 SynAttackProtect

The default setting for SynAttackProtect of 0 provides no synattack protection. A setting of 1 results in reduced retransmission retries and delayed route cache entry (RCE) creation if the settings for the registry keys TcpMaxHalfOpen and TcpMaxHalfOpenRetried are satisfied. A setting of 2, which is the recommended setting, is similar to the effect of a setting of 1 but, in addition, results in a delayed indication to Winsock being made. By setting the key value to 2 you reduce the amount of retransmissions for the SYN-ACKS in the 3-way handshake, which in turn reduces the time for which resources have to remain allocated. By delaying the allocation of a RCE until a connection is made you reserve resources until the 3-way handshake is complete. Thus, key resources will not be consumed until a verifiable connection occurs. Note that this protection mechanism only goes into effect if TcpMaxHalfOpen and TcpMaxHalfOpenRetried settings are exceeded.

7.5.2 TcpMaxHalfOpen

This key controls the number of connection in the SYN-RCVD state allowed prior to SYN-ATTACK protection (SynAttackProtect) going into effect. Microsoft recommends using the default value of 100 for Professional and Server versions of Windows and 500 for Advanced Server.

7.5.3 TcpMaxHalfOpenRetried

This key parameter controls the number of connections in the SYN-RCVD state for which there has been at least one retransmission of the SYN sent, prior to SYN-ATTACK protection (SynAttackProtect) begins to operate. Microsoft recommends accepting the default value for this registry key, which is 80 for Professional and Server versions of Windows and 400 for the Advanced Server version of Windows.

7.5.4 EnablePMTUDiscovery

This registry key setting governs whether TCP will attempt to discover the Maximum Transmission Unit (MTU) over the part to the remove site or fixes the MTU size at 576 bytes for all connections. Microsoft recommends an entry of 0 to select a fixed 576 byte MTU which limits resources expended on bogus connections. However, when you do this you eliminate the potential of eliminating fragmentation resulting from a discovery of an MTU. This in turn will result in a greater potential for network congestion and is one reason why many attack prevention measures can be two-edged weapons.

7.5.5 NoNameReleaseOnDemand

This registry key parameter determines whether the host will release its NetBIOS name when it receives a name release request from the network. The default value of this key is 0 and Microsoft recommends a setting of 1 to protect the host against malicious name-release attacks.

7.5.6 EnableDeadGWDetect

When this key value is set to its default of 1, TCP is allowed to perform what is referred to as a dead-gateway detection function.

That is, TCP can ask IP to change to a backup gateway if a number of connections are experiencing difficulty. It appears that Microsoft believes that under a DoS or DDoS attack there is no advantage to be gained by allowing TCP to ask IP to change to a backup gateway, and recommends the setting should be changed to 0. This is one Microsoft recommendation this author does not necessarily agree with, since it is possible that you can have a backup gateway with a different set of filters that could allow packets to and from predefined blocks of IP addresses to continue to flow when under attack. Thus, being from Missouri in spirit, this author would state that you should consider your network configuration and the filters on backup gateways prior to deciding whether or not to use the recommendation value of 0.

7.5.7 KeepAliveTime

This registry key parameters controls the frequency by which TCP attempts to verify that an idle condition is still intact, by transmitting a keep-alive packet. If the remote system is both reachable and functioning it will acknowledge the keep_alive transmission.

The default registry setting is 7,200,000 milliseconds, or two hours. Microsoft recommends a setting of 300,000 milliseconds or approximately 5 minutes. Although this is a significant improvement from a default of two hours, this author believes that a lower default setting, perhaps on the order of 200,000 milliseconds or approximately 3.33 minutes, might be a more desirable default setting.

7.5.8 PerformRouterDiscovery

This register key value controls whether Windows 2000 attempts to perform router discovery according to RFC 1256 on a per-interface basis. The default setting for this key value is 2, which is DHCP-controlled but off by default. Other values supported are 0 (disabled) and 1 (enabled). Microsoft recommends that this registry key value should be set to 0.

7.5.9 EnableICMPRedirects

The last registry key that Microsoft recommends you consider to hinder the effect of DoS and DDoS attacks is the EnableICMPRedirects key. Prior to discussing the setting of this registry key a brief review of ICMP redirect behavior may be in order for some of us. Thus, let us digress a bit and quickly examine the concept of ICMP redirect.

In an IP networking environment it is assumed that IP hosts only require a minimal amount of routing information and thus rely upon routers having knowledge of the topology of the internetwork, including routes to connect different locations. Thus, IP hosts are normally configured with the IP address of a default gateway, a term used to refer to a default router. If an IP host has traffic to transmit that is not on the current network, it will forward the traffic to the default gateway or router. Because many networks have multiple routers, the transmission of all remote traffic to the same router can result in one router being overloaded while other routers have excessive CPU cycles to burn, a situation referred to as non-optimum host routing. To alleviate this situation IP routers have the ability to dynamically update the routing tables of hosts via the use of an ICMP redirect message.

To illustrate the manner by which an ICMP Redirect message would be transmitted, consider Figure 7.2 which illustrates an internetwork consisting of two routers (R1 and R2) and several network segments tied to the Internet. Let us assume host A on LAN A

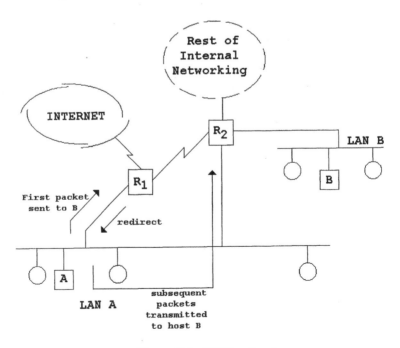

Figure 7.2 ICMP redirect

is to transmit a packet to host B on LAN B. Suppose host A's default IP router is R1. Because host B is not on the same network, host A forwards the packet for host B to its default router, R1. Router R1 checks its routing table and notes that the next hop for the route to the network where host B resides is router R2. Thus, it forwards the first packet to R2. However, router R1 notes that host A and router R2 are connected to the same Internet. Thus, instead of having to traverse two hops, packets from host A could be sent to router R2 and avoid one hop to their ultimate destination. Thus, R1 sends an ICMP Redirect message to host A that R2 is the better route when transmitting to host B. Host A then adds a host router to its routing table for host B's IP address, using router R2's IP address as the forwarding address. Then, all subsequent datagrams other than the first transmitted from host A to host B are forwarded via router R2.

An ICMP Redirect message has a Type value of 5. Its code value can range from 0 to 3, with the meaning of each code value indicated below:

Code value   *Meaning*

0	Redirected datagrams for the network (obsolete)
1	Redirected datagrams for the host
2	Redirected datagrams for the Type of Service and the network
3	redirected datagrams for the Type of Service and the host.

Under Windows a host route learned by means of an ICMP Redirect will be added to the host route table for a period of 10 minutes, after which time it is automatically removed and must be relearned through another ICMP redirect.

Now that we have an appreciation for ICMP Redirects, it is easy to envision how a hacker could use this tool to redirect traffic to a location where he or she could monitor traffic. Due to this, Microsoft recommends changing the default registry key value of 1 (true) to 0 to turn off ICMP Redirects. It should also be mentioned that under Windows NT you must have at least Service Pack 5 installed to obtain the ability to disable ICMP Redirects.

7.6 OTHER REGISTRY CHANGES TO CONSIDER

In addition to the previously described registry settings designed to impede DoS and DDoS attacks, some of the items covered in Table

7.1 also require registry changes. In this section we will describe and discuss some of those potential registry changes.

7.6.1 Displaying a legal notice

The following registry key can be changed to specify specific legal information concerning the use of the host.

> Hive HKEY_LOCAL_MACHINE\SOFTWARE
> Key \Microsoft\WindowsNT\CurrentVerions\winlogon
> Name LegalNoticeCaption
> Type REG_SZ
> Value The title of the message box

Once the preceding is set, you would change the LegalNoticeText name value to the legal text you want to be displayed in the message box.

7.6.2 Remove OS/2 and POSIX subsystems

There are four key settings that must be operated upon to remove OS/2 and POSIX support from a Windows platform. To do so you would perform the following registry actions:

1. Hive HKEY_LOCAL_MACHINE\SOFTWARE
   Key \Microsoft\OS/2 Subsystem for NT
   Action Delete all sub keys

2. Hive HKEY_LOCAL_MACHINE\SYSTEM
   Key \CurrentControlSet\Control\SessionManager\Environment
   Name Os2LibPath
   Action Delete

3. Hive HKEY_LOCAL_MACHINE\SYSTEM
   Key \CurrentControlSet\Control\SessionManager\SubSystem
   Name Optional
   Action Delete values

4. Hive HKEY_LOCAL_MACHINE\SYSTEM
   Key \CurrentControlSet\Control\SessionManager\SubSystems
   Action Delete entries for Posix and OS/2

Once the pervious actions have been accomplished, you would then delete the \winnt\system32\os2 directories and all sub-directories. These changes will then come into effect upon the next reboot.

7.6.3 Remove all net shares

You can easily delete all net shares other than administrative shares via the use of the command line net share/d. However, this action still leaves such administrative share (C$, D$ and ADMIN$) available for exploitation. You can prevent the use of those shares through the following registry key.

Hive HKEY_LOCAL_MACHINE\SYSTEM
Key \CurrentControlSet\Services\LanmanServer\Parameters
Name AutoShareServer
Type RG_DWORD
Value 0

7.6.4 Remove the Shutdown button at logon

You can change the following value in the Registry to remove the shutdown option at logon.

Hive HKEY_LOCAL_MACHINE\SOFTWARE
Key \CurrentControlSet\Control\SessionManager
Key \Microsoft\WindowsNT\CurrentVersion\winlogon
Name ShutdownWithoutLogon
Type REG_SZ
Value 0

7.6.5 Restrict anonymous network access

Included in Windows is a feature that enables non-authenticated users to enumerate users on a Windows NT domain. You can remove this functionality by setting the following in the registry.

Hive HKEY_LOCAL_MACHINE\SYSTEM
Key CurrentControlSet\Control\LSA
Name RestrictAnonymuos
Type REG_DWORD
Value 1

7.7 OTHER ATTACK METHODS TO CONSIDER

In concluding this chapter we will turn our attention to several additional attack methods that arose over the past two years and some preventive measures you can consider to counter such attacks. The examples presented in this section are only included to provide a small representation of the ingenuity of hackers, as well as to illustrate the fact that no matter how hard our effort against attack is, it may never be complete. Thus, similarly to a boy scout it is important to remember the motto 'Be prepared'.

7.7.1 Trojan horse attacks

One of the more popular methods of recent hacker attack is a Trojan horse attack. Under this attack method one or more programs are embedded in a file that is sent to a user via email. When the recipient double-clicks on the icon for an attached program, it may first generate an innocent message, while it performs its dirty work in the background unknown to the computer user. That dirty work can include modifying itself to capture the user's password when they logon to a server and email the results without the target being aware that they were attacked.

Another common attack method is programs that break the hashing algorithm used by the Windows Security Account Manager (SAM). According to trade press articles, several hackers were successful in developing a Trojan horse attack that emailed the contents of SAM where passwords reside. This allowed the hackers, at their leisure and without the threat of a lockout, to run dictionary attacks to determine user passwords. The obvious solution to email based Trojan horse attacks is both scanners and education. Many email scanners have an option that can be used to prevent program attachments. If this is not acceptable due to the normal email of programs within an organization, employee education may be an important tool that can prevent this attack from being successful.

7.7.2 RPC denial of service

Just when it appeared we were familiar with different types of denial of service attack, a hacker came up with a new twist on this attack method. The new twist a hacker developed was based upon an attack on the Remote Call Procedure (RPC) component in Windows NT, using named pipes transport. This attack method results in a gradual increase in a Windows RPC system process until it consumes 100 percent of CPU time, leaving no processing available for other functions and thus denying service. During late 1999 several variations of this RPC DoS attack method were targeted at the Spoolss.exe or the Lsass.exe files. Each of these attack methods was based upon the transmission of random data to the target. The RCP service would then attempt to respond to each request, resulting in the service cycling into a 100 percent CPU usable loop as it closed invalid connections, only to be faced with additional false connection requests.

In November 1999 Microsoft's release of Service Pack 4 contained a fix for this attack method. Thus, this attack reinforces the key fact that on a periodic basis you should visit the Microsoft Web site. In addition, you should subscribe to the Microsoft Security Notification listserv to obtain via email the notification of security related issues with respect to different Microsoft products.

7.7.3 Malformed FTP requests

In perhaps a never-ending quest to find methods to bring computers to their knees, a person found that special malformed FTP requests can create a denial of service in the Microsoft FTP service. This in turn can result in the Microsoft Internet Information Server ceasing to respond to requests, generating an Access Violation error message.

The malformed FTP request attack occurred during 1999. Microsoft provided a hot fix to alleviate the potential of this attack and incorporated the fix into Service Pack 5 for Windows NT Version 4.0.

7.7.4 Screen saver vulnerability

Because of the complexity of Windows there are hidden vulnerabilities that can be unknowingly or knowingly exploited. One such vulnerability is the use of a screen saver under certain versions of Windows NT.

Windows NT will start a screen saver in the local system context and then immediately change the context to match that of the logged-on user. Until a hot fix was posted, Windows would not verify that the change completed successfully. If the change failed, the screen saver is then running in a privileged state that allows a specially programmed screen saver to use these privileges to elevate the level of security of the logged on user.

Microsoft issued a hot fix for the previously described vulnerability during 1999. The hot fix was then incorporated into Service Pack 5 for Windows TN Version 4.0.

7.7.5 Last user logon

Perhaps a carryover from the era of mainframes, by default Windows displays the name of the last person to log on in the user name space of the Logon Information dialog box. While this might not appear to be much of an attack, it provides a potential hacker with a requirement to guess the last user's password instead of both the user name and associated password. You can change the registry key DontDisplayLastUserName from a default value of 0 (false) to a value of 1 (true) to ensure the Username space is always blank with the Logon Information dialog box appears. After all, why make life easier for potential hackers?

8

WORKING WITH WINDOWS

While the title of this chapter is a bit vague, you must remember that the focus of this book is upon bulletproofing a TCP/IP network, including Windows hosts on the network. Thus, the primary focus of this chapter is upon key areas of Windows, including Windows NT and Windows 2000 that have a major role in promoting a high level of host security as well as providing key vulnerabilities that can be exploited by hackers. Those areas that we will examine in this chapter include the following:

- User Manager—the administrative tool for establishing user accounts;

- The System Policy Editor, which allows an administrator to specify the computers and programs a user can operate;

- The NT File System (NTFS), which provides much more file control than the legacy FAT system; and,

- FTP and IIS, because it is commonly used by many organizations and provides two key areas of vulnerability.

However, prior to turning our attention to these topics some general comments concerning Windows NT and Windows 2000, which we will collectively refer to as Windows in this chapter, are warranted.

8.1 GENERAL SECURITY-RELATED CONSIDERATIONS

Windows represents the coding of hundreds, if not thousands, of programmers. According to various trade publications, there are tens of millions of lines of code in Windows. Due to the volume of code you can always expect program bugs to occur. If a hacker discovers a bug that can be exploited, what was a program bug becomes security vulnerability. For example, several years ago a hacker discovered that the TCP/IP protocol stack implemented on an early version of Windows NT would 'blow up' if it received a datagram longer than 65,535 bytes. Apparently the Microsoft implementation of the TCP/IP protocol suite did not check the length of the datagram to ensure it was within specification. When an abnormal length datagram was received, the resulting attempt at processing it resulted in the operating system shutting down. Granted, this situation was initially obscure. However, when it became known, this minor bug became an exploitable vulnerability.

8.1.1 Tracking known fixes

The point made above is that there can be other bugs lurking in the OS, waiting to be found and exploited. Thus, it is extremely important to periodically check the Microsoft Web site for known fixes to security problems and, if they are applicable to the software used on your hosts, to apply those fixes.

8.1.2 Applying service packs

It should also be noted that the previously mentioned fixes are not the same as service packs. A service pack represents a collection of fixes, patches and periodically improvements to an operating system. Whereas a fix can be released at almost any time to hopefully correct a pressing and just discovered problem, a service pack is infrequently released. For example, at the time this book was written Microsoft had released Service Pack 6 for Windows NT as well as approximately 100 or more fixes. While it is important to upgrade to the latest service pack available for a particular operating system, it is also worth mentioning that periodically the upgrade to a new service pack can fix some old problems as well as create some new ones. Thus, the old adage that an 'explorer is the one with an arrow in his back' has some merit concerning service packs. That is, you may wish to consider waiting a period of time after a service pack is released prior to applying it. In addition, you should also view new fixes to determine if one or more should be applied after the new service pack. Now that this author has thrown his nickel into the ring concerning fixes and service packs, let us turn our attention to the key topics of this chapter. However, prior to doing so a few words concerning the locations of different tools are in order.

In describing a series of security related screen operations, this author will attempt to avoid referring the manner by which a screen is initiated. Under Windows NT most screens contained in this chapter are invoked from Start>Administrative Tools. In comparison, under Windows 2000 most of the tools described in this chapter are accessed via the Management Console. Rather than use a considerable amount of space describing how to bring up a specific screen under different versions of Windows, we will simply note that you can enter the name of the tool under Help to obtain information concerning how to invoke the tool.

8.1.3 NT versus 2000

While Windows NT and Windows 2000 are very similar with respect to many security-related screen options, there are certain differences between the two that deserve mention. Under Windows NT the ability to work with multiple computers and other network resources involved the use of domains. Setting up trust relationships between domains could be quite cumbersome and there were restrictions on security groups that span domain partitions. Under Windows 2000 the ability to work with multiple computers and other network resources can be accomplished through Active Directory. Active Directory uses the Domain Name System (DNS) as a locator mechanism to find network resources. Under Active Directory Windows 2000 domain controllers function as peers and replicate Active Directory information to all domain controllers within an organization. This permits true centralized control and allows all network information to be stored in the Active Directory. This also allows authentication for domain users to occur based upon user accounts in the Active Directory.

8.1.4 User Manager

The User Manager provides you with the ability to add, change and delete accounts for both individuals and groups. Because those accounts have a considerable bearing upon the ability of remote users to access different applications and even to take control of your computer, it is important to understand both the capabilities and limitations associated with the User Manager.

To start User Manager you can select Start>Administrative Tools>User Manager (User Manager for Domains on the server) or type USRMGR.EXE in the command line box. This action will result in the display of the main window of User Manager, which will appear similar to Figure 8.1. Note that the User Manager screen is divided into two parts. The upper portion of the screen lists previously defined accounts while the lower portion of the screen lists predefined groups. You can add or delete both user accounts and groups.

Because the focus of this book is upon security, we will describe and discuss User Manager functions and features with respect to this topic. In a network environment there are several functions you should consider performing to make it more difficult for persons to break into your hosts.

Built-in accounts to consider

There are two built-in accounts you should consider modifying from the get-go. First, the Administrator account, which by default has all system privileges, is similar to the red cape used by a bullfighter. That is, it is a favorite place for an attacker to begin his

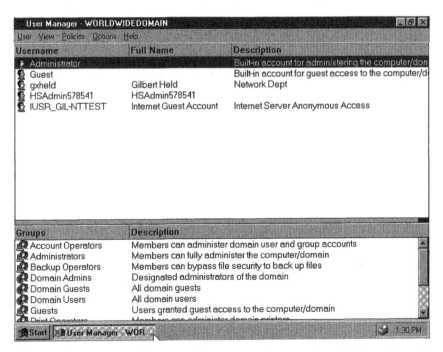

Figure 8.1 The User Manager provides the ability to create, delete and modify user accounts and groups as well as to assign users to one or more groups

Figure 8.2 Using the Rename dialog box to change the name of the Administrator account

or her effort. Why wave a red flag at a hacker? Instead, add a bit more difficulty to an attack by renaming the built-in administrator account. Figure 8.2 illustrates the Rename dialog box after the Rename option was selected from the User menu. Note that this action provides you with the ability to rename the Administrator account. In doing so you should consider changing the name to one that may not be distinguishable from hundreds or thousands of other conventional accounts.

A second action you should immediately consider when working with the User Manager is to disable the Guest account. We can 'kill two birds with one view' by examining the User Properties dialog box for the Guest account, so let us do so. Figure 8.3 illustrates the previously mentioned display. This box is displayed by selecting the User Properties entry from the User menu shown in the top left portion of Figure 8.1.

If you need to provide guest access for some reason, you would then elect not to check the box to the left of 'Account Disabled'. However, if there is no reason to have a guest account, it is suggested that you disable this account. Otherwise, if you maintain this account and are a bit loose on permissions, you might wake up one day to determine that one or more of your organization's hosts were participants in a Distributed Denial of Service attack on a third party.

Password assignment

In examining the options shown in Figure 8.3 note that the password is case-sensitive and can be up to 14 characters in length. This means you have considerable flexibility in assigning passwords to accounts.

To avoid leaving your hosts open to a dictionary attack you should select passwords that represent an alphanumeric mix of characters, and encourage your employees to continue in this manner when they need to change their passwords. This can either

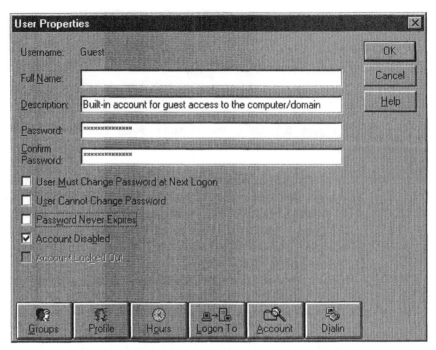

Figure 8.3 The User Properties dialog box provides a mechanism to control passwords and remove an account lock out situation, as well as to control the ability of the user to perform different activities

be accomplished by policy or enforced via the use of third party software (available from several vendors) that places constraints upon the composition of a password.

Because some intelligent hackers have been known to develop brute force attacks against passwords, the selection of alphanumeric passwords does not represent a foolproof method against such attacks. Given enough time to try different combinations of characters, an attacker will eventually discover the password used for different accounts. This means that you must take steps to limit the number of logon attempts by enabling an account lockout for each user. Thus, the bottom entry, which is gray in color and cannot be selected, deserves mention. If an account should become locked out due to a user or hacker attempting a series of unsuccessful log in attempts, the Account Locked Out entry will appear checked and you can click on it to allow the legitimate user to regain access to his or her account. As we will note shortly, there are several selections that govern account lockouts that you should consider. If you do not select an appropriate setting and assign users via an easy-to-determine user name convention, you can be setting your organization up for an early morning disaster. For example, assume your user naming convention is to place the initial of an employee's first name and middle initial before their last name, using 'X' as the middle initial if the employee has no middle name. If a person obtains the directory for your organization, they could create a script over a weekend that could attempt user logons until each of your legitimate accounts are locked out. If your lockout restrictions allow temporary or permanent lockouts, the script executed at 8:00 a.m. on a Monday morning can have a rather dramatic effect on the productivity of your employees, as well as on the administrator that may have to remove the lockout from hundreds or thousands of accounts.

Group membership

If you click on the button labeled 'Groups' at the bottom of a user account screen, you obtain the ability to assign a particular user to membership in one or more predefined groups. Each group has a set of access privileges and rights ranging from a minimum set for the Guest group to a maximum set for Administrators. Figure 8.4

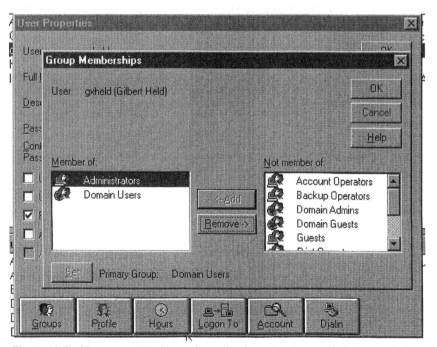

Figure 8.4 You automaically assign all relevant access privileges and rights associated with a group to a user when you add a user to a group

illustrates the display of the dialog box labeled 'Group Member-ships' resulting from clicking on the button labeled 'Groups'. To add a user to a group you would select one or more groups from the Not member of list area and click on the button labeled 'Add'. Similarly, to remove a selected user from a group you would select the group from the Member of list area in the left portion of the dialog box and click on the button labeled 'Remove'. Due to the capabilities associated with different groups with respect to their access rights and privileges, it is important to carefully think about assigning users to different group memberships and to do so only when a particular requirement exists for a user being assigned to a particular group.

Profile

The second button in the User Properties screen previously shown in Figure 8.3 is labeled 'Profile'. When you click on this button, the resulting dialog box (shown in Figure 8.5) provides you with the ability to associate several predefined items to a network user. The profile associates a log-on script name and home directory with a particular user account. Although it is theoretically possible to write a script that can alter permissions, the key function of a profile is to facilitate the logon process of a user.

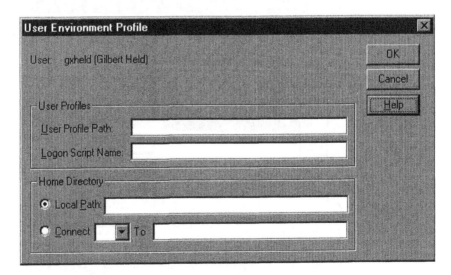

Figure 8.5 The User Profile dialog box facilitates the logon process based upon the association of a script and home directory to a user

Logon hours

The third button on the bottom of a user's main display is labeled 'Hours'. You can select this button to control the portion of time within a week that a user can log onto a host. Figure 8.6 illustrates the initial Logon Hours display for one user. In this example, the user gxheld is initially provided with full access during each week.

If you need to operate a guest account, it is suggested that you consider limiting the period of time for which users can access that account. This is especially true if you have automated intrusion detection scanning software but do not operate a 24/7 technical control center. In this situation the notification generated via software that something is amiss may sit in an email inbox for hours or even possibly a day or more until your employees begin their normal shifts.

Workstation access

The fourth button along the lower portion of Figure 8.3 is labeled 'Logon to'. The resulting dialog box displayed when that button is click on is shown in Figure 8.7.

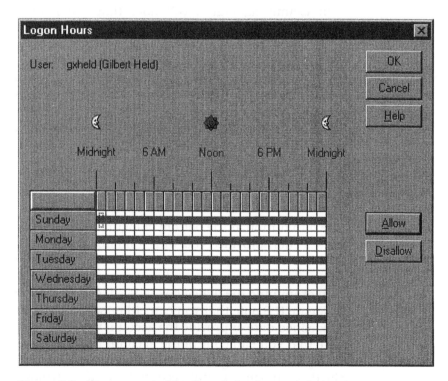

Figure 8.6 You can control the time during the week that a user can access a host through the Logon Hours dialog box

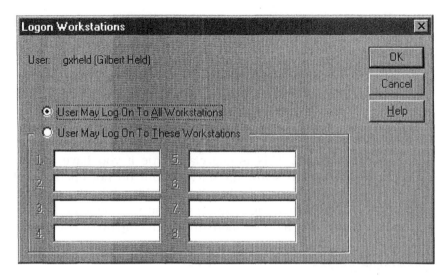

Figure 8.7 You can control attempts of server users to logon to workstations through the Logon Workstations dialog box

In examining Figure 8.7 note that the resulting dialog box provides you with the ability to let a user with an account on a server gain access to either specific workstations or all workstations. Although the user still needs to have an applicable account and password, a play on the old adage 'too many guest accounts spoil the brew' can be made. Thus, it is important to consider both guest accounts on servers and workstations, as well as granting or excluding the ability for users to access one or more workstations.

Account control

The fifth button at the bottom of Figure 8.3 is labeled 'Account' and its selection provides you with a limited ability to control a user's account. As we will note later in this chapter, there are far more comprehensive controls that you can place on a user's account.

In examining the dialog box labeled 'Account Information' shown in Figure 8.8 note that you can either set an account to expire on a predefined date or provide the account with permanent status. Also note that you can control the account type through the use of this dialog box. In doing so, a global account is an account for a user of the domain while a local account is used for users from untrusted domains.

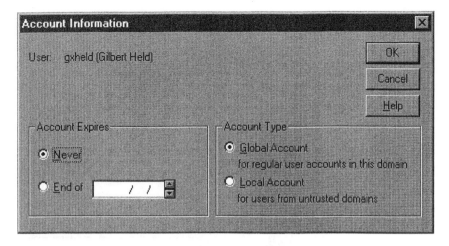

Figure 8.8 The Account Information dialog box provides you with the ability to control the account expiration and account type for a user

Dialin control

Continuing our examination of the buttons along the lower portion of Figure 8.3, note the one labeled 'Dialin'. Clicking on this button provides you with the ability to control a user's ability to access a server via the switched telephone network.

Figure 8.9 illustrates the Dialin Information dialog box. In examining Figure 8.9 note that you can significantly secure dial-in access to your host by presetting callback. When you click on the bottom button in Figure 8.9 and enter a telephone number, a dialin connection inbound results in the host terminating the call and then dialing the preset telephone number. This action in effect authenticates the user via their telephone number.

The key problem associated with callback to a predefined number is if your user population travels. In this situation it is rather difficult, if not impossible, to use a present telephone number for callback. However, for persons that work at home and need dial-in access, it is highly suggested that you consider the use of the preset callback option for dial-in access.

Managing security policies

We previously examined the result obtained by clicking on the button labeled Account in Figure 8.3, noting that it was useful for

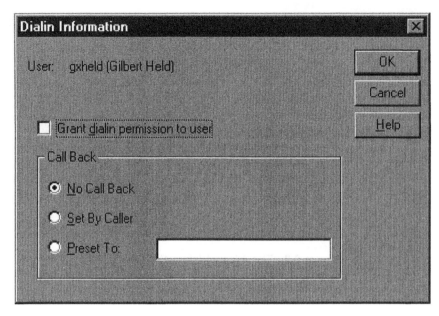

Figure 8.9 The Dialin Information dialog box provides you with the ability to control dial-in access to your host to include the use of several callback options

providing a limited control of the user account selected. At that time we indicated that there are other options within User Manager that have a far more profound effect upon the security of an account. In this section we will examine how we can define and configure the manner by which passwords are used, control user rights, and perform other security-related tasks.

Controlling password use

From the Policies menu in the User Manager display you can select the Account menu entry to control the manner by which passwords are used. Figure 8.10 illustrates the resulting Account Policy screen display.

In examining Figure 8.10 note that through the use of this screen you can control not only the password age, length and uniqueness, but, in addition, account lockout parameters. In Figure 8.10 the account lockout is enabled and set to occur after five bad logon attempts. Note that the lockout duration is also set for 30 minutes and not forever. The advantage to this setting, rather than a permanent lockout, is the fact that at the very worst over a weekend (48

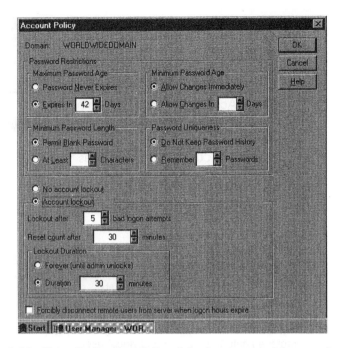

Figure 8.10 Using the Account Policy dialog box to control the use of passwords and account lockout for a user

hours), a hacker is limited to 48 × 2 attempts, each of which permits five guesses. Thus, at the most, a hacker is limited to 480 password guesses. On the positive side, if your network was attacked by a script that attempts to lockout all legitimate users, a 30 minute duration can save you the major effort of removing lockouts from each user account on a Monday morning or another period of time.

In addition to thinking twice about a lockout that lasts forever, it is also important to consider periodic password changes. Although Figure 8.10 has the button checked for permitting a blank password, it is strongly suggested you should forego this setting and require a minimum length password.

8.2 SETTING USER RIGHTS

A second key Windows security related policy is effected through controlling user rights provided to a particular group of host users. To set user rights you would select the User Rights entry from the Policies menu in User Manager. Figure 8.11 illustrates the resulting dialog box with the Right menu pulled down. In examining

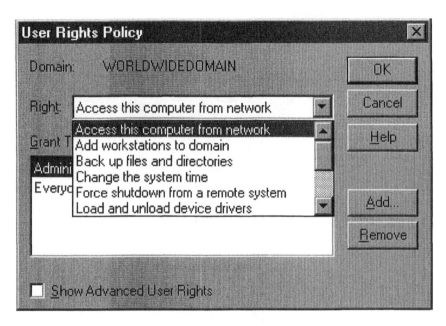

Figure 8.11 Through the User Rights Policy dialog box you can assign and remove rights to groups or individual users

Figure 8.11 note that only some of the available user rights are shown.

User rights can be set to both groups and individual users. While it is more efficient to assign a set of rights to a group, upon occasion you may have one or a few users with special requirements and elect to tailor a set of rights to those users.

There are several user rights you should carefully consider for both their default values and auditing. For example, default permissions for log on locally and shut down the system may not obviously be in the best interest for a key server. Table 8.1 lists the default user rights to include a description of the function the rights permit and their initial group assignment.

There are several key differences with respect to default permissions between Windows NT and Windows 2000. Under Windows 2000 members of the Everyone and Users groups do not have broad read/write permissions by default as they had under Windows NT 4.0. Under Windows 2000 normal users have read-only permissions to most areas of the operating system, with read/write permission limited to their own profile folders. Another interesting change between Windows NT and Windows 2000 concerns interactive logon to domain controllers via the network.

Although this was not permitted via default rights under Windows NT, under Windows 2000 normal users now have this capability.

Returning to Figure 8.11, note that you can only access what are considered to represent advanced user rights by clicking on the box in the lower left corner of the dialog box. If you do so, user rights such as 'Act as part of the operating system' and 'Bypass traverse clicking' will appear in the scroll list.

One of the problems associated with any modern operating system is the fact that it is based on the premise that all users access the system remotely. If you examine Table 8.1 and look at the first entry, you will note that the members of the groups Administrators, Everyone and Power Users by default have the user right to access the server via the network. While changing the name of the administrator account represents a good step for enhancing the security of a server, you may also wish to consider removing remote access capability from administrators and power users if the server is in the same building, easily accessible to those that need access, and represents a production environment with few changes occurring. In this type of operational environment there may be no need to provide key accounts with a remote access capability. In fact, for three years this author managed a very high volume (multi-millions of hits per week) trio of Web servers where remote access to the Administrator account was disabled. Although this required two trips into the building to correct some problems, it also resulted in 156 worry-free weeks since it was impossible for an outsider to gain administrative access.

8.2.1 Auditing

You can construct a very good defense through the application of many of the points raised in this chapter. Unfortunately, the best defense is no substitute for the insomniac hacker that may decide to attack your hosts in the middle of the night or over a long weekend. For this reason, as well as the fact that it is simply a good policy to be able to track significant events that affect the operation of your computer, you should consider setting applicable audit policies.

You can manage events that are added to the audit log via the Audit entry in the Policy menu. Selecting the Audit entry results in the display of the dialog box shown in Figure 8.12. In examining Figure 8.12 note that Windows provides you with a mechanism to record each time a successful or failed event, or both, occur. Table 8.2 lists the events that can be audited, including a brief description of the meaning of each event. It should be noted that you can obtain third

Table 8.1 Default User Rights.

Right	Description	Initial assignment
Access this computer from the network	Allows remote access to the computer	Administrators, Everyone, Power Users
Act as part of the operating system	Allows a process to perform as a secure, trusted part of the operating system	None
Add workstation to the domain	Allows workstation to be added to domain but has no effect on the server	None
Backup files and directories	Allows user to back up files and directories	Administrators, Backup Operations
Bypass traverse checking	Allows a user to change directories and access files and subdirectories even if the user has no permission to access the parent directory	Everyone
Change the system time	Allows a user to set the clock of the computer	Administrators, Power Users
Create a page file	Allows the user to create a page file	Administrators
Create a token object	Allows a process to create action tokens	None
Create permanent shared objects	Allows a user to create permanent shared objects	None
Debug programs	Allows a user to debug low-level objects	Administrators
Force shutdown from a remote system	Allows a user to shut down a remote system	Administrators
Generate security audits	Permits a process to generate security-audit log entries	None
Increase scheduling priority	Permits a user to boost the execution priority of a process	Administrators, Power Users

Continued

Table 8.1 *Continued*

Right	Description	Initial assignment
Load and unload device drivers	Allows a user to install and remove device drivers	Administrators
Lock pages in memory	Allows a user to lock pages in memory so that they cannot be paged out to the Pagefile.sys file	None
Log on as a service	Permits a process to register with the system as a service	None
Log on locally	Permits a user to log on at the computer via its keyboard	Administrators, Backup Operators, Guests, Power Users, Users
Manage auditing and security log	Allows a user to specify the types of resources to be audited as well as view and clear the security log	Administrators
Modify firmware environment	Permits a user to modify environmental variable stored in nonvolatile RAM	Administrators
Profile single process	Permits a user to perform profiling (performance sampling) on a process	Administrators, Power Users
Profile system performance	Permits a user to perform profiling on the system	Administrators
Replace a process-level token	Permits a user to modify a process's security-access token	None (System Only)
Restore files and directories	Permits a user to restore backed up files and directories	Administrators, Backup Operators
Shut down the system	Permits a user to shut down the system	Administrators, Backup Operators, Power Users, Users
Take ownership of files and other	Allows a user to take owner-ship of objects files, directories, printers and other resources	Administrators

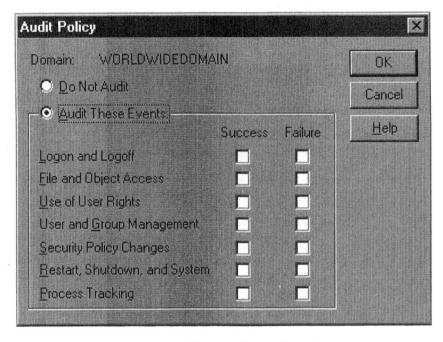

Figure 8.12 The Audit Policy dialog box

Table 8.2 Events that can be audited.

Event	Meaning
Logon and Logoff	Log into or log off a host or connect to a network.
File and Object Access	Access a directory, printer or file set.
Use of User Rights	The use of a user right.
User and Group Management	The addition, modification or deletion of a user or group account, renaming, disabling or creating a user account, or the changing of a password.
Security Policy Change	Changes to the rights of a user or to audit policies.
Restart, Shutdown and System	The restart or shutdown of the host or the triggering of an event that has an impact on the security log or security of the host.
Process Tracking	A change in a process, such as starting or stopping a program.

party software to inform an appropriate person by email or pager of the occurrence of certain critical events, such as so many failed logons, the shutdown of the system, or a change in a security policy.

8.2.2 Shares

One of the key reasons for the deployment of a network involves the ability of users on hosts connected to the network to share resources. Among those resources that can be shared are directories and their contents, with the term directory commonly meaning a folder under a Graphic User Interface (GUI) operating system.

Although sharing can be a considerable boost to employee productivity, it can also represent a potential security problem. This is because an improper permission on a share can result in the placement of a file that can be a ticking time bomb. Thus, for many organizations that run Web servers a common decision is to ensure that the server does not support file sharing. In actuality, this might represent a mistake for there are some good reasons, such as remote administration, for the use of file sharing. However, to ensure that no hole in your file sharing is exploited you can prohibit the flow of NetBIOS through your organization's router and firewall via the untrusted connection side. Because share information is transported via NetBIOS this action will allow sharing on the local internal private network while blocking attempts to gain resource control via sharing from the untrusted side of the network.

If you need to have shares, it is important to understand the permissions associated with share access. You can create, view and change share access via Server Manager as illustrated in Figure 8.13. In examining Figure 8.13 you will note a series of windows, with Server Manager being in the remote background. From Server Manager you would select Shared Directories from the Computer menu. If you want to create a share you would select as an applicable button the dialog box labeled Shared Directories. This would result in the display of the dialog box labeled New Shares, which is also in the background of the screen. Note that the share name is fy2000 and it is located in the path C:\budget. From the New Share dialog box you can define access permissions to the share for one or more users. This is illustrated in the foreground dialog box labeled 'Access Through Share Permissions'. Note that the type of access through the drop down menu is restricted to four options: Read, No Access, Change and Full Control.

When working with shares it is important to note that the permissions control network access to the shared directory, its subdirectories and their files. Thus, it is important to consider all of

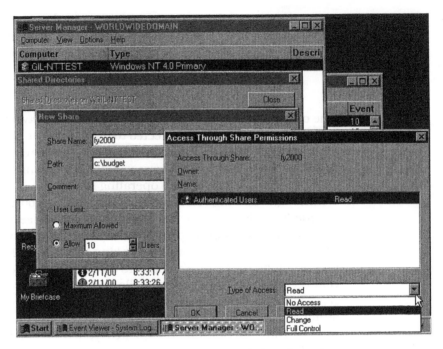

Figure 8.13 Creating permissions for a share

the files you have or plan to place within a shared directory. Another important item to consider is the file system on which a share resides.

Under the NTFS (NT file system) you can also restrict access to files as well as enjoy the potential use of additional access permissions. Table 8.3 lists the access permissions you can consider employing based upon the type of folder selected and the type of file system used. It is important to note that when using FAT volumes you cannot set permissions on individual files and folders. The only security available on such volumes is share permissions that are set for the share and which affect all files and folders on that share. Thus, the use of NTFS provides you with the ability to better control folder and file permissions and represents a far better mechanism for restricting access to data on your server than the use of the legacy FAT system.

8.2.3 Auditing files and directories

In war there is no substitute for victory. In the field of communications security we can modify the famous saying of a well-known

Table 8.3 Folder and File Permission Options.

Access right	Description
Basic folder permission	
No Access	No access to folder
Read	Ability to display name of folder owner, permissions of folder and move to any subfolders in the folder
Change	Provides the ability to add files to folder, display a folder's files and attributes, delete the folder or any subfolder and move any subfolder within the folder
Full Control	Provides all rights associated with Add, Read and Change permissions, as well as ability to change permissions for a folder or delete subfolders and files in the subfolders
Additional permissions for local folders	
List	Provides ability to display a folder's files and attributes as well as to move to any subfolder within the folder
Add	Provides same capabilities as list plus ability to add files to the folder
Add and Read	Provides all rights from Read permission plus ability for user to create subfolders, add files to the folder and change
Permissions for files	
Standard	Access allowed
No Access	None
Read	Display a file's data, view its attributes
Change	Adds to Read permission ability to launch program files, change a file's attributes, display the file owner and permissions assigned to the file
Full Access	Adds ability of users to change or append data to a file to Read and Change permissions
Special access permissions	
Delete	Provides ability to delete a file
Take Ownership	Provides person with all file permissions except ability to change ownership
Change Permissions	Provides ability to change file permissions
Write	Provides ability to modify a file
Execute	Provides ability to execute but not alter a file

general and note that a trail of events can be critical for understanding what happened and who did what. To obtain this understanding we can invoke Windows auditing, which can be used to obtain a view of the users or user groups that are using files or directories. Similar to the ability to obtain extended rights, auditing is only applicable for files on an NTFS volume.

If you have critical files or directories on your host you should consider enabling auditing. To audit a file or directory you would select the folder or drive and right-click to bring up its context menu. You would then select Properties to bring up the Properties dialog box.

The left portion of Figure 8.14 provides an illustration of the Properties dialog box for the directory budget on drive F. Note that by selecting the Security tab you display options that allow you to view or set permission information, view or select auditing information, or view or take ownership of the selected file or directory. Because the focus of this section is upon auditing, we would select the middle option in the background portion of Figure 8.14, which will result in the foreground display.

In examining the foreground screen shown in Figure 8.14 note the two boxes at the top portion of the screen. You would set the

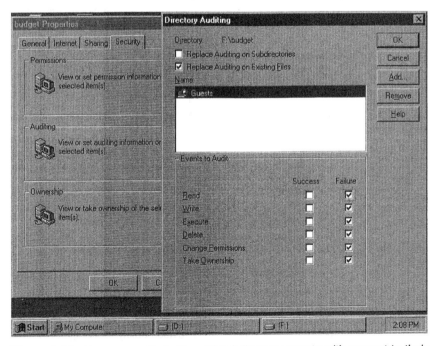

Figure 8.14 You can audit six file and subdirectory events with respect to their success, failure, or their success and failure

Replace Auditing on Subdirectories or the Replace Auditing on Existing Files check boxes if you want to audit existing directories and/or files. You would leave the check boxes empty if you only want to audit new files and subdirectories.

As indicated in the window area of the foreground screen, you can select groups or individual users that you want to audit. Once this has been accomplished you would then select the events you want to audit. To do so you would place a check in a box to inform Windows to audit a specified event. As indicated in the lower portion of Figure 8.14, you can audit the following actions for success, failure or for both success and failure.

Read
Write
Execute
Delete
Change permissions
Take ownership

8.2.4 Working with logs

While viewing the results of auditing represents an 'after the fact' display of information, many times it can provide a valuable insight concerning actual or potential adverse operations. Windows has three different event logs that you can view through the operating system's Event Viewer. In the area of security as you would expect the security log to provide key security related information. However, it is important to note that if improperly configured, it is quite possible that your ability to view previous events, that could shed light upon a particular problem, may no longer exist. Thus, instead of focusing attention upon different entries in Windows logs, since they can considerably vary based upon your server's facilities and logging options selected, let us turn our attention to the settings associated with each type of log.

Figure 8.15 illustrates the event log settings dialog box, which is similar for each event log supported by Windows. Note that the default setting for each log is a maximum log size of 512 Kbytes with the overwriting of events older than 7 days. If you operate a very active server, it is important to carefully consider both the size of the log and the method of log wrapping. If your organization views log entries on a daily basis you can consider the overwrite of events set for older than 7 days. However, if your organization is like many organizations for which good intentions turn to

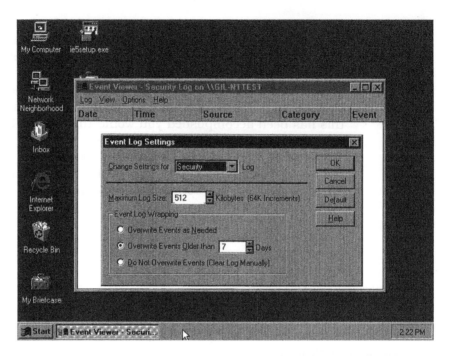

Figure 8.15 Examining the potential changes to different Windows logs

complacency when operations are normal, you may not be able to view log information, for example, to trace a security-related event that occurred greater than a week ago. Due to this, it is suggested that a good standard operating procedure should archive your log entries rather than overwrite them. In fact, during the beginning of the year 2000 when a series of distributed denial of service (DDoS) attacks occurred, a key problem faced by the FBI in attempting to trace the originators of the attacks was a lack of logs to view. Thus, setting applicable events to view as well as keeping logs for a reasonable period of time at the very least may be helpful in allowing law officials to investigate security-related problems.

8.3 WORKING WITH FTP

One of the key problems with respect to security is the fact that FTP passwords are passed in the clear. Because of this it is strongly suggested that you supplement any use of FTP for specific account support via public network access with a third party authentication method. Otherwise, you must live with the fact that it is possible for UserID-password combinations to be observed and used against your computer. However, prior to having a panic attack it should be noted that the author of this book operated a high profile Web server for a three-year period. That server was updated remotely via FTP without a problem. Well . . . almost without a problem. When a new home page was placed on the server, it would not go into effect until access to the server was temporarily suspended. Other than this repeating need for manual intervention whenever a new home page was to be placed on the server, FTP worked very well and without problems. However, if applicable funds were available it would have been obviously much more secure to have used a third party authentication system to supplement FTP access to the server.

In this section we will focus our attention upon the screens associated with the configuration of FTP, noting when applicable various options you can consider that can affect the level of security of your server.

8.3.1 TCP port use

Figure 8.16 illustrates the main FTP screen display with the Service tab placed in the foreground. In examining the screen display note that by default TCP port 21 is used for FTP. Some organizations without anonymous FTP access will attempt to hide FTP by selecting a different port number, typically a high number, such as 6021. While this action makes it more difficult for a casual user to discover the fact that FTP is operating on your server, the ready availability of port scanners provides persons that wish to discover applications operating on a host with the ability to do so. Thus, while port hiding could keep your FTP service hidden from view, it does not actually provide security for the application.

8.3.2 Anonymous connections

The checkbox labeled 'Allow Anonymous Connections' should only be used when you need to provide the general population of public access users with FTP access to your server. Similarly, the checkbox labeled 'Allow Only Anonymous Connections' should be carefully considered as its selection precludes your ability to allow FTP access to specific user accounts on the server.

8.3.3 User session control

If you click on the button labeled 'current sessions' you obtain not only a view of user sessions, but, in addition, you gain the ability to terminate user connections. If you operate a popular FTP server and

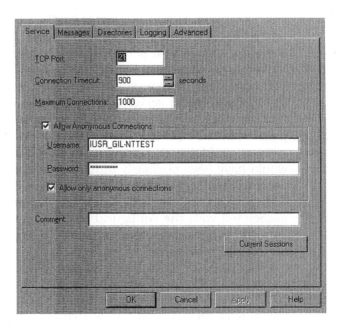

Figure 8.16 Through the use of the FTP Service tab you can change the TCP port number for the application as well as enable and disable anonymous access

have a relatively high time-out value and low number of maximum connections allowed, you may get calls from users that cannot access your server. If you receive such calls, you can either tell them to wait or select the Current Sessions button and terminate one or more users to allow new users to access your facilities.

8.3.4 Messages

The second tab on the FTP dialog box is labeled Messages. Through the use of this tab you can specify three types of message. Figure 8.17 illustrates the display of the Messages tab.

In examining this tab note that the majority of space is allocated for a Welcome message. The applicable use of this space is highly recommended, as it is extremely important to have an appropriate message to be able to legally take action against persons that abuse access to your host. For example, if your organization's welcome message simply says 'Welcome to our server', it could be very difficult to attempt to prosecute persons that constantly pull files from your server to tie up your organization's transmission facilities. In comparison, if your Welcome message lists the name of your organization and states that it is available for 'Official Use

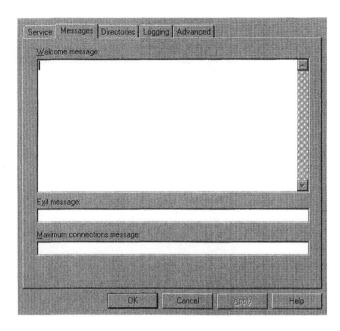

Figure 8.17 The Messages tab provides users with the ability to specify three types of message that are associated with FTP access

Only' and 'Violators will be prosecuted', it will be easier to take legal action against unauthorized users.

The exit message can range from a simple 'Thank You' to a reference to your organization's Web site location. The maximum connections message can be used to inform a potential user of a heavily trafficked location that they should retry at a later time. Thus, from a security perspective, the welcome message represents the most important message to place on your server.

8.3.5 Directories

The third tab on the FTP control dialog box is labeled 'Directories'. This tab, which is shown in Figure 8.18, provides you with the ability to define the directories associated with FTP access. By default, the home directory is the directory path InePub\ftproot on the C drive. You can click on that directory path and then click on the Remove button to delete that directory. You can also add one or more directories and in doing so control the type of access permitted to files within a directory.

Assuming you click on the button labeled Add in the Directories tab, you will obtain the ability to select additional directories as well as specify access permissions for the directory selected. Figure 8.19

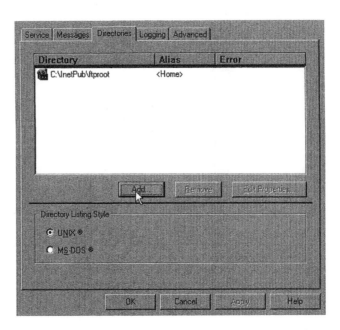

Figure 8.18 The Directories tab provides you with the ability to specify directories that can be accessed via FTP as well as the type of access permitted to files within selected directories

illustrates the dialog box labeled Directory that is displayed in response to selecting the button labeled Add in the FTP tab labeled Directories. Note that you can use the button labeled Browse to scan your volumes and directories. If you did not previously select anonymous user access you can use the Account Information portion of Figure 8.19 to provide specific access to a specific user.

Although both Read and Write access are shown enabled in Figure 8.19, if you are supporting anonymous access, you will note that you have no control over specific FTP commands, such as mget and mput. As previously discussed when we covered the use of firewalls, if you believe your site could be subjected to the abusive use of one or both commands, you should consider the use of a firewall FTP proxy service to limit any potential attack via the use of those commands.

8.3.6 Logging

The tab labeled 'Logging' provides you with the ability to control logging activity associated with the use of FTP. Figure 8.13 illustrates the display of the FTP Logging tab.

In examining Figure 8.20 note that you can enable or disable FTP logging, control when a new log should be opened, and control the

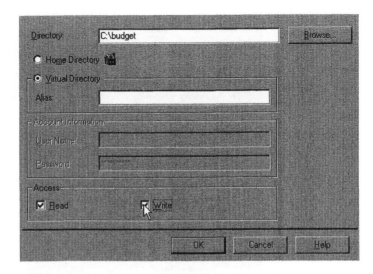

Figure 8.19 Although you can control Read and Write access, you cannot control the use of individual FTP commands

location of the log file via the use of this display. Similar to our previous discussion concerning logging, it is extremely important to maintain logs for a period of time in the event your host is attacked. These logs can be considered as evidence in a court and their absence can prove detrimental in attempting to build a case against an actual or blocked penetration attempt.

8.3.7 Controlling access via IP address

The last tab in the FTP dialog box provides you with the ability to add a degree of protection for narrowing the scope of permitted access to your server. Figure 8.21 illustrates the display of the Advanced tab and the selection of the Deny Access On box.

In examining the background portion of Figure 8.21 note that you can by default either grant or deny access to specific computers. For either situation you can specify either a single computer or a group of computers as illustrated by the foreground dialog box. If you select the single computer button you must enter a specific IP address. In comparison, if you select the Group of Computers button you can then enter a subnet mask, obtaining the ability to specify a network or a portion of a network if you so desire.

Although the concept of restricting access via user accounts from defined IP addresses would appear to provide a good technique to

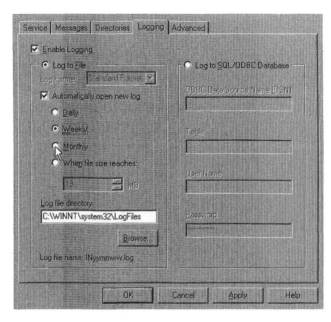

Figure 8.20 Logging FTP usage can be an important piece of your evidence in the event your host is attacked

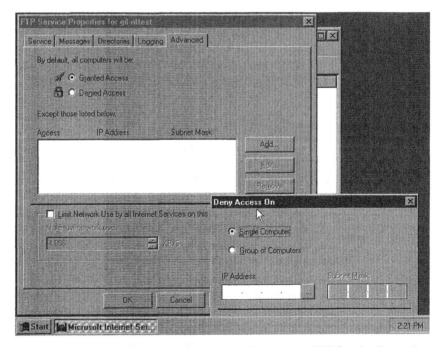

Figure 8.21 Through the use of the Advanced tab on the FTP Service Properties screen you can control access based upon a specific IP address or a group of IP addresses

enhance security, in actuality there is a key problem with this method. That problem is the fact that dynamically assigned IP addresses provided by Internet Service Providers or via network address translation effected by routers and firewalls are hard to support. For example, if you have one or more employees that require FTP access to your server and you want to restrict access via IP address, you might have to allow the address block used by the ISP. This would obviously open a wide range of permissible IP addresses that would be allowed to access your server; however, at least it provides some limitations on access. Similarly, if a remote site employs network address translation you might select the Group of Computers button and allow any IP address in the group used by your organization. While the previously mentioned controls are not as good as having the ability to specifically restrict access to a particular IP address, they do allow you to limit FTP access and at the very least should be considered when you want to restrict FTP access to specific user accounts.

8.4 INTERNET INFORMATION SERVER

In concluding our examination of Windows security related items we will turn our attention to Microsoft's Internet Information Server (IIS). In doing so we will focus upon the security aspects of IIS and defer to other authors and books the setup and utilization of the Web server software program.

When this book was being prepared the latest version of IIS was 4.0. At the time IIS Version 4.0 was made available, Microsoft also made available its Management Console, referred to as the MMC, as a tool for server administration and management that is now an integral part of Windows 2000.

Figure 8.22 illustrates the use of the Microsoft Management Console to access the properties associated with IIS installed on the author's computer. In examining Figure 8.22 note that to display the properties for a selected service operating under the MC you would first select the computer in the left portion of the screen and then select the service in the right portion of the screen. Once the preceding has been accomplished you would right-click on the service whose properties you wish to view or adjust. Note that right-clicking brings up a menu from which you would select the Properties entry as shown in the lower right portion of Figure 8.22. Also note that under the MMC you would perform a similar operation to view or adjust FTP settings, selecting the FTP site entry instead of the Web site entry in the upper right portion of Figure 8.22.

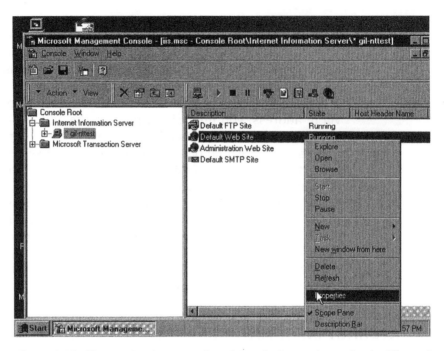

Figure 8.22 To examine the properties of a particular service under the Microsoft Management Console you would select the service, right-click your selection, and select the Properties entry from the pop-up menu

8.4.1 Web site properties

Once you have selected the Properties option from the pop-up menu Windows will display a dialog box that has nine tabs. Figure 8.23 illustrates the Web Site Properties dialog box. Note that the name of the dialog box commences with the term 'Default' as at the present time no description as been entered for the Web site.

In examining the Web Site tab shown in the foreground in Figure 8.23, note that many of your basic options are very similar to the setup for FTP. That is, you can use the default TCP port, which is 80, for a Web server or change the port to a different value if you wish to hide the presence of the Web server from casual surfers. Similar to our discussion concerning the hiding of FTP, the hiding of a Web server's port can easily be ascertained via the use of port scanning software and can be considered more as a privacy mechanism than a security measure.

Continuing our examination of Figure 8.23, note you can either support an unlimited number of connections or click on the button 'Limited to' to set a connection limit. In an era of frequent denial of service attacks it is suggested that you use a router or firewall to limit TCP open connections instead of attempting to use the Web server. Thus, for users with protection in the form of a firewall or router access list with TCP intercept enabled, you would then more than likely use the unlimited connection setting. However, the default 900 second connection time-out value appears to be quite excessive and you may wish to consider adjusting this value downward.

8.4.2 Multiple site support

If you click on the button labeled Advanced shown in Figure 8.23 you obtain a relatively new capability added to ISS that allows you to host multiple sites with 'host headers'. Figure 8.24 illustrates the Advanced Multiple Web Site Configuration dialog box in the background which is displayed when you select the button labeled Advanced previously shown in Figure 8.23. By clicking on the button labeled Add, the dialog box labeled Advanced Web Site Identification is displayed in the foreground. In examining the foreground and background displays shown in Figure 8.24 you will note that these screens provide you with the ability to configure

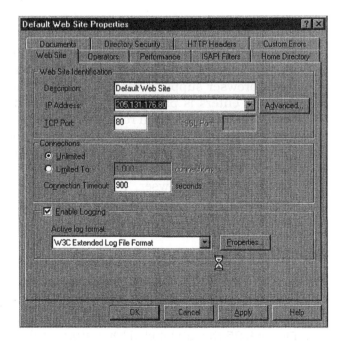

Figure 8.23 The Web Site tab in the Web Site Properties dialog box provides you with the ability to control connections to the Web server

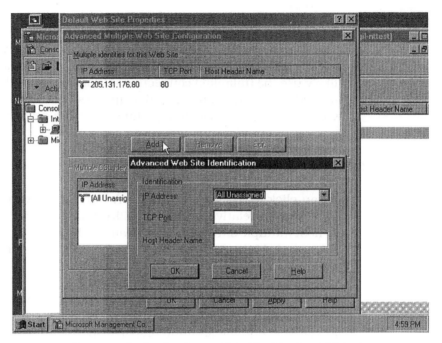

Figure 8.24 Configuring multiple identities for a Web site

multiple Web sites to share a common IP address. Note that the host header name entry is equivalent to a domain name and allows multiple names to be associated with a common IP address. If a client browser supports the use of host header names, the name the user enters is passed in the HTTP header as the destination host. The server will then route the client to the correct Web site. If the browser does not support the use of host header names the server will then respond with the default Web site, assuming the default Web site is enabled. Otherwise, an error message is returned to the browser. If the Web site requested in the host header is stopped, the default Web site is used to service the client.

8.4.3 Operator control

If we return to the Web Site Properties screen and continue our focus upon security, we can click on the tab labeled 'Operators' to obtain a display similar to the one illustrated in Figure 8.25. In Figure 8.25 the tab labeled 'Operators' is shown in the background portion of the screen. Note that through this screen you can control operator privileges to the Web site. By default, permission is granted to those users that are members of the Administrators group. If you click on the button labeled 'Add' the foreground dialog box labeled 'Add Users and Groups' will be displayed. Through this dialog box you can grant additional operator privileges.

As discussed at the beginning of this chapter, care should be taken when considering the users and groups you want to allow to operate your Web site. Because the key administrator account represents a red flag for attack, it is probably best to forgo using that built-in account. Instead, consider making up a name or series of names for your key users that will have operator privileges and then assigning them to the Administrators group. This technique, while obviously not foolproof, will result in the hiding of those employees with Web site operator privileges from the basic public as well as removing a frequent target of hacker attacks.

8.4.4 Directory security

As you might surmise, the tab labeled Directory Security plays a vital role in the ability of an organization to secure access to pages on their Web server. Figure 8.26 illustrates the display of the Directory Security tab in the Web Site properties dialog box. In examining the

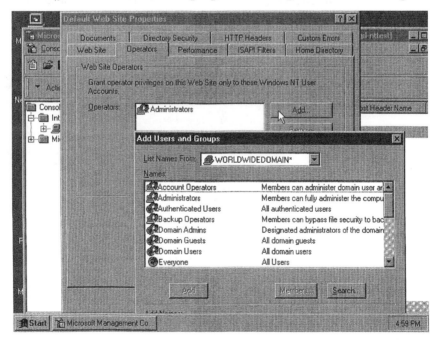

Figure 8.25 Assigning operator privileges to your Web site should be carefully considered

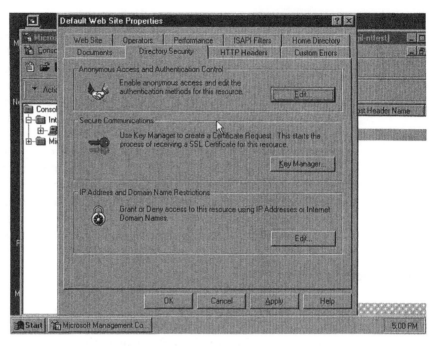

Figure 8.26 The Directory Security tab provides you with the ability to implement authentication and encryption as well as to restrict access to your server based upon IP address or domain name

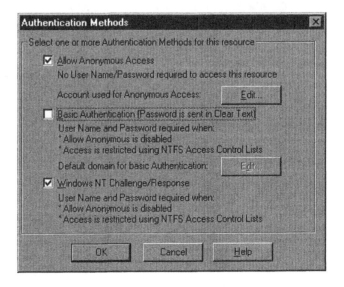

Figure 8.27 IIS supports three native authentication methods

display you will note that it is divided into three sections. The top section provides you with the ability to restrict access to the Web server to persons that have an account on the server. The middle portion of the display provides you with the ability to create and manage SSL key pair files for establishing encrypted communications with remote users. In addition, you can access the Key Manager via the middle portion of Figure 8.26 and generate a request for a server certificate. Because the operation of public and private keys requires a server certificate, you must obtain a certificate and attach it to your server's key pair to implement its SSL security features.

The third portion of Figure 8.26 provides you with the ability to allow or prohibit access to your server based upon IP address or domain name. Thus, you should consider the use of the Directory Security tab if you wish to implement authentication, encryption, or domain or address checking.

8.4.5 Authentication

Figure 8.27 illustrates the authentication methods supported natively by IIS. By default IIS is set up to allow anonymous access.

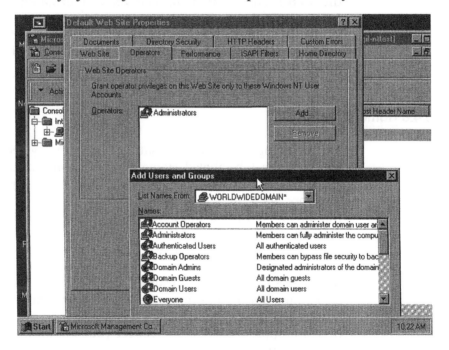

Figure 8.28 The Home Directory tab controls where the content for the server comes from as well as various permissions associated with the files in the directory

When set up to support anonymous access, no user name and password combination is required to access the server. Although we think of anonymous access as unrestricted access, in actuality the only lack of restrictions concerns the ability of any person to access Web pages. Because the server can be configured to use an account for anonymous access, such as the guest account, that account has security restrictions that go into effect and limit the type of Web content that anonymous users can access.

By default your Web server will create and use the account IUSR_computername, which is automatically granted a minimum set of rights. If you want to use basic authentication for access to the Web server, you must disable anonymous access. As the warning message on the screen image shown in Figure 8.27 indicates, this method of authentication results in the transmission of passwords in the clear. While it provides a degree of protection, it is also vulnerable to the use of a sniffer since passwords are transmitted in the clear and can easily be captured.

A third method of authentication supported by IIS is the Windows Challenge/Response method. This method results in the Web server exchanging encrypted information with a user's Internet Explorer Web browser, which limits the potential vulnerability of this access method. However, similarly to basic authentication, the challenger/response method only works when anonymous access is disabled.

8.4.6 Home directory

In concluding our brief examination of IIS security-related items we will view the tab labeled Home Directory, shown in Figure 8.28. Note that you can control both read and write capability to the directory, as well as the associated several types of permission to the directory. One of the key reasons many Web sites have been defaced has been traced to the inadvertent check of the Write permission box, which allows a person to download the page, make one or more changes to a file, and upload the changes, to the chagrin of the organization operating the server. Thus, in concluding our brief examination of IIS permissions, it is important to note that you should always check your permissions to ensure they are appropriately set to reflect your organization's operating environment.

9

THE ROLE OF THE SCANNER

In previous chapters in this book we examined an assortment of methods that could be used to attack both network facilities and hosts residing on a network. In addition, we have devoted a considerable amount of space in this book to describe and discuss the use of hardware and software that could prevent or mitigate the effect of such attacks. If you remember a scene in the movie *The Lion in Winter*, you might feel a bit perplexed like the king who told the queen to 'know the facts', only to receive the response 'Which ones—there are so many!' In security, like in the movie, we are faced with a large number of facts that we must consider. In addition, we have to consider changes in technology as well as the improper use of both old and new technology as mechanisms by which hackers could develop new methods of attack. Due to this, no network or host on a network can really be considered fully secure. In addition, to err is human and there always exists the possibility that despite our best intentions we may overlook one or more actual or potential security settings that could be exploited by a hacker. Due to this fact of life a relatively new software industry was developed that focuses attention upon developing products that check your network and host against potential vulnerabilities. Referred to as scanning software, such products are the focus of this concluding chapter.

In this chapter we will first focus our attention upon the difference between intrusion detection and scanning software. Once this has been accomplished we will turn our attention to the use of scanners and examine several products you can use to considerably automate the process, associated with examining your network and networked hosts for potential vulnerabilities.

9.1 INTRUSION DETECTION VERSUS SCANNING SOFTWARE

A popular misconception some persons have is an association of intrusion detection with scanning. To alleviate any possible misconceptions we will briefly review the differences between the two types of software prior to turning our attention to scanning software.

9.1.1 Intrusion detection operation

Intrusion detection software operates passively, monitoring traffic and looking for repeated sequences of activities that could indicate the possibility that a network or host on a network is under attack. The host running intrusion detection software sets an adapter to operate in the promiscuous mode, reading every frame flowing on a network. As the software examines each packet, it dynamically constructs table entries which denote source and destination IP addresses and layer 4 ports. In addition, depending upon the type of intrusion detection software product obtained, it may examine the packet content when it notes a series of repeated packets flowing between two locations.

To determine that the flow of packets being examined is an irregular occurrence and not a planned operation, the software will probably include a packet length field in the table it creates. Then, if the flow of a long sequence of packets between two locations consists of similar length packets, it is quite possible that something non-kosher is occurring. This is because the download of a Web page that has several graphics would, at a minimum, contain several dissimilar length terminating packets for each graphic being downloaded. Thus, it becomes possible for some intrusion detection software products to avoid having to examine the actual contents of each packet. Other intrusion detection products compare the contents of packets against predefined operations, such as an attempted logon to a server or even a router. Once a predefined threshold is reached the intrusion detection software will normally generate an alarm in the form of an email message or pager call.

9.1.2 Limitations

Unlike a firewall that can block the flow of information, unless intrusion detection software operates on a firewall it is limited to an alarm generation capability. Thus, most intrusion detection software provides a reactive capability via alarms and does not actually provide protection.

A second limitation of intrusion detection software is the location of the host where it operates. If intrusion detection operates on a firewall at the entryway to a network, it can examine all packets flowing onto the network or networks located behind the firewall. In comparison, if intrusion detection software operates on a stand-alone computer host on one segment and the firewall defends two segments, it is possible an attack limited to one segment will go undetected. If you are a bit confused as to why you might supplement the use of a firewall with a stand-alone host operating intrusion detection software, the reason is similar to the rationale for purchasing insurance. That is, although the firewall is specifically designed to provide a high level of network security, the employees of the company marketing firewall software may have overlooked one or more possible security vulnerability holes. By purchasing intrusion detection software from another vendor, it is quite possible that the software may detect an unexpected flow of packets through the firewall and alert you to this fact.

9.1.3 Scanning software

In comparison to intrusion detection that operates passively, a scanner is anything but a passive monitoring tool. Instead, a scanner actively checks your network and hosts connected to your network. In doing so, the software either runs through a series of predefined checks and operations or permits you to select those operations you want to test against your network and hosts on the network. Examples of scanning operations include simple port scans looking for openings in your equipment, to numerous types of denial of service attack that can be used to test the ability of your network to withstand such attacks. Other operations performed by scanners can include attempting to crack passwords to creating benign viruses that are transmitted to a target. It should be noted that some scanners specifically warn you not to target a production server when you run a series of denial of service attacks as it is quite possible you might bring down the server. Instead, you should either run the scanner modules that could cause disruption of equipment either in the evening or against a duplicate server whose potential crashing may not result in the 'egg on the face' syndrome. Now that we have a general appreciation for the differences between intrusion detection and scanners, let us turn to the primary topic of this chapter and examine the operation and utilization of scanning software.

9.2 BINDVIEW HACKERSHIELD

The first scanning program we will examine in this chapter is HackerShield from BindView Development Corporation of Houston, TX. HackerShield is a software program that probes devices on a network for vulnerabilities. The program uses a predefined series of hacker techniques to probe for weaknesses in a network but does not actually exploit the hole to gain access to a network device. The program can be used to probe servers, workstations, routers and firewalls. In addition to finding holes in a network, the program will provide detailed information on the vulnerabilities it locates, as well as instructions for closing each hole. For organizations operating Windows NT a side benefit of the program is its ability to close certain Windows holes.

9.2.1 Device discovery

The initial use of HackerShield is based upon the discovery of devices. To accomplish this task the program has a built-in scan wizard that allows you to enter a network address and subnet mask as the first step towards locating all operating devices on a target network. Figure 9.1 illustrates the use of the program's scan wizard. In this example we will first attempt to locate all devices on the 205.131.176.0 network.

Depending upon the type of network, the initial scan time can range from a minute for a Class C network with a maximum of 254 devices to a considerably longer period of time for networks with more hosts. Once the scan has been completed the scan wizard will display the hosts located on the target network, including any resolved host names determined by the scanning process. Figure 9.2 illustrates the display of the potential targets located on the 205.131.176.0 network. Note that the boxes to the left of two IP addresses were checked as we will scan for security holes for those two devices.

9.2.2 Working with groups

Because the HackerShield program is based upon the concept of groups, even if you want to scan one device you must place your

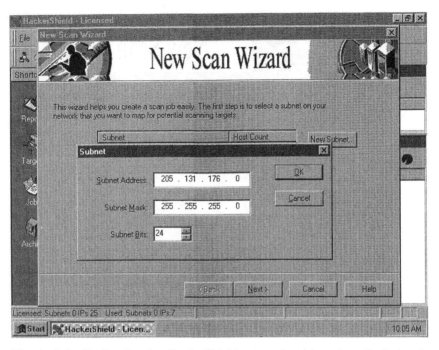

Figure 9.1 Configuring the HackerShield scan wizard to automatically locate devices on a target network

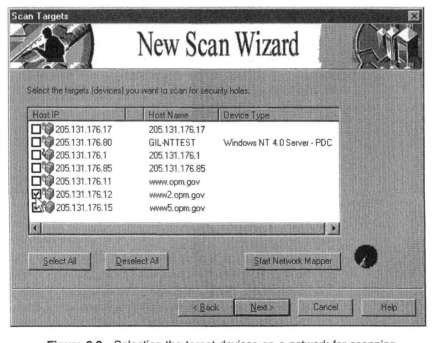

Figure 9.2 Selecting the target devices on a network for scanning

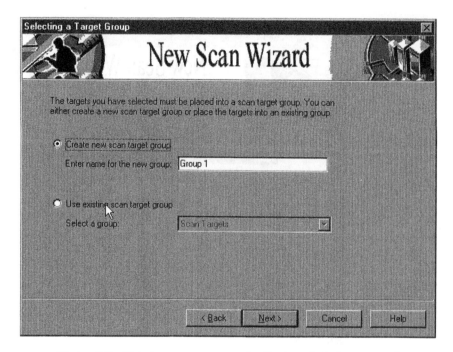

Figure 9.3 Entering a group name for the targets to be scanned

single target into a group. In Figure 9.3 we used the name Group1 to assign the two target IP addresses we wish the program to scan.

Once you have entered a group name you can instruct HackerShield to initiate its scanning operation. This scanning process may take a considerable amount of time so you may wish to experiment with one or two targets prior to selecting every device on a network as a target.

Figure 9.4 illustrates the initial display of the program's Scan Progress dialog box. As a matter of possible interest for persons considering the use of this program a total of 28 minutes was required to run the scan against two hosts. Thus, running the scan against a large number of hosts could require a considerable amount of time. This also indicates the value in being able to schedule scans to be run in the evening or on weekends. Since HackerShield's probing is basically non-intrusive you do not have to be concerned about a disruption and stay on site to watch the horizontal progress bar expand to the right.

In examining Figure 9.4 note the lower left box in which the two target devices are listed. As the program cycles through its security checks, it displays the name of each check. While you can sit in front of the screen and watch the cycling of security checks

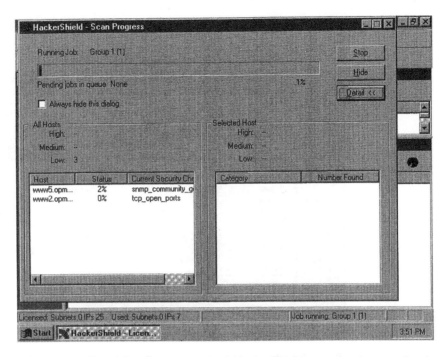

Figure 9.4 Examining the progress of HackerShield scanning two previously selected targets

performed by HackerShield, you can also generate a full report that will summarize the finding associated with each security check.

9.2.3 Viewing reports

Once HackerShield has completed its scan you can display and print several types of report concerning the scan operation. Figure 9.5 illustrates a portion of the scan summary for Group 1 that consists of the two target devices we previously selected. Note that the program found what it defines as five 'high risk' security holes and six 'low risk' security holes for a total of eleven security holes.

Although a network manager might develop heart palpitations by viewing a display that notes 'high risk' security holes, before you have a panic attack it is worth noting that what the program defines as 'high risk' and its effect upon your network environment may not necessarily correlate. For example, as we will shortly note HackerShield considers the use of cgi scripts to be a high risk. While this is certainly true if your organization uses some rather loose programming techniques, if you previously

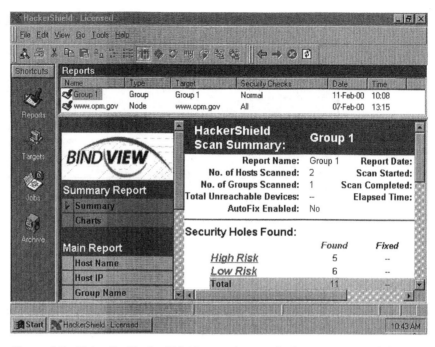

Figure 9.5   Using the HackerShield report icon to display a summary of the scan

checked your cgi scripts you may be able to obtain a good night of sleep instead of having to watch or manage a midnight software recovery effort.

Because it is quite normal to be concerned about high-risk holes, we will view a few first. To do so we can simply click on 'high risk' to view the portion of the report concerning holes that fall into this category. Figure 9.6 illustrates a portion of the high-risk holes report display.

In examining Figure 9.6 note that the fourth column labeled 'security hole' defines in broad terms the type of security hole. If we click on a security hole definition we can display additional information, so let us do so.

9.2.4 cgi script considerations

Because the first security hole noted is for cgi_htmlscript, let us click on that entry. Doing so results in the display of security hole information as illustrated in Figure 9.7. In examining Figure 9.7 note that the program simply informs us that it is possible to enter non-valid information into a poorly designed cgi script. In fact,

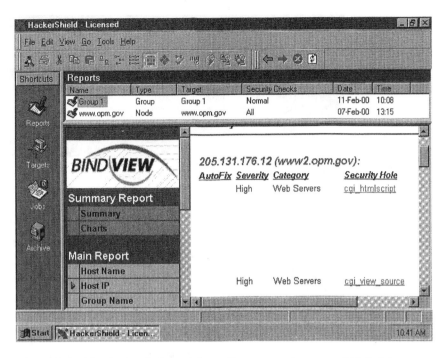

Figure 9.6 Viewing preliminary information concerning several high-risk security holes

several well-publicized server crashes over the past few years were traced back to the innocent entry of incorrect data into a cgi script which caused the program to crash, adversely affecting the operation of the server. While it is nice to note that scripts can cause a potential problem, you may wish to consider the acquisition of a program that scans your server for all cgi scripts and actually tests those scripts. Thus, while scanning is important it may not be sufficient by itself and may need to be supplemented by testing.

9.2.5 Open ports

Another common type of security hole reporting by the Hacker-Shield program involves layer 4 TCP and UDP ports. Many devices that support the TCP/IP protocol stack either by default or design support the operation of certain ports whose operation could be harmful to the health of your network. For example, as we noted earlier in this book, echo and character generation (CHARGEN) could be used by a hacker to initiate a random stream of characters

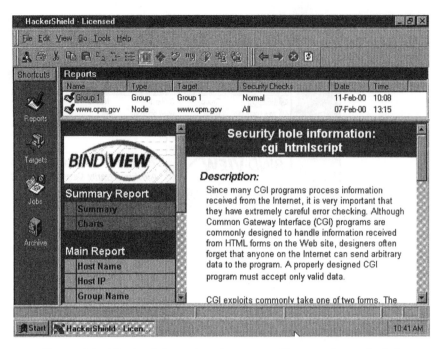

Figure 9.7 Viewing information about a specific type of security hole

from one device to another via address spoofing. If the spoofed address supports echo then the random stream of characters would be returned to the originator. If a hacker finds one computer with CHARGEN enabled and another with echo enabled, the hacker will spoof the address of the device supporting echo as he or she sends requests to the device supporting CHARGEN. Then the hacker can sit back and relax as the two network devices flood the network with extraneous information to the detriment of persons attempting to perform productive work.

Returning to the use of HackerShield, Figure 9.8 illustrates a portion of the security holes previously summarized in an earlier display. In Figure 9.8 we note four low risk security holes associated with TCP ports. The program obtains this information during the initial scanning process during which it checks each port from 0 to 1023. If it receives a response to a probe packet on a specific port, the port is then considered to be open. We can obtain additional information concerning the TCP open ports and the TCP open reserved ports shown in Figure 9.8 by clicking on either entry.

Figure 9.9 illustrates a display that provides summary information concerning the two TCP open port entries contained in Figure 9.8. In examining Figure 9.9 note that the two low risk entries

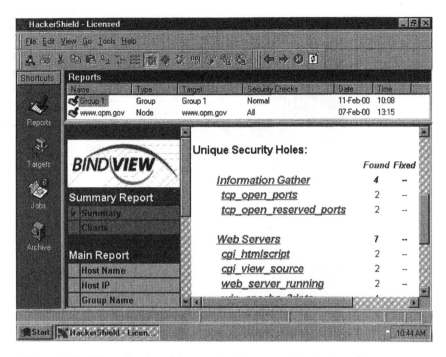

Figure 9.8 Observing low risk security holes associated with TCP open ports

summarized in Figure 9.8 for TCP open ports correspond to each target that was scanned. You will also note that the description for each host is the same. Whether or not we have a security hole and if the hole is a true area of concern will depend upon the ports that are open and the services you need to provide on a particular host. For example, if you are operating a Web server you will obviously have to respond to queries on port 80 which is the port used by HTTP. Thus, the fact that port 80 is open is not significant since there is nothing you can do about its status other than disabling Web service. In actuality, you can hide certain services from the general public by moving such services to a different port number. However, a half-decent hacker can easily discover this type of situation, and other than discouraging casual snoopers, this action is not really a security measure.

If you click on the security check output link for either host listed in Figure 9.9, you will obtain a display of open ports found on the target host. Figure 9.10 illustrates the display of open TCP ports. Note that because the scanned device supports both FTP and WWW it came as no surprise that ports 21 and 80 were open. Similarly, there was a good reason for port 135 and 139, with the latter being used to support file sharing between hosts. While this scan did not

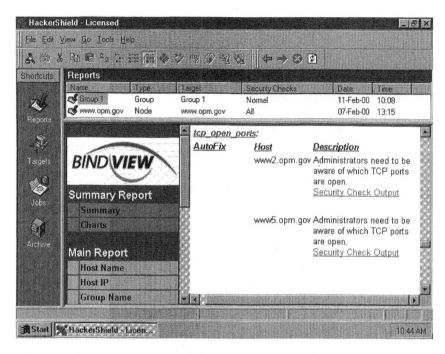

Figure 9.9 Observing a description of the low risk TCP open port condition

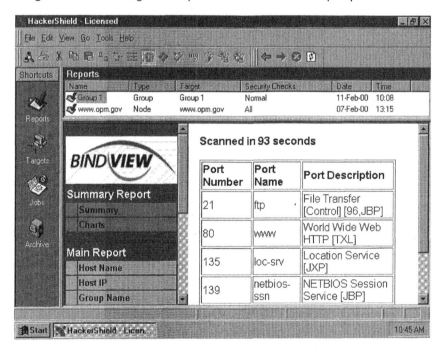

Figure 9.10 Viewing the open ports found by the scanning process

result in any extraordinary information concerning the vulnerability of the two targets, at the very least it provides some peace of mind.

If the program indicated that other ports were open that were not required, the obvious solution to the problem is to close those ports. However, prior to doing so you should carefully consider whether or not you need to close those ports. For example, your organization may support Finger for internal use and block outside access via a router or firewall. Thus, instead of turning off this application you would allow it to continue. This indicates that you need to examine the entire network infrastructure prior to making a decision concerning the wisdom of having a particular port open on a scanned device.

9.3 OTHER TYPES OF SCANNING PROGRAMS

It should be noted that there are several types of scanning program to consider. The program we just examined is a non-intrusive external program that does not actually examine the settings of the operating system of different network platforms. A second type of scanning program you may wish to consider operates on different network platforms with administrator privileges. This type of program focuses its attention upon the internal settings of a computer that govern its level of security. For example, this type of program would examine the status of each account on a computer to determine if a password was associated with each account, if the password will expire after a predefined period of time, whether or not an account lockout was enabled for each account, and similar information. Other characteristics of this type include examining file permissions and logging of different types of security-related condition. One example of this type of program is the Kane Security Analyst.

Readers can obtain an evaluation copy of HackerShield by visiting the BindView Development Web site whose address is http://www.bindview.com. In addition, you can request information about the program via email using the address info@bindview.com.

9.4 THE INTERNET SCANNER

A second scanning program that operates externally to hosts that we will examine in this chapter is the Internet Scanner, a product of Internet Security Systems, Inc. of Atlanta, GA. The Internet Scanner can be classified as similar to HackerShield as a vulnerability assessment product that analyzes the security of devices on a network. Although it is difficult to compare the two products, the Internet Scanner provides more flexibility as it includes built-in policies that contain specific types of scans applicable to different devices. As we will note later in this section when we examine the use of the policy selection dialog box, the Internet Scanner supports predefined policies for scanning routers and switches, Unix Servers, Unix Web Servers, NT Servers and other devices. In addition, you can create your own policy and select one or more applicable scans you wish to execute against an applicable target. Thus, this program provides users with a significant level of customization capability.

Prior to using the Internet Scanner it is important to note that the program includes many types of scan that push the limits of a system's operating system when looking for potential vulnerabilities. Due to this it is best to notify individual users and administrators ahead of time when their effect on your organization's hosts will minimize production operations.

9.4.1 Creating a scan

The capabilities of the Internet Scanner are very comprehensive, allowing you to use the program to not only scan for vulnerabilities but, in addition, to collect information about your network and develop an inventory of hosts, operating systems, IP addresses, DNS names and other network-related information. In this section we will primarily focus our attention upon how we can use the Internet Scanner to create a scan.

Once you install the Internet Scanner you would initiate its operation via the Windows NT Start menu, selecting Programs>ISS>Internet Scanner. Figure 9.11 illustrates the main ISS Internet Scanner window. Note that this opening window initially provides only two options the first time you use the program. You can either create a new session or open an existing session file. Once you run the program you can load a prior session from the database generated by the use of the program, and use the opening menu to generate a report. Because this is the first time we will use the program, we will select its initial default, which is to create a new session.

At the time this author used the Internet Scanner there were several restrictions concerning the platform it could be operated on. The program version used by this author was restricted to operating under Windows NT workstation with at least service pack 4 installed. If you are interested in using this program, information concerning obtaining an evaluation copy is presented at the end of this section.

When you click on the button labeled OK shown in Figure 9.11, the program will generate the use of a wizard that walks you through series of screen displays required to select a policy. As briefly mentioned earlier in this section, the Internet Scanner is a policy-driven program. You can either select one of many predefined policies developed to test the vulnerabilities of certain types of host or create a specific policy tailored for a particular networking environment.

Figure 9.12 illustrates the initial display of the program's New Session Wizard. Note that there are a series of graphic icons with labels within the scrollable window of the dialog box shown in Figure 9.12. Some of the icons represent predefined policies for different types of generic equipment, such as routers and LAN switches, while other icons represent predefined policies for different types of Unix and Windows NT servers. To illustrate some of the potential capabilities of the Internet Scanner we will focus our attention upon creating a new policy. However, we will also examine, when appropriate, a portion of the policy proper-

Figure 9.11 The first time the Internet Scanner is executed you can either create a new session or open an existing session file

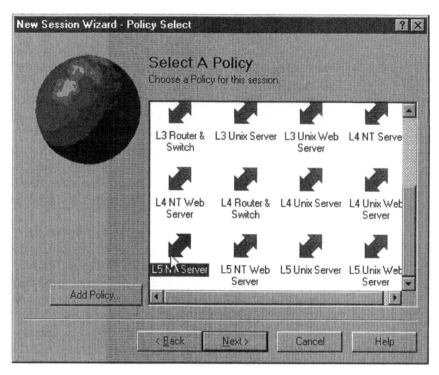

Figure 9.12 The Internet Scanner provides a series of predefined scans for different devices that are referred to as policies

ties supported by the program for Windows NT and router scanning.

9.4.2 Policy creation

If you decide to create a new policy, the program will display directions that indicate the three-step process you must follow. Those steps include selecting an existing policy to clone, editing the properties for the new policy and then naming the new policy. Assuming you selected an existing policy to clone and named the policy 'server', the program's policy editor screen display would then be similar to that shown in Figure 9.13. Note that the left portion of the display shown in Figure 9.13 can be expand downward by clicking on each plus sign to display a series of activities the program will perform if so selected. By default all activities are disabled for a newly created policy. As we will shortly note, care must be taken when you select some scans to be performed as their

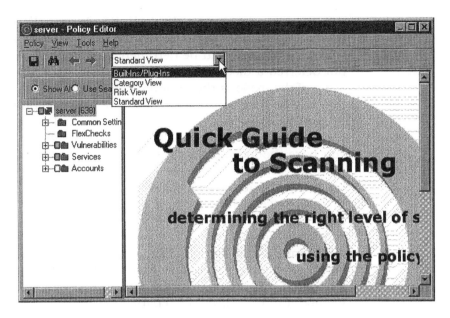

Figure 9.13 The Internet Scanner policy editor provides you with the ability to select certain predefined activities to be performed by the program

use could result in system lockouts. Also note that you can alter the manner by which information is displayed in the left portion of the screen via the use of the pull-down menu. When you move down by clicking on several plus signs you can considerably focus your view of items by selecting a specific menu entry from the pull-down menu.

9.4.3 Policy properties

Prior to moving forward with our examination of the use of the program, let us digress a bit and examine a few of the series of policy properties associated with two of the many policies supported by the program. When we first decided to create a new policy we had to select an existing policy to clone. To provide an indication of the capabilities of the program, this author selected the Windows NT server policy to clone. Thus, Figure 9.14, which indicates a portion of the policy properties for the policy named 'server' that was previously created, in actuality lists Windows NT Server Properties.

If you examine the list of exploits shown in Figure 9.14 you will note that the policy is very comprehensive. If you select every exploit the policy will attempt to guess different types of account password, access shares, check the Windows registry and perform other operations too numerous to mention. We previous mentioned some operations could be detrimental to the health of your hosts but deferred a discussion as to why. Thus, now that we can view some of the exploits the program can conduct, let us discuss how they can be hazardous to the health of your computer.

Note the NT Password Checks shown in Figure 9.14. As the program guesses passwords for different accounts, let us assume you have the lockout option set for those accounts. Then, as the scanning process progresses to guessing passwords, it will either break into the account or lock out the account. Thus, you may wish to think twice about password guessing. In fact, as we will shortly note, the Internet Scanner will provide us with several options concerning lockouts.

Continuing our examination of policy properties, Figure 9.15 lists those for a router-switch. Note that if you run this scan against a router, it will attempt to break into a Cisco router via a brute force method to determine the enable password. The router policy properties include two SNMP-related exploits. Note that the program will attempt to determine if the device supports the 'public' community name. If not the program will cycle through a list of

Figure 9.14 Examining some of the exploits that could be performed by the policy named server, which is based on a Windows NT server predefined policy

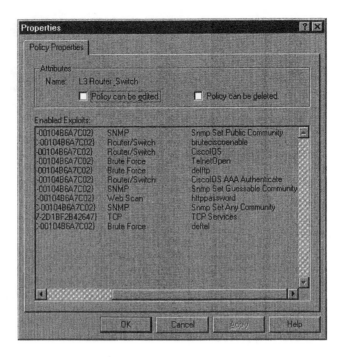

Figure 9.15 Examining the policy properties supported by the Internet Scanner for scanning a router

possible settings to determine a list of possible settings to determine if a previous SNMP community name is able to be guessed. The program also will determine what TCP services are supported as well as performing a brute force entry to access the router via a Telnet connection and other exploits. However, note that the program does not perform a UDP scan which would uncover whether or not echo or CHARGEN was active, a common security hole that hackers like to use. Thus, although the exploits are significant they are not all-encompassing.

9.4.4 Selecting exploits for the scanner

Now that we have digressed a bit to examine some of the exploits that can be performed by two different policies, let us return to the program's policy editor. In Figure 9.16 we selected the policy editor's Risk View after moving down the vulnerabilities setting previously shown in the left portion of Figure 9.13. In examining entries in the left portion of Figure 9.16 note that we both high-

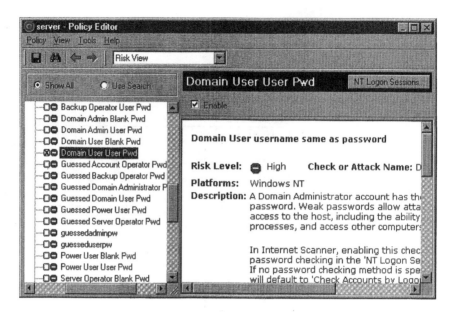

Figure 9.16 Selecting a potential vulnerability for testing during the scanning process

lighted and selected via a click on the box of the entry labeled 'Domain User User Pwd'. Selecting the entry results in a description of the entry being displayed in the right portion of the screen. This particular vulnerability that was selected will result in the scanning program attempting to gain entry into a targeted server by using the domain user username as the password. By clicking on the box to the left of the entry we select it for use by the scanning program. Thus, the Internet Scanner provides users with a considerable degree of flexibility for determining what exploits should be attempted.

9.4.5 Considering account lockout

If you click on the button labeled NT Logon Sessions located in the upper right corner of Figure 9.16 the program will provide you with the ability to control additional NT logon exploits. Figure 9.17 illustrates the resulting NT Logon Sessions dialog box with its default settings shown. Note that you can set the program via this screen to enable or preclude account lockouts as well as to allow a permanent account lockout. This means that in the wrong hands this program could become a rather interesting tool to lock out

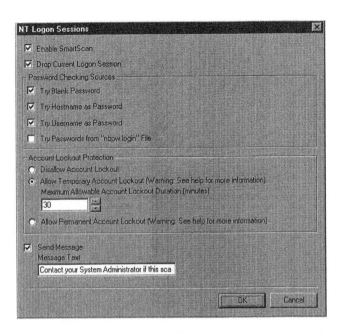

Figure 9.17 The Internet Scanner's NT Logon Sessions screen provides you with the ability to control lockouts

legitimate users. Perhaps for this very reason the company supplies a special key that must be used to activate both evaluation software as well as a full functional program. In addition, the key restricts the use of the program to predefined network addresses which hopefully eliminates the possibility of this program being used against a third party target network. This also means that if you are doing the scan in the wee hours of the morning and inadvertently click on the button associated with allowing permanent account lockouts, a few hours later when employees report to work your technical control center or help desk facility will begin to receive some rather interesting calls. Thus, the use of the Internet Scanner is similar to the use of other scanners in that you must carefully consider what you are attempting to do before you do it.

9.4.6 Scanning a local host

One of the more interesting aspects of the Internet Scanner is its ability to scan a local host. Because the IP address of 127.0.0.1 results in a loopback to the current host, you can use this address to scan the host the software is operating on. Figure 9.18 illustrates

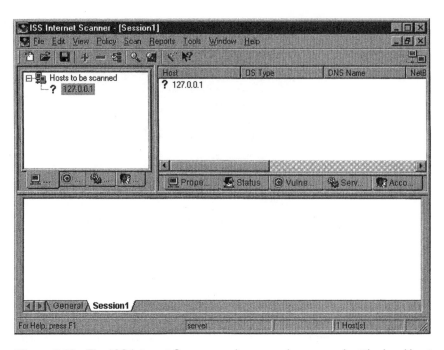

Figure 9.18 The ISS Internet Scanner main menu when you select the local host for scanning

the ISS Internet Scanner window when you set the program to scan the local host.

Although the configuration of the program assumes the user knows what he or she is doing, the Internet Scanner assumes otherwise. That is, prior to executing the configured scan the program displays a list of denial of service checks enabled for the scan to be performed. Figure 9.19 illustrates a portion of the comprehensive list of denial of service checks the program can perform. As the warning in the dialog box indicates, running one or more of the checks can result in a target crashing. While you obviously want to check the vulnerabilities of your hosts, it is highly recommended that you do so with the full knowledge of your network managers and their supervisors. In addition, instead of testing the DoS checks against each device in a network, you should probably run the test against your router and firewall first to determine how they handle such checks. If the router and firewall cannot prevent such attacks from reaching the hosts on a network, you would then want to consider running the DoS checks against individual hosts on your network.

Readers are referred to the ISS Web site whose address is http:solutions-iss.net for information about Internet Scanner as

Figure 9.19 The Denial of Service Warning issued by the Internet Scanner

well as to download an evaluation copy of this program. For security purposes and due to the powerful nature of ISS's Internet Scanner product, the company requires that in order to evaluate this product you utilize an encrypted license key. To obtain an extended evaluation key from Internet Security Systems (ISS), you can email the company with your request at sales@iss.net. In the email include your name, contact information including mailing and email address and phone number as well as the IP address range of your network.

INDEX

Printed and bound by CPI Group (UK) Ltd, Croydon, CR0 4YY

27/10/2024

14580297-0001